Nurturing Self-Reg in Early Childhood

Nurturing Self-Regulation in Early Childhood explores how young children develop self-regulation and offers practical guidance on helping them to manage their feelings and behaviour. It considers the skills, attitudes and dispositions children need to be able to self-regulate and how their wellbeing and self-esteem can affect their ability to do this.

Grimmer and Geens show how schools and settings can adopt an ethos where self-regulation permeates their whole provision. Considering the broad and multifaceted nature of self-regulation and how this key area of development shapes children and their learning, the chapters cover:

- developing empathy

- emotion coaching

- the practitioner as a co-regulator

- executive function and the sense of self and wellbeing

- international approaches to promoting self-regulation

- the role of the adult and environment in encouraging skills for self-regulation

- working effectively with parents and carers to ensure a consistent approach

With a focus on developmentally appropriate expectations, this book is essential reading for all early childhood educators who want to develop their understanding of self-regulation and embrace an approach that underpins their practice and changes children's lives.

Tamsin Grimmer is director of Linden Learning and a Senior Lecturer in Early Years Teacher Education at Bath Spa University. An experienced consultant and trainer, she has written several books, including *Developing a Loving Pedagogy in the Early Years* and *Calling All Superheroes*.

Wendy Geens is an experienced Early Years Teacher, Primary Teacher and Senior Leader who is currently a Senior Lecturer in Early Years Teacher Education at Bath Spa University. Wendy is a Fellow of the Higher Education Academy, and her research interests are in early years mathematics and self-regulation.

Nurturing Self-Regulation in Early Childhood

Adopting an Ethos and Approach

Tamsin Grimmer and Wendy Geens

Routledge
Taylor & Francis Group

LONDON AND NEW YORK

Cover image: © Shutterstock

First published 2023
by Routledge
4 Park Square, Milton Park, Abingdon, Oxon, OX14 4RN

and by Routledge
605 Third Avenue, New York, NY 10158

Routledge is an imprint of the Taylor & Francis Group, an informa business

British Library Cataloguing-in-Publication Data
A catalogue record for this book is available from the British Library

Library of Congress Cataloging-in-Publication Data
Library of Congress Cataloging-in-Publication Data
Names: Grimmer, Tamsin, author. | Geens, Wendy, 1967- author.
Title: Nurturing self-regulation in early childhood : adopting an ethos and approach / Tamsin Grimmer, Wendy Geens.
Description: First edition. | Abingdon, Oxon ; New York, NY : Routledge, 2023. | Includes bibliographical references and index. | Identifiers: LCCN 2022011860 (print) | LCCN 2022011861 (ebook) | ISBN 9780367753924 (paperback) | ISBN 9780367753894 (hardback) | ISBN 9781003162346 (ebook)
Subjects: LCSH: Early childhood education—Psychological aspects. | Self-control in children. | Emotions in children. | Child development.
Classification: LCC LB1139.23 .G747 2023 (print) | LCC LB1139.23 (ebook) | DDC 372.21—dc23/eng/20220425
LC record available at https://lccn.loc.gov/2022011860
LC ebook record available at https://lccn.loc.gov/2022011861

ISBN: 978-0-367-75389-4 (hbk)
ISBN: 978-0-367-75392-4 (pbk)
ISBN: 978-1-003-16234-6 (ebk)

DOI: 10.4324/9781003162346

Typeset in Bembo
by codeMantra

This book is dedicated to children across the world.
Thank you for inspiring us, challenging us and guiding us.
You are our future.

Contents

Acknowledgements

As authors it has been our pleasure to work with colleagues across the sector who on a daily basis provide exemplary education and care for children.

We'd like to express our thanks to those colleagues and parents who have generously given their time, expertise and thoughts, which have been instrumental in shaping this book. In particular, we'd like to thank headteacher Julie Way for her thought-provoking discussions about education, the future and what we can do now for our children.

Finally, our thanks also go to all our families and friends but, in particular, our mums for their never failing support and enthusiasm.

We are grateful to the following providers for sharing their inspiring stories:

Barrowford Primary School

Brentford Day Nursery & Pre-School

Charlton Nursery & Preschool

Chewton Mendip Primary School

Childminders

Cinnamon Brow CE Primary School Nursery

Colerne Old School Playgroup

College Green Nursery School & Services

Denmead Infant School

Happitots Boddam Nursery, Thrive Childcare and Education

Hillocks Primary Academy

Holyrood Nursery Salford Royal, Thrive Childcare and Education

Holyrood Nursery Swinton, Thrive Childcare and Education

Hua Hin International School

Malthouse Nursery School

Milford Lodge Nurseries

Moorlands Infant School

Mulberry Bush Pre-School

Noah's Ark Nursery

Pebbles Childcare

St Andrew's Church School

St John's Pre-School

Taipei European School

Thrive Childcare and Education

Widcombe Infant School

In addition, we would like to name the following educators for contributing to this book through discussion, sharing case studies and helping us to reflect upon self-regulation:

Linda Adamson, Nancy Andrews, Nikki Arbreu, Kate Bate, Lynn Blakemore, Megan Bowkett, Sarah Brady, Elaine Brown, Tracy Clark, Sarah Dunn, Melanie Ellis, Nawal Filali, Sarah Fisher, Laura Gee, Lisa Gibbons, Jess Gosling, Cassie Hartley, Jennie Holloway, Amy Hunter, Jenna Jefferies, Marlis Juerging-Coles, Ursula Krystek-Walton, Sue Martin, Sarah McDonald, Rachel Meehan, Ruby Moxey, Gemma Rowlands, Jane Sale, Amy Skinner, Charlie Swan, Alena Szczuczko, Allie Thorne, Lisa Tidy, Rachel Tomlinson, Julie Way, Chloe Webster, Laura Whitall, and Juliet Young.

Introduction

Tamsin Grimmer and Wendy Geens

Self-regulation is a term now used frequently within Early Childhood Education and Care (ECEC), partly due to the emphasis given to self-regulation in the current EYFS curriculum in England (DfE, 2021). Whilst self-regulation is not a new concept, it remains difficult to explain or unpick what is meant by this term. Most people would say they understand what it means, however when asked to elaborate, some found themselves floundering or oversimplifying it. Self-regulation is complex. It involves how we think, how we feel, how we make decisions, how we respond to others and how we respond to ourselves – it is no wonder it is difficult to explain. To help put self-regulation into context, we will explain it through a story, as this might help to provide an example of some of the skills and dispositions involved.

Imagine the scene: you have been out to get groceries and, as you don't need much, rather than take the car you decide to get the bus. You wait at the bus stop longer than you expected but think it's okay – you have plenty of time before your afternoon meeting. The bus arrives and it's full. You have to stand and, as you try to put your ticket in your bag, you drop it on the floor. Whilst trying to hold on to the rail, you manage to pick it up. No one offers to help. At your stop you wait your turn to get off, then someone pushes in front of you. You head to the store only to find they don't have two of the five things you came out for, so as you shop you begin to adapt the original meal you've planned. As you pay for the goods and head back to the bus stop, you notice that much time has passed, and you are aware that you need to be back by a certain time. There is a long queue, but you remain patient. The bus arrives and, just as you are about to get on, three children run ahead and jump on the bus before you. Although you have to stand, you think to yourself that it's okay – you were not left waiting for the next bus and will soon be home.

We all have times in our lives when our days do not go as planned. There are days when we need to be extra patient, more forgiving of others and ourselves. We need to plan in more detail or think ahead or be more considerate of others – after all, we don't know what has gone on in other people's lives. Being able to think and behave in this way requires us to have empathy, good organisation, social confidence, and resilience.

DOI: 10.4324/9781003162346-1

These are some of the disciplines that form our dispositions, which are shaped by the experiences we encounter and begin in early childhood.

Part of children's development is learning to understand powerful thoughts and feelings, to maintain attention, to respond to others, to wait their turn, to keep trying when something is hard to understand or do and to resist the temptation to give in. Our role as educators is to provide opportunities for them to make sense of what and how they are feeling and doing. We support them to understand and regulate their emotions by becoming a co-regulator and actively listening and being attuned to children's emotional states. This book aims to explore and explain the many different sides of self-regulation and offer ideas and strategies that adults and educators can use to support children in this key area of development.

It is through relationships with others that children learn to self-regulate. Whilst part of this process is learning about our emotions and understanding of social situations and etiquette, it is also about our ability to respond to others, overcome challenges, persist when learning gets tough and sustain a sense of calmness. This is a developmental process, and children learn through their experiences, which increase as they grow. Bodrova and Germeroth (2013) suggest this is about mature and immature play, with children growing in maturity with age and experience. Research informs us that children with high levels of self-regulation achieve more in school and have better life chances than those who have not developed this skill (Robson et al., 2020; Vink et al., 2020; Eisenberg et al., 2011), therefore the role of self-regulation cannot be underestimated.

Defining self-regulation

There are many definitions of self-regulation, and we could have filled a whole book just exploring the similarities and differences between these definitions. The term has been used in over 400 different ways in the psychological literature alone (Shanker, Hopkins & Davidson, 2015) and is now more of an umbrella term covering a cluster of concepts. Despite it being a complex concept, it is helpful if we attempt to define what we perceive it to be, at least for the purposes of this book. We are viewing self-regulation as the capacity of a person to both cognitively and emotionally cope with the ups and downs of daily life as well as the dispositions and skills needed to do this. It includes being in control of our emotions, adjusting our behaviour, planning our actions, empathising with others and developing social confidence, all of which promote good wellbeing.

Other definitions that are helpful to consider include Rosanbalm and Murray's simple definition, which views self-regulation as "the act of managing thoughts and feelings to enable goal-directed actions" (2017:1), and the summary that Asquith has adopted,

> Self-regulation is the ability to manage our own energy states, emotions, behaviours and attention, in ways that are socially acceptable. Self-regulation enables us to

understand, monitor and control our own behaviour and adjust the way in which we behave according to where we are and what is happening.

(2020:8)

Conkbayir defines self-regulation as

one's ability to manage one's own emotional responses and consequent behaviour and knowing how to control those big, overwhelming feelings such as anger or fear, in order to get on with the serious business of play, building relationships and learning.

(2020)

She has written an excellent online course about self-regulation, which we highly recommend and which is available from the link in the References at the end of the Introduction (Conkbayir, 2021).

Conkbayir (2021) views self-regulation as broadly covering these ten attributes:

- Controlling own feelings and behaviours.

- Applying personalised strategies to return to a state of calm.

- Being able to curb impulsive behaviours.

- Thinking before acting.

- Being able to concentrate on a task.

- Persisting in the face of difficulty.

- Being able to ignore distractions.

- Behaving in ways that are pro-social.

- Planning.

- Delaying gratification.

These definitions show that self-regulation is an active concept and the term describes a way of being, which is possibly why it is so difficult to pin down. Shanker sees self-regulation as how we cope with and manage stress and how well we recover from being stressed. "When a child's stress levels are too high, various systems for thinking and metabolic recovery are compromised. The signs of dysregulation show up in the child's behaviour, mood, attention, and/or physical well-being" (Shanker, Hopkins & Davidson, 2015:16). This book explores emotional dysregulation and the implications of this for educators whilst also considering strategies we can use to help children develop their cognitive and emotional self-regulation.

How are emotions made?

When Tamsin delivers training about emotional regulation, she sometimes shares a clip from the film *Inside Out* that depicts our brains as being controlled by our emotions and having five characters inside representing joy, anger, fear, sadness and disgust. This analogy has been criticised by neurologists as being incorrect and is based on several assumptions, many of which are untrue (Adolphs & Anderson, 2018), although it can be helpful in sharing how easily the adult's responses can escalate a situation without meaning to. In our understanding, scientists are still figuring out how emotions are made and the impact they have on our behaviour and cognition.

Many specialists study emotion from different angles – for example, neurologists might be interested in how the neurons fire up when in a certain emotional state, and psychologists may want to observe the behaviour and thought processes when a person feels a specific emotion. These experts often use a different professional language, and when attempting to read papers from both fields of study, we often find ourselves disappearing down a rabbit hole of thought and rarely come to a conclusion!

Despite our difficulties in fully following the scientific arguments, we understand emotions to have evolved out of reflexes: the simple freeze, fight or flight responses that determined our survival as a species (Adolphs & Anderson, 2018). However, behaviour is influenced by our emotions but not purely driven by them. It also relies upon these reflexes, our planned actions and our thought processes. Emotions are part of the story of behavioural responses but do not account for every response we make. Therefore, self-regulation is not purely about emotions – it is also about cognitive responses, executive function, pro-social behaviour and the way we interact with others. This book aims to consider all elements of self-regulation, and the thread running through will be how we, as educators, can support children with this. There is no quick fix. Instead, educators will need to reflect upon their practice and review their whole approach to how they support children and respond to them.

The Early Years Foundation Stage

Self-regulation now forms part of the Early Years Foundation Stage (EYFS), which is the statutory framework that all settings in England need to comply with and abide by (DfE, 2021). The revised Early Learning Goal (ELG) has a very narrow focus in terms of self-regulation and implies that the skills involved are all about children controlling themselves, waiting their turn and paying close attention to the teacher. It reminds us of 'Sit down, sit still and shut up!' This book does not make many references to the EYFS or educational programmes, however, we would like to explain why we feel the goal to be limiting and unhelpful.

The revisions for the EYFS came about after a review of assessment and were first published for use by several pilot schools who were trialling the revised EYFS Profile, which is the end of EYFS assessment in England. All the previous ELGs were reworded and in some places changed drastically, causing critics to suggest that this was a complete curriculum overhaul through the back door, and English settings and schools found themselves in the unfortunate position where their end-of-phase assessment was driving the curriculum.

The ELG for self-regulation is listed below, and it includes several components of self-regulation – for example, showing an understanding of feelings, focusing attention, waiting for a turn and inhibiting impulses – but they are not the whole story. The way this goal is described sounds like a very formal approach, which is not how we should support children with their feelings and behaviour.

ELG: Self-regulation

Children at the expected level of development will:

■ Show an understanding of their own feelings as well as those of others and begin to *regulate their behaviour accordingly*;

■ Set and work towards simple goals, *being able to wait for what they want* and *control their immediate impulses when appropriate*;

■ Give focused attention to what the teacher says, *responding appropriately* even when engaged in activity, and show an ability to follow instructions involving several ideas or actions.

(DfE, 2021:12, emphasis ours)

There are several key words and phrases which are contentious. What does 'regulate their behaviour accordingly' mean? According to whom? This vague statement is unhelpful and open to interpretation. The next bullet point says, 'control their immediate impulses when appropriate' – when is it appropriate to control them? From a child's perspective, is it when the teacher is talking? When my friend takes my toy? Or when I want to run around inside? This sounds more like compliance! Assessing if children are able to 'wait for what they want' might open the doorway to some children being made to wait inappropriately at times, and if a teacher needs to assess if they can respond 'appropriately even when engaged in activity', the easiest way to check this is to interrupt the children's play even when they are deeply involved. Fisher (2016) warns against this – she suggests adults should be interacting not interfering. So the ELG, sadly, feels like a very top-down model focused on traditional chalk-and-talk methods.

In addition, children will 'show an understanding of their own feelings and those of others' – this in itself is a very difficult task. It requires a high level of empathy and the ability to know that others have thoughts and feelings that are different to the child's own. We know adults who find this difficult! When considered in the light of child development, this is assessing them on something that could be developmentally beyond the reach of many children.

The good news – and an important point to note – is that the ELGs should not be used as a curriculum in themselves. There are so many more rich experiences that are crucial to child development. So educators can and must focus on what we believe is right for young children and not feel constrained to teach to the ELGs. In addition, as the end of phase assessment, those teaching younger children should not be referring to the goal at all. It is our hope that this book will widen educators' understanding about self-regulation and help them to define it in a much broader way and ensure their practice is developmentally appropriate.

Redefining 'self' in self-regulation

A key thing to understand is that, although the term *self-regulation* has the word *self* in it, understanding the concept in terms of 'self' is misleading because it implies that it is something that children do alone or for themselves. It is not and, actually, it is the opposite of that! Imagine that as an adult you joined a class that aimed to raise your self-esteem. One evening you attend the class and admit to feeling unworthy and having a poor self-image. The leader of the group responds by saying to you, 'Please leave this class and wait outside until you can recognise the beauty in yourself – then you can rejoin the group!'

We may laugh at the preposterous notion of this scenario, but this is what is happening on a daily basis in our schools and in settings when children find self-regulation difficult. Children are being told to leave or given time on the sidelines to watch their peers for a couple of minutes until they are calm enough to rejoin the group. This is totally inappropriate practice and has no place in early childhood education. So, in the same way that we wouldn't dream of asking someone to raise their own self-esteem, we shouldn't be expecting children (or adults) to be able to fully develop self-regulation on their own. Supporting the development of children's self-regulation is part and parcel of the adult's role, which is linked with children's social development and explored more throughout the book. We need to redefine the 'self' part of self-regulation in order to emphasise the role of others, and we need to adopt a whole new ethos around how we, as educators, respond to children.

Outline of book

Self-regulation can be misunderstood by early years educators and those working within early childhood education when it is only equated with managing behaviour or self-control, and this is not the whole story. This book aims to explore the many facets of self-regulation, linking with research and offering ideas of how it may look in practice. Each chapter is organised to include case studies, practical application and a conclusion with three reflective questions to enable critical reflection on our practice.

For the purposes of this book, we are using the term *settings* very broadly to encompass all schools as well as private, voluntary and independent settings and childminding establishments, and we are referring to all adults who work alongside children as *educators*, regardless of their level of qualification or experience. If we refer to *parents* we mean to be inclusive of birth parents and the main carers of a child, which could refer to foster carers, grandparents or step-parents, to name a few.

In order to include examples of what each aspect of self-regulation might look like in practice, we have gathered stories, anecdotes and case studies from colleagues, parents and early years educators who have an interest in this area. We are aware of the ethics involved with using material written about children and, unless we have specific permission to use real names, we have used pseudonyms to protect their identities. Wherever possible, children and their parents have also been consulted about the use of any case-study material or photographs. We have attempted to consider representation so that this book contains not only our own viewpoints but shares the perspectives and lived-experiences of others. We have also respected anonymity when colleagues have asked not to be named.

It is widely documented that stress has a negative impact on our brains and ability to function. The way we react and learn to respond when stressed may make all the difference to a child. Chapter 1 considers the development of self-regulation and puts it in the context of neurological development and other research. It considers emotional dysregulation in more detail and how we can promote emotional literacy in our settings and schools. It also briefly outlines the clear benefits for children in developing self-regulation.

Chapter 2 considers self-regulation within ECEC from a variety of international perspectives. It would be impossible to consider how self-regulation is developed in every country, so this chapter provides a flavour of this and shares an interesting case study about how one child was supported in an international school. The clear message from reading different international perspectives is the importance of embedding self-regulation into a whole school/setting approach.

In terms of their sense of self, children need to have high self-esteem and self-awareness, which is not really a skill but more a way of being so that they feel OK in themselves and ready to learn. This links with wellbeing and will be partly determined by their previous experiences and the way adults have responded to and met their needs in the past. Therefore, we need to be aware if children have experienced any Adverse Childhood Experiences (ACEs) and how we can use a trauma-and-attachment-aware approach to support them. Chapter 3 links to wellbeing, emotional development, a loving pedagogy and emotional warmth and attachment. It considers how children develop self-esteem and become self-aware, which in turn helps them to self-regulate.

Young children experience many big feelings and emotions and do not always know what the feelings are and how they should respond. They can be impulsive and reactive or lose control easily – in fact, we all can at times! We need to support children to help them understand their feelings and emotions and teach them how to react and respond when they feel that way. So we can use an emotion-coaching approach to label, acknowledge and validate their feelings whilst role-modelling or coaching to help them know how to cope. Teaching a child, for example, that it's OK to feel angry, but it's not OK to lash out and hit someone when they feel that way. Chapter 4 builds on Chapter 3 as it links with understanding feelings and emotional resilience and explores behaviour in terms of control and inhibiting responses.

Executive function is a term that has been around for a while and is now being used more and more in association with self-regulation. It relates to skills like decision-making or formulating and executing plans. It involves having a good working memory and being able to problem-solve, organise and prioritise. The ability to delay gratification or wait for a reward is also part of executive function, and research has demonstrated links between children who can delay gratification and cognitive development and intelligence. Chapter 5 explores executive function, Theory of Mind (ToM) and metacognition, and it considers expectations placed upon children whilst linking to theory and research. It also looks at how developing self-regulation can improve metacognition and offer opportunities for children to make decisions and problem-solve.

Chapter 6 thinks about skills relating to listening, maintaining focus and attention and questions the developmental appropriateness of insisting on this. We need to teach children to listen to others in an active way, which requires a response from the listener. A great way to teach this is by role-modelling active listening ourselves and allowing children a voice in our settings and schools. If children feel listened to, they are more likely to learn how to listen themselves. In addition, maintaining focus and attention as well as being able to ignore distractions are important skills – they are about children's levels of engagement and involvement in play. Chapter 6 expands on the idea that if we want children to maintain focus and attention, we need to start with their interests and fascinations and get them engaged in learning through our provision. We also need to foster the characteristics of effective teaching and learning and help children to be resilient, have a 'can do' attitude and persist in the face of difficulty, which will also help them to maintain focus and attention so that, even when they face challenges, they will endure, persevere and keep going.

Children grow up as part of a family, community and society. Chapter 7 puts self-regulation in the context of social development and developing social confidence. It links to theory in terms of social constructivism and sociocultural approaches and offers ideas of how to practise self-regulation skills through play and playful interactions, such as role play, sociodramatic play and rough and tumble. It also explores how young children develop empathy and offers ideas of how we can promote empathy through our interactions.

Research has shown that developing secure attachments and building strong relationships is an essential part of the role of the educator within ECEC. Chapter 8 explores the role of the adult in supporting children's self-regulation and focuses on the importance of becoming a co-regulator in addition to providing an enabling environment. It also considers how low arousal environments may support children when they feel overwhelmed. The chapter finishes by sharing about one school that has adopted a restorative ethos as part of their approach to co-regulation.

Parents have a difficult job in raising children in today's society. Despite living in a social world, parenting can be isolating, and many parents are unsure of the best approach to adopt when supporting their children's behaviour. Chapter 9 considers how we can enable parents to support their children in developing self-regulation. It offers some specific strategies and shares various ideas from a number of different perspectives.

The final chapter sums up the book, summarising our key findings and drawing themes together. Lastly, this chapter offers ways forward for practitioners and recommendations in relation to policy and ethos. It is our hope that this book will enable us, as educators, to better understand the complex skills and aspects that make up self-regulation so that we have developmentally appropriate expectations for our children, feel confident in our roles as co-regulators and adopt an ethos within which children will thrive.

Our mission

Self-regulation is sometimes narrowly framed within the way we approach behaviour in our schools and settings. We argue that, although our ability to self-regulate will have an impact on our behaviour, it is broader and wider than this. All behaviour is communication, and the way we respond and react to children is key – whether they are trying to solve a problem, they are learning how to turn an error into something more intentional or good or they are recognising that their actions and words have an impact on others. Educators are there to enable children to express their feelings as well as to support their needs and wants, and, as such, self-regulation is more about an approach to education or an ethos that underpins our whole practice, which should not be limited within discussions around behaviour. Tamsin links our ethos with adopting a loving pedagogy (Grimmer, 2021), because part and parcel of this approach is being child-centred, which is explored a little more in Chapter 3.

The more we have researched self-regulation, the more we believe we should invite educators to review their whole ethos and raison d'être. Although there are skills involved in relation to how children develop self-regulation, it isn't really about the children – it's about how the educators respond and facilitate the ethos they foster. Are we a school or setting where children feel able to make mistakes, nurtured, accepted, free to ask questions and express their feelings and learn to discover who they are? Do we encourage children to develop resilience and persist when the going gets tough? Are we role-modelling how to act and react when we face challenges or when we do not get our own way? Chapter 2 shares the story of an international school whose ethos from kindergarten upwards is grounded in self-regulation. They are seeing the advantages and benefits of this methodology unfold in older classes in terms of how children approach their own learning.

In their book on emotion coaching, Gilbert, Gus and Rose remind us that we are building the citizens of tomorrow:

> It is important that today's children, who will be tomorrow's society, have the skills and knowledge to understand that we all have emotions and they are natural and

normal. They need to recognize emotions in themselves and others and in doing so manage emotions more effectively to problem-solve and engage with others.

(2021:12)

For the sake of our children's futures and for wider society as a whole, we must support children in developing self-regulation. This book aims to equip us, as educators, so that we are ready, willing and able to respond to this challenge. This is our mission, should we choose to accept it!

References

Adolphs, R. & Anderson, D. (2018) *The Neuroscience of Emotion: A New Synthesis.* Princeton, NJ: Princeton University Press.

Asquith, S, (2020) *Self-regulation Skills in Young Children: Activities and Strategies for Practitioners and Parents.* London: Jessica Kingsley.

Bodrova, E. & Germeroth C. (2013) 'Play and Self-Regulation Lessons from Vygotsky', *American Journal of Play, 6*(1), pp. 111–123.

Conkbayir, M. (2020) 'Self Regulation in Early Years'. *Foundation Stage Forum.* Available at https://eyfs.info/articles.html/personal-social-and-emotional-development/self-regulation-in-early-years-r283.

Conkbayir, M. (2021) '*Self-Regulation in Early Years* course'. *Mine Conkbayir Consultancy.* Available at https://mineconkbayir.co.uk/online-programme/self-regulation-in-early-years.

Department for Education (DfE) (2021) *Statutory framework for the Early Years Foundation Stage.* Available at https://assets.publishing.service.gov.uk/government/uploads/system/uploads/attachment_data/file/974907/EYFS_framework_-_March_2021.pdf.

Eisenberg, N., Smith, C., & Spinrad, T. (2011) 'Effortful control – relations with emotion regulation, adjustment, and socialization in childhood', in K. Vohs & R. Baumeister (Eds.), *Handbook of self-regulation* (pp. 263–283). New York: Guilford Press.

Fisher, J. (2016) *Interacting or Interfering?: Improving interactions in the early years.* London: Open University Press.

Gilbert, L., Gus, L., & Rose, J. (2021) *Emotion Coaching with Children and Young People in Schools: Promoting Positive Behavior, Wellbeing and Resilience.* London: Jessica Kingsley.

Grimmer, T. (2021) *Developing a Loving Pedagogy in the Early Years: How Love Fits with Professional Practice.* London: Routledge.

Robson, D., Allen, M., & Howard, S. (2020) 'Self-regulation in childhood as a predictor of future outcomes: A meta-analytic review', *Psychological Bulletin, 146*(4), pp. 324–354.

Rosanbalm, K. & Murray, D. (2017) *Promoting Self-Regulation in Early Childhood: A Practice Brief.* OPRE Brief #2017-79. Washington, DC: Office of Planning, Research, and Evaluation, Administration for Children and Families, US Department of Health and Human Services.

Shanker, S., Hopkins, S., & Davidson, S. (2015) *Self-Regulation: A Discussion Paper for Goodstart Early Learning in Australia.* Peterborough, ON: The MEHRIT Centre LTD.

Vink, M., Gladwin, T., Geeraerts, S. Pas, P., Bos, D., Hofstee, M., Durston, S., & Vollebergh, W. (2020) 'Towards an integrated account of the development of self-regulation from a neurocognitive perspective: A framework for current and future longitudinal multi-modal investigations', *Developmental Cognitive Neuroscience, 45*, pp. 1–9. doi: 10.1016/j.dcn.2020.100829.

1 Development of self-regulation

Tamsin Grimmer

Introduction

Young children are learning how to respond when they have big feelings and emotions – for them, this is a marathon not a sprint. It will take a lifetime of learning, and even when they are adults there will be times when they lose control or feel overwhelmed with emotion. Our role in the early years is to help children as they embark on this journey of self-regulation and to walk alongside them helping to prepare them for independence.

At birth, babies find it difficult to regulate their emotional states, although they may be able to turn their heads away and cry to express discomfort, they predominantly rely on their primary caregivers to soothe and calm them through rocking, stroking and holding (Hrabok & Kerns, 2010). However, by about three months a baby can begin to be distracted when upset, and after four months they can usually self-soothe by calming themselves down, allowing themselves to fall asleep, sucking their thumb/fingers, rubbing their eyes or using a dummy/pacifier, special toy or blanket. This is the beginning of self-regulation, and there is a correlation between babies who are able to self-soothe and predictable caregiving with responsive parents, who are often mothers due to the ages of the children involved (Mohr et al., 2019). By the end of a child's first year, babies can distract themselves and maintain attention, which also fits under the umbrella term *self-regulation*. As they are generally on the move by this stage, they can also physically remove themselves from any stimuli they find unpleasant and move towards things they like or are attracted to.

During their preschool years, as they grow and develop their physical, cognitive and language skills, children become more intentional in their behaviour and perhaps less reliant on the influence of their carers (Hrabok & Kerns, 2010). They gain more understanding about their emotions and are increasingly able to use language to express their feelings as well as their needs and wants. They also start to problem-solve and begin

DOI: 10.4324/9781003162346-2

to develop Theory of Mind, recognising that other people have thoughts and feelings too.

There is a misconception that self-soothing means leaving a baby to cry so that they can soothe themselves. However, research has found that children need to be responded to quickly and consistently in order to learn that they are safe and well (Richter, 2004). Recent research by Bilgin and Wolke (2020) questions this, as they found no adverse behavioural development and attachment at 18 months of age if a child was sometimes left to 'cry it out' within the first six months of life. However, their research has been widely critiqued and challenged, and the long-term impact of a 'cry it out' strategy as well as their methodology are questionable due to the wealth of contradictory research available (Davis & Kramer, 2021; Mohr et al., 2019). There is also an abundance of research that indicates the negative impact that both stress and insecure attachments have on our brains (Jarvis, 2020), and allowing a child to cry could contribute to toxic stress. It is our view that educators need to respond to babies and children promptly and consistently, demonstrating warmth and love, to help co-regulate their emotions and avoid them feeling dysregulated and stressed.

Emotional dysregulation

We've all had days when something happens on our way to work – perhaps we have a difficult phone call, or we have to wait in a queue for ages when trying to ring our bank, or we have just heard some bad news about a friend's diagnosis – and we become dysregulated ourselves. This rubs off on others too. When we've had a difficult day, we can sometimes come home and snap at our children, or we can be oversensitive and overreact to something our partner says, which might cause a row. All of us – children and adults alike – are not immune to feeling emotionally dysregulated.

When a child is able to self-regulate, they are calm, feel at ease, tend to have a higher sense of wellbeing and generally feel OK. They are also ready to learn. The opposite of this is when a child is dysregulated and does not feel calm or OK. They may appear 'out of sorts', angry, upset, fearful, worried or perhaps even unbalanced. They will also have a lower level of wellbeing. Understandably, they will not be ready to learn.

Emotional dysregulation is a term sometimes used within the mental-health community to refer to people whose responses do not lie within the usual range of emotive responses. Emotional dysregulation in childhood is often associated with mental-health issues later in life – for example, attachment disorder, Autistic Spectrum Condition, ADHD, bipolar disorder or PTSD. There are also specific groups of children who might have experienced trauma or ACEs or who have neurodevelopmental disorders that will struggle with emotional dysregulation. However, all of us are emotionally dysregulated at times, and young children in particular find it difficult to deal with their emotions. So, for the purposes of this book, we are thinking about emotional dysregulation broadly with the intention of supporting children with or without a specific diagnosis.

When we feel dysregulated we are unable to think rationally and feel overwhelmed with emotion. This is true for all of us, adults included. It's important to distinguish that we are not talking about a group of children who are disobedient or who cannot sit still. We can all be dysregulated at times, and it is really important to begin with this premise. This is not misbehaviour. It is a natural response to feeling overwhelmed, out of control or emotional. Everyone feels like this sometimes. When we consider how to respond, we are thinking about strategies to support all of the children and adults in a setting or school – ourselves included.

This is not something to feel guilty or worried about. In fact, our brains all respond to stress in the same way. If we can better understand some of the causes of emotional dysregulation in our everyday lives, we can think more preventatively, and we can be proactive rather than reactive in our responses.

Ways of responding to dysregulation in children:

- Remain calm.

- Acknowledge, accept and validate the child's feelings.

- Label the emotions involved.

- Become a behaviour detective (Grimmer, 2022) and try to find out why the child is feeling this way.

- Consider how to help the child feel calmer.

- Adopt an emotion-coaching, problem-solving approach.

What is going on in our brains?

The part of our brain that is mainly responsible for emotions is the limbic system. It is sometimes referred to as the 'emotional brain' (OECD, 2007). The limbic system consists of several structures, including the amygdala, basal ganglia, cingulate gyrus, hippocampus, hypothalamus and thalamus. Conkbayir (2017) points out that when we begin to consider the limbic system, the link between our emotions and our brain becomes really clear. The OECD explains that emotions are "complex reactions generally described in terms of three components: a particular mental state, a physiological change and an impulsion to act" (2007:25). Emotional dysregulation is actually the way that our brains respond to feeling stressed.

When we are calm and we experience the world using our senses, this information is received by the thalamus, the part of the brain that acts like an air traffic controller, and it sends the information to the thinking part of the brain, called the cerebrum, then on to the amygdala, which translates this thinking into actions and emotions. Siegel and Bryson (2012) call this the 'upstairs brain'. At this point we are able to think before we act, make decisions, have empathy for others and, most importantly, we are in control.

When we are stressed, we are undergoing changes or transitions or we are in a conflict situation, the brain reacts differently. We go into survival mode and the freeze, fight or flight response kicks in. What is happening is our thalamus is receiving information as usual, but it goes on red-alert and straight into action. So, information is sent directly to the amygdala, bypassing the thinking part of our brain! Goleman (1996) calls this the 'amygdala hijacking', as it has taken control. The downstairs brain (Siegel & Bryson, 2012) is now in control. We act before we think and have overpowering emotions. Physiologically, we also have increased adrenaline and cortisol. It is not possible to rationalise and think in this high emotional state. It is worth pointing out that some research (Feldman-Barrett, 2017) challenges the simplistic view of a two-system brain (one where we are in control and another where we are not); however, we find it helpful in making a difficult concept relatable and easier to comprehend.

Everyone's brains react in this way, and, as adults, we have many opportunities to learn strategies for how to respond – for example, we become practised at taking a deep breath or ringing our best friend to let off steam. However, most young children will not have learned how to deal with these feelings yet, so they can appear emotionally dysregulated more often than others. Children who are emotionally immature, who have experienced Adverse Childhood Experiences (ACEs) or who are neurodiverse – for example, those who have autism, ADHD, dyspraxia or dyslexia – will also appear more dysregulated than others. We need to recognise that this is a natural response and use calming techniques with children before we can begin to resolve any issues.

The best way to calm children down is to get to know them really well – then we will know how to respond appropriately. Some children may need time and space away from others to calm down, whilst others may need us to cuddle up and read them a story. When we know our children emotionally, we will interact and respond sensitively.

Here are a few calming techniques to try:

- Provide calm spaces, dens, tents or cosy corners where children can escape busy settings.

- Teach children breathing exercises, such as counting whilst breathing in and out, blowing out candles on a birthday cake or tracing a spiral whilst breathing in and out.

- Encourage children to lie down on their backs with a teddy on their tummy and invite them to watch the teddy rise and fall as they breathe – can they make teddy go even higher?

- Sing songs or engage in action rhymes to help children breathe regularly and regulate their heart rate.

- Count together, as this also necessitates regular breathing and offers distraction and something to focus on.

- Play calming music and allow the children to move about or lie down to listen.

- Provide resources that have a calming effect, such as fiddle toys, liquid timers, lava lamps or bubble tubes.

- Encourage children to talk about how they feel using stories, books or photos of emotions.

- Cuddle up for a story or offer a big hug if a child needs one – being held closely helps us to feel calm, safe and secure.

- Engage in sensory activities, such as playing with lavender-scented playdough or making potions in a mud kitchen.

- Encourage children to play outside, where they can be as active and noisy as they please.

- Teach children grounding techniques, such as think about 5 things we can see, 4 things we can touch, 3 things we can hear, 2 things we can smell and 1 thing we can taste.

- Engage in mindfulness or yoga activities, which help children feel calm.

- Provide worry dolls or worry monsters that children can use to share any concerns they have with others (see Chapter 8).

- Help children talk about their feelings and emotions as well as how we can act when we feel a certain way.

- Dim the lights and limit the noise in the room, as this can help everyone feel calmer.

Yoga – Marlis Juerging-Coles, St John's Pre-School

We practice yoga at the pre-school, supporting children to become aware of their own bodies, their breathing and paying attention to how their environ-ment feels. The teacher also shares some sessions via the pre-school's Facebook page so that children can watch again at home. This little girl is using one of the yoga lessons to practice her breathing and self-regulation.

Theory of constructed emotion

Tamsin recently read an interesting book called *How Emotions are Made* (Feldman Barrett, 2017), which looks at emotions in a different light. Rather than emotions being like a reflex, with physiological effects based on past experiences and designed for survival, emotions are constructed by our brains. Or, rather, our brains are constructing the way we experience emotions. Feldman Barrett explains that we experience the same sort of symptoms for different types of emotions – for example, we might have an increased heart rate, flushed face and knots in our stomach when we feel very sad, but we could also experience the same thing when we feel really happy or nervous! Emotions and emotional responses do not have some sort of universal fingerprint that is understood across all international boundaries and cultures, instead they are created and constructed as the child grows and develops.

Feldman Barrett's research suggests that if we hear a loud bang, rather than a triggered response causing us to feel fear, our brain is actually making predictions based on past experiences, helping to explain what we experience with our senses (2017). Just like a scientist making a hypothesis, our brain is continually making best guesses and testing these predictions. Sometimes the prediction is correct, which reinforces the prediction, and sometimes our brain makes an error, and we learn from that too. Another important point that Feldman Barrett makes is that it is through naming these emotions that we aid learning. Our brains learn emotion concepts by grouping together ideas relating to a particular word. For example, when a child looks upset because another child has taken a toy, we might say, "You look upset" or "Is everything OK? I wonder if you are upset because Sarah is playing with your car?" So, we're naming the emotion, and the child's brain will then categorise that information, remembering the feeling, facial expression, tone of voice and behavioural actions so that in the future they will recognise the combination as 'upset'. As children grow older they will develop their concept of 'upset' to include other manifestations, e.g., crying or feeling sad.

With this in mind, the theory of constructed emotions suggests that there is a wealth of variation in how emotions are experienced. For example, we might love our own children very differently compared to how we love our partners or how we love the children we care for, but these different types of love are no less loving than each other (Grimmer, 2021). Feeling afraid of a large dog growling is a very different than feeling afraid whilst on a rollercoaster. They are both the same emotion – fear – despite differences in facial expressions, autonomic nervous system responses and the way we react. In order to construct an emotion, our brain is using knowledge of past experiences, in terms of how we felt and reacted, and then predicting and categorising the new sensory input in a best-fit way to assign it to an emotional category (Siegel et al., 2018).

Children are learning that there is variation in how we experience emotions and that there are varying degrees of emotions and words to describe emotions. They learn the subtle differences within an emotion category – for example, rage, scorn, vengeance or irritation could all come under the umbrella of 'anger' (Feldman Barrett, 2017). "Emotion words hold the key to understanding how children learn emotion concepts" (Feldman Barrett, 2017:102). Every time we label emotions and provide a running commentary of how we are feeling, we help our children better understand these emotions. This fits with Siegel's 'Name it to tame it' idea (Siegel & Bryson, 2012). He suggests that we can use storytelling and words to help children cope with their big emotions. He shares ideas such as talking about the emotional event, drawing a picture, writing about it (if the child is old enough) or simply naming and explaining the emotions involved. "It's important for kids of all ages to tell their stories, as it helps them try to understand their emotions and the events that occur in their lives" (Siegel & Bryson, 2012:29). So, if a child watches a television programme and feels scared, rather than dismissing the emotions and saying, "Don't worry you're safe," we would say, "That was a bit scary, I don't think you liked that part of the programme." Likewise, if a child falls over while playing outside, instead of saying, "Up you get, you're OK," we would acknowledge their feelings and say, "Oh no! You fell over, that must have hurt." We consider these ideas in more detail in Chapter 4 when we look at emotion coaching.

Supporting a child – Lisa Tidy, Mulberry Bush Pre-School

I spotted a child who had taken himself off to a quiet corner on the carpet. He looked sad and had his knees tucked up to his chest. Another member of staff then explained to me out of the child's earshot that the child was upset because the snack table was full.

I went and laid down on the carpet in front of the child and said, "I can see you look sad." He nodded. "Is it because the snack table is full?"

"Yes," he replied.

I then demonstrated I understood by saying, "Feeling like there is no room for you at the table has made you feel sad." He relaxed his legs and crossed them.

"Would you like to have your snack when there is room at the table?" I asked him.

"Yes," he replied.

I then spotted a space that had become available. "Look, now there is a space. Would you like to go and wash your hands and have your snack now?"

"Yes," he said with a small smile. He got up, washed his hands and had his snack.

I recently read a book called *Creating Loving Attachments* (Golding & Hughes, 2012), and it talks through the importance of using PACE [playfulness, acceptance, curiosity and empathy] to help understand and work with children and their emotions. It made me aware of how important it is to not automatically go into 'sort out the problem' mode but to first take time to understand how the child is feeling and acknowledge their emotions before dealing with the issue.

In the case study Lisa shares how she acknowledged the child's feelings before attempting to deal with the child's problem. She talked through the situation and named the child's emotions, and once she did so, she saw that he began to relax and eventually joined in with the group again. Lisa's strategy used playfulness, acceptance, curiosity and empathy – or, PACE, an acronym coined by Hughes (Golding & Hughes, 2012) and an approach used regularly in attachment and trauma-aware practice, particularly in the field of fostering and adoption. The PACE concept is explored further in Chapter 4.

Research is growing daily in the area of neuroscience and how it relates to emotions, and we do not claim to understand these difficult concepts. We are trying to relate – to the best of our ability – what we are learning to practice, however, as Adolphs and Anderson (2018) remind us, there is still so much to learn and understand about how emotions are created in our brains.

Vagus nerve

The vagus nerve is actually the longest nerve in the body, and its primary function is to convey information from our brain to most of our vital organs. Interestingly, the term *vaga* comes from the Latin for 'wandering', and we could see the vagus nerve as wandering from the brain stem to many different parts of the body. This nerve is the main component of the parasympathetic nervous system, which, amongst other things, is in charge of helping us rest and relax. It helps to calm our heart rate and breathing when we are under stress. Researchers talk about increasing our vagal tone, which enables our bodies to relax faster after experiencing stress:

> We use the term "vagal tone" to describe a person's ability to regulate the involuntary physiological processes of the autonomic nervous system. Just as kids with good muscle tone excel at sports, kids with high vagal tone excel at responding to and recovering from emotional stress. The heart rates of such autonomic athletes will temporarily accelerate in response to some alarm or excitement, for example. But as soon as the emergency is over, their bodies are able to recover quickly. These children are good at soothing themselves, focusing their attention, and inhibiting action when that's what's called for.
>
> (Gottman, 1997:39)

Gottman's research, which we will return to in Chapter 4 when considering emotion coaching, found that children with a high vagal tone were good at self-soothing, calming themselves, inhibiting impulses if necessary and focusing their attention, which are all elements of self-regulation. This has implications for us as educators, as these children will be able to bounce back after difficulties, persevere in their learning or cope with any arguments that naturally arise during the day.

Educators need to teach children to be emotionally literate and talk through conflicts using an emotion-coaching approach. Of course, there are other influences that will impact on a child's ability to cope with life, such as their temperament and their home environment, including their interactions with parents and carers (Gottman, 1997), however, educators can have a direct impact on children by teaching discrete skills and providing an emotionally literate environment. Chapter 8 expands on these ideas and explores the role of the adult in supporting children's self-regulatory skills.

Interoception

When we feel big emotions, it is our sense of interoception – the body's internal system responsible for interpreting our senses and sensory input – that helps us feel this way. The vagus nerve is involved, however, if we are hungry or tired, our sense of interoception helps us interpret the feeling. Interoception also enables us to feel pleasure, pain or discomfort, notice when we are full after a meal or need the toilet, and this sense is still developing in young children. Schaan et al. (2019) noticed that very little research had investigated the development of interoception in young children, so they studied whether children between the ages of four and six years could consciously notice their increased heart rate after completing ten jumping jacks. This was to ascertain interoceptive accuracy. Their findings suggest that the older the child, the more accurately they could sense an increased heart rate and, thus, the more in touch they were with their interoceptive sense. Interestingly, they also looked into children's emotional regulation and whether or not children with a better interoceptive sense could also better regulate their emotions. They found that "children who are oversensitive to internal bodily changes, as suggested by higher self-reported changes in heart rate, may also experience emotions more intensely, thus requiring particular effort to regulate their emotions" (Schaan et al., 2019:53). This means that if a child is overly sensitive to sensory input, they will find self-regulation more difficult.

This makes sense because children who have sensory processing issues may find it more difficult to tell whether they are hot or cold, or they may experience pain differently. They are often the children who are dysregulated and find it hardest to know how to deal with their big emotions. This is also true for some neurodiverse children – for example, if Tamsin brushes past one of her daughters (diagnosed with Autism Spectrum Condition), she will exclaim, "Mummy, why did you push me?"

Her interoceptive sense is not responding in a typical way, and she is very sensitive to touch.

Many of the children we work with will be sensitive to sensory input, whether noise, light, touch or even smell. They may – or may not – have additional needs or a diagnosis, but they will all need educators who are sensitive to their needs and who try to help them with their sensory awareness. The Department for Education in South Australia (2021) published some interesting materials for educators about interoception, so their website is worth a look.

One strategy we can use to help children develop their interoceptive skills is to encourage them to notice what happens to their bodies when they feel a certain way. Many educators and parents use a scale with the children, which can be displayed or referenced when the child is overly emotional. These scales are easily adapted to suit the ages and stages of development of the children in our care – for example, by adding pictures. Tamsin references one of these – aimed at supporting a younger child with anger – in her book *Calling All Superheroes* (Grimmer, 2019).

My emotional responses scale – Childminder

We created this scale to use with children in our setting who struggle to regulate their emotions. It covers how they feel and what is happening in their bodies. It also reminds us how we can help and what children can do to help themselves. In the past we have used similar scales with younger children that include pictures and fewer words.

Scale	How do I feel?	What is happening to my body?	What can I do and how can you help me?
5	I am out of control. I feel like I am going to explode. I want to scream and hit or run away.	I am in freeze, flight or fight mode and my downstairs brain has taken control. I cannot feel my body's signals. My hands are clenched. I might lash out or run away.	I need to calm down. I need to move into a safe space or hide. Dim the lights, reduce noise. Give me space and time.
4	I am getting very emotional and am starting to lose it.	My body is tense, I might go red in the face and breathe faster. I will find it difficult to listen.	Take 10 deep breaths. Help me focus on breathing. I need to walk away or hide to have a break.
3	I feel a little out of control or over excited.	Heart rate increases. My voice gets louder and my words more urgent.	I need to do something calmer. A drink and snack may help. I may want to cuddle my favourite soft toy or blanket.
2	I feel a little worried or frustrated.	My breathing gets shallow and my heart starts pumping faster.	I need to be careful not to get overwhelmed. I might need to take a break.
1	I feel good. I'm completely in control. I'm happy.	I am relaxed and my body is calm. My upstairs brain is in control. My breathing and heartbeat are regular.	I can have fun, smile and enjoy myself.

Stress and stressors

If we accept that, generally speaking, self-regulation is about how we respond to the many stresses we encounter in everyday life, it is helpful to consider what these stressors are and when we might feel stressed. Shanker (2021) suggests stressors exist in five domains: biological, emotional, cognitive, social and pro-social. In an educational context biological stressors include a lack of natural light, bright lights, loud noises, having to sit too still, sensations of hunger or tiredness or simply being in the busy classroom environment. Emotional stressors include feelings of overexcitement, fear or anxiety or changes to routine. Cognitive stressors that might arise include experiencing information overload or a lack of intellectual stimulation leading to boredom, having a poor working memory, feeling confused or unable to grasp concepts, being interrupted or learning something new. Stressors in the social domain include being told what to do, disagreeing with others, being left out or rejected, bullying or being bullied, missing or misunderstanding social cues, experiencing peer pressure or having no one to play with. Lastly, pro-social stressors could include finding it hard to cope with the stress of others, feeling empathy or a lack of empathy, trying to please others, being late, having a strong sense of injustice and feeling unable to help to solve problems.

Shanker (2021) suggests we adopt the following five-step process in order to deal with these stressors and help children self-regulate:

1. Read the signs of stress and reframe the behaviour.

2. Recognize the stressors.

3. Reduce the stress.

4. Reflect: enhance stress awareness.

5. Respond and restore energy.

These five steps remind us of the import role that adults play in supporting children through stressful situations and talking to children about their feelings and ways of responding. The five domains of stressors help us to view children more holistically so that we consider all aspects of their environments as well as their individual situations.

When considering the various stressors that a child may be subject to, we need to think about the child, their family circumstances and the environment around them (home and setting). In Tamsin's book, *Supporting Behaviour and Emotions* (Grimmer, 2022), she talks about becoming a behaviour detective – reflecting on children's behaviour and trying to work out why they behave the way they do. She uses the iceberg analogy, which suggests that, for any behaviour, we only really see the tip of the iceberg, and underneath the surface there is a lot more going on. Therefore, we need to try to unpick the behaviour and work out what the child might be trying to communicate.

This iceberg shows the visible behaviours on the surface that express themselves in behaviours, such as screaming, throwing, biting, etc., and the unseen needs under the water level. It suggests possible reasons why children behave the way they do and what they might be communicating – for example, I feel overwhelmed, misunderstood or unhappy.

Tamsin suggests we ask the following questions to help unpick the behaviour:

- Have their basic needs been met, e.g., is the child hungry or tired?

- What is the child trying to tell me?

- Is this child communicating something with us through the way they behave, either consciously or not?

- Why do they do what they do?

- Could this behaviour be evidence of schematic play (repetitive play)?

- Could they be attention/attachment seeking?

- Does their emotional cup need refilling?

- Do they enjoy behaving that way?

- Do they like my response?

- Are they frustrated or feeling misunderstood?

- What is this child hoping to achieve through this behaviour?

- Has this behaviour been triggered by anything?

- What happened prior to this child behaving in this way?

- Has anything different happened at home?

- Is this behaviour a result of social interaction?

- Can we try to unpick why this child has acted or reacted in this way?

(Grimmer, 2022:73)

An important starting point, as already mentioned, is knowing our children really well. Early childhood educators can talk fluently about their children, sharing favourite colours, toys, names of pets and so on. However, how many of us know the emotional needs of our children? For example, do we know what helps them calm down or if anything frightens them? When might they get overexcited or anxious? Do they have any objects or resources they use to help themselves feel safe and secure, or is there a particular member of staff they appear to have a strong attachment with? Finding out more of these emotional details will help educators respond sensitively and individually to each child.

Supporting challenging emotions – Early Years Teacher

I previously supported a boy aged between three and four in a foundation-stage class who started presenting some very challenging emotions. We noticed some inconsistencies when he behaved this way. After speaking to each of his divorced parents, they could not think of a reason why some days he was more angry and upset, whilst other days he was fine.

We then began a log of the days he would spend at his mum's house and the behaviour the following day and the behaviour that followed after staying with his father. We found that on the nights he stayed with his mother, his behaviour the next day was very challenging from the minute he stepped foot in the class – for example, he would immediately throw things and knock things off tables, hurting and lashing out at anyone who got in his way. This behaviour was consistent throughout the day until he went home with his dad. On the days following staying with his dad, he would come in like a different child – caring, helping other children, engaging in the lessons and learning.

This finding led us to involve the safeguarding team, and we discovered that the boy did not like his mum's boyfriend. It transpired that her boyfriend often joked around and, thinking it was funny, provoked the boy, which was clearly having an impact on his behaviour.

We then developed a wide range of strategies to try and help him to have a better day and manage his emotions, working with him to help him understand how he can help himself to regulate these. We created a "calming box" containing a range of toys, such as a squidgy stress ball, a fluffy teddy and a few other sensory toys that he could squeeze and manipulate. This was stored in the book corner where there was also a mirror and, displayed on the wall, pictures demonstrating different emotions. He was encouraged to point to the emotion he was feeling. Once he was calm, a member of staff asked him about his feelings, using the pictures as a prompt.

After doing this a few times, the boy was able to take himself to the corner and to use the calm-down box to regulate his own emotions until he felt able to return and join in the lesson. On a number of occasions he would put his hand up and say, "I need to go to the book corner," and take himself there. This was a big step, as before he would just get overwhelmed, and it would have passed the point of return with his anger and upset.

At the start of the year he was a very upset and angry little boy. After he was taught how to recognise and control his anger, he was able to use these strategies to self-regulate himself and join in with the learning, something that will help him through the years. What could have been put down as a child simply being naughty was found to be much deeper than that, and it was the emotions underneath that were making him do these things. We helped him identify and understand the emotions and then control them throughout the day.

In addition to the stressors mentioned above, a number of different factors will inhibit children's learning and prevent them from feeling OK – for example, family circumstances, illness and, sadly, abuse and neglect. Children may have life-changing experiences during their time with us – for example, they may move house, have a new sibling, lose a loved one or need to deal with parental separation or divorce. Many of these experiences could be described as ACEs – Adverse Childhood Experiences, which are explored in more detail in Chapter 3. As educators, we support children through these challenges and do our best to equip children with the skills necessary to recover, which is where supporting self-regulation comes into play.

Emotional intelligence

Goleman defines emotional intelligence as "abilities such as being able to motivate oneself and persist in the face of frustrations; to control impulse and delay gratification; to regulate one's moods and keep distress from swamping the ability to think; to empathize and to hope" (1996:36). This reads in a very similar way to our understanding of self-regulation, and we propose that emotionally intelligent people are self-regulated people and vice versa. Goleman moves beyond thinking about intelligence in terms of cognitive development or IQ and suggests that we also have an emotional dimension to our intelligence that determines how we feel about situations. As educators, we have a role to play in growing the emotional intelligence of our children through promoting their understanding of emotions, naming and labelling feelings and providing an emotionally literate environment (as discussed in Chapter 8).

Promoting emotional intelligence – Nawal Filali, College Green Nursery School & Services

Our vision at College Green is to inspire a life-long love for learning and empower children to be compassionate, resilient and distinctively remarkable.

One of the ways we support children to understand their emotions is to use stories, such as *The Colour Monster* (Llenas, 2015). In the book black is associated with fear, and we change this to grey because we really didn't want black to be associated with negative language.

We created an interactive display on emotions, linking to the children's interests in superheroes. We extended language by introducing alternative emotions, and then children copied the facial expressions using mirrors. This was also teaching them how to read the emotions of others.

The children helped make this display by choosing those facial expressions and labelling the emotions together.

Supporting self-regulation

There are many ways we can support children to develop self-regulation skills and become more emotionally intelligent. The following chapters explore many of these ideas in more detail, however, this general list provides an overview of the key strategies we can use:

- Developing a loving pedagogy and being trauma and attachment aware.

- Being proactive not reactive.

- Becoming a behaviour detective and trying to work out what children are communicating.

- Acknowledging, validating and labelling children's feelings.

- Using gestures and signs to aid communication and comprehension.

- Adopting an emotion-coaching and problem-solving approach.

- Providing an emotionally literate environment and access to sensory resources and spaces.

- Using calming strategies and mindfulness techniques.

- Role-modelling how to act and react when we feel certain ways.

- Sharing stories and books about emotions.

- Using photographs and images that depict emotions.

- Role-playing scenarios and using puppets and soft toys to express feelings.

Supporting self-regulation skills – Lisa Gibbons, Denmead Infant School

In general, each day is based around supporting all children to develop their self-regulation skills. My last class was unusual, attaining well in the specific areas of learning but not the prime areas of learning. This was a possible result of COVID-19, lockdowns and a lack of opportunities to mix socially and develop emotional skills. We will never know for sure, but we had some work to do with regard to this. Helping the children to understand their emotions and regulate their feelings was not going to happen overnight, and we couldn't expect it to. This was about supporting key parts of their development, and it takes time. Something we found really useful was commenting on our own feelings as adults about a range of situations. Explaining when we felt sad or cross and modelling what to do when we have those feelings. Attuning to the children's feelings and validating them has also been very powerful – labelling and recognising children's feelings for them as well as supporting them in making the right choice. For example, "I can see you are getting cross sharing with Izzy. Sharing is hard. What can we do to make it better?" Having a calm-down space in the classroom has also been supportive for some children – safe space to go and work through some of those feelings. Sometimes we do something else – for example, play with a busy box – until they are calm, then later we come back to the problem and help them work through it. Having clear but simple expectations for behaviour is also helpful – for example, kind hands, kind feet and kind mouth. I'm pleased to say that through a mixture of discrete and incidental teaching of self-regulation we have made big steps forward.

The benefits of self-regulation

There is a wealth of research that demonstrates the positive implications of developing self-regulation – from increased academic achievement to better life outcomes and improved mental health (Robson et al., 2020; Vink et al., 2020; Eisenberg et al., 2011). This may be because self-regulation encompasses many positive dispositions and life skills. For example, children who resist the impulse to lash out when angry and instead use words to express their emotions will learn to manage their big feelings in a peaceful way. And children who are resilient will fare better when faced with adversity because they know how to persevere and get up, brush themselves down and try again. These dispositions are further explored in later chapters. One longitudinal study found that when prevention and early intervention strategies help children with building quality relationships, developing self-control and fostering a positive self-concept, they can better cope with any adverse family circumstances that arise, and this supports them into adulthood (Miller-Lewis et al., 2013).

In addition, as explored in Chapter 5, part of self-regulation is about executive functioning skills that help us operate in everyday life – for example, being organised, able to plan and carry out plans or able to work towards goals. Developing these skills has a positive impact on our lives because they allow us to prioritise and manage our time and the resources available to us to the best of our abilities. Children who are organised fare better in school as they are able to meet the many demands placed upon them (Pozuelos et al., 2019; McClelland & Cameron, 2012).

From reading various research papers (including Robson et al., 2020; Vink et al., 2020; Eisenberg et al., 2011), we listed several of the many benefits that developing self-regulation can bring throughout a child's life into adulthood:

- Increased academic achievement.

- Increased social competency.

- Increased engagement in school.

- Improved mental health.

- Decreased aggression and delinquency.

- Less likely to smoke or abuse substances and alcohol.

- Less likely to engage in criminal activity.

- Less likely to be unemployed.

- Less likely to be obese.

This is an incredible list and almost difficult to believe! However, there is a wealth of research backing up these findings time and time again. As educators, when we support our children in developing self-regulation, we can celebrate that it will have so many added benefits!

Summary

Everyone has days when they feel out of sorts or dysregulated. As adults, we generally know how to cope and overcome these feelings. Young children are still learning what these feelings are and how to respond when they feel that way. This chapter considered aspects of the growing area of neuroscience to help us understand what is happening in our brains and bodies and how we can relate this to our teaching and practice. Although we do not claim to fully understand all aspects of this research, we can see the huge benefits for children who develop self-regulation at a young age, and acknowledge the implications for educators. We can attempt to minimise the various stressors children might experience throughout the day and ensure our practice helps increase vagal tone by offering rest, relaxation and recovery from any stressful moments. In this way we are helping our children develop self-regulation and fulfilling our role as co-regulators. The next chapter considers self-regulation within early childhood education and care from a variety of international perspectives.

Questions for reflection

1. How does our understanding of emotional development impact our practice?

2. To what extent do we explore and understand what children's behaviour is communicating to us?

3. Have we considered the various stressors that our children may experience and taken steps to minimise these?

References

Adolphs R. & Anderson, D. (2018) *The Neuroscience of Emotion: A New Synthesis.* Princeton, NJ: Princeton University Press.

Bilgin, A. & Wolke, D. (2020) 'Parental use of "cry it out" in infants: No adverse effects on attachment and behavioural development at 18 months', *Journal of Child Psychology and Psychiatry, 61*(11), pp. 1184–1193.

Conkbayir, M. (2017) *Early Childhood and Neuroscience: Theory, Research and Implications for Practice.* London: Bloomsbury.

Davis, A. & Kramer, R. (2021) 'Commentary: Does "cry it out" really have no adverse effects on attachment?: Reflections on Bilgin and Wolke', *Journal of Child Psychology and Psychiatry, 62*(- 12), pp. 1488–1490. doi: 10.1111/jcpp.13223.

Department for Education, South Australia (2021) *Applying interoception skills in the classroom.* Available at https://www.education.sa.gov.au/schools-and-educators/curriculum-and-teaching/curriculum-programs/applying-interoception-skills-classroom.

Eisenberg, N., Smith, C., & Spinrad, T. (2011) 'Effortful control – relations with emotion regulation, adjustment, and socialization in childhood', in K. Vohs & R. Baumeister (Eds.), *Handbook of self-regulation* (pp. 263–283). New York: Guilford Press.

Feldman Barrett, L. (2017) *How Emotions Are Made: The Secret Life of the Brain.* London: Macmillan.

Golding, K. & Hughes, D. (2012) *Creating Loving Attachments: Parenting with PACE to nurture confidence and security in the troubled child.* London: Jessica Kingsley.

Goleman, D. (1996) *Emotional Intelligence: Why it can matter more than IQ.* London: Bloomsbury.

Gottman, J. (1997) *Raising an Emotionally Intelligent Child.* New York: Simon & Schuster.

Grimmer, T. (2019) *Calling All Superheroes: Supporting and Developing Superhero Play in the Early Years.* London: Routledge.

Grimmer, T. (2021) *Developing a Loving Pedagogy in the Early Years: How Love Fits with Professional Practice.* London: Routledge.

Grimmer, T. (2022) *Supporting Behaviour and Emotions in the Early Years: Strategies and Ideas for Early Years Educators.* London: Routledge.

Hrabok, M. & Kerns, K. (2010) 'The Development of Self-Regulation: A Neuropsychological Perspective', in B. Sokol, U. Müller, J. Carpendale, A. Young & G. Iarocci (Eds.), *Self- and*

Social-Regulation: Exploring the Relations Between Social Interaction, Social Understanding, and the Development of Executive Functions (pp. 129–154). Oxford: Oxford University Press.

Jarvis, P. (2020) 'Attachment theory, cortisol and care for the under threes in the twenty-first century: Constructing evidence-informed policy', *Early Years: An International Journal of Research and Development*, pp. 1–15. doi: 10.1080/09575146.2020.1764507.

Llenas, A. (2015) *The Colour Monster*. London: Templar Publishing.

McClelland, M. & Cameron, C. (2012) 'Self-Regulation in Early Childhood: Improving Conceptual Clarity and Developing Ecologically Valid Measures', *Child Development Perspectives, 6*(2), pp. 136–142.

Miller-Lewis, L., Searle, A., Sawyer, M., Baghurst, P., & Hedley, D. (2013) 'Resource factors for mental health resilience in early childhood: An analysis with multiple methodologies', *Child and Adolescent Psychiatry and Mental Health, 7*(6), pp. 1–23.

Mohr, C., Gross-Hemmi, M., Meyer, A., Wilhelm, F. & Schneider, S. (2019) 'Temporal Patterns of Infant Regulatory Behaviors in Relation to Maternal Mood and Soothing Strategies', *Child Psychiatry & Human Development, 50*, pp. 566–579.

OECD (2007) *Understanding the Brain: The Birth of a Learning Science*. Paris: OECD.

Pozuelos, J., Combita, L., Abundis, A., Paz-Alonso, P., Conejero, Á., Guerra, S., & Rueda, M. (2019) 'Metacognitive scaffolding boosts cognitive and neural benefits following executive attention training in children', *Developmental Science, 22*(2), pp. 1–15.

Richter, L. (2004) *The importance of caregiver–child interactions for the survival and healthy development of young children: A review*. World Health Organization: Child and Adolescent Health and Development. Available at https://www.who.int/publications/i/item/924159134X.

Robson, D., Allen, M., & Howard, S. (2020) 'Self-regulation in childhood as a predictor of future outcomes: A meta-analytic review', *Psychological Bulletin, 146*(4), pp. 324–354.

Schaan, L., Schulz, A., Nuraydin, S., Bergert, C., Hilger, A., Rach, H., & Hechler, T. (2019). 'Interoceptive accuracy, emotion recognition, and emotion regulation in preschool children', *International Journal of Psychophysiology, 138*, pp. 47–56.

Shanker, S. (2021) *Self-Regulation: 5 Domains of Self-Reg*. Peterborough, ON: The MEHRIT Centre. Available at https://self-reg.ca/wp-content/uploads/2021/05/infosheet_5-Domains-of-Self-Reg.pdf.

Siegel, D. & Bryson, T. (2012) *The Whole-Brain Child: 12 Proven Strategies to Nurture your Child's Developing Mind*. London: Robinson.

Siegel, E., Sands, M., Van den Noortgate, W., Condon, P., Chang, Y., Dy, J., Quigley, K. & Feldman Barrett, L. (2018) 'Emotion fingerprints or emotion populations? A meta-analytic investigation of autonomic features of emotion categories', *Psychological Bulletin, 144*(4), pp. 343–393.

Vink, M., Gladwin, T., Geeraerts, S. Pas, P., Bos, D., Hofstee, M., Durston, S., & Vollebergh, W. (2020) 'Towards an integrated account of the development of self-regulation from a neurocognitive perspective: A framework for current and future longitudinal multi-modal investigations', *Developmental Cognitive Neuroscience, 45*, pp. 1–9. doi: 10.1016/j.dcn.2020.100829.

2 International perspectives

Wendy Geens

Introduction

Earlier this year Wendy and a friend who works in an international school were debating the skills that students need to be successful when taking examinations. As well as noting that children need to develop their knowledge across a number of curriculum subjects, the discussion centred around the students' dispositions and how they approached their exams. Naturally, within the conversation they talked about barriers as well as strategies to enable learning, such as resilience, empathy and organisation, and they considered how children develop these qualities. It is no surprise that the discussion quickly focused on the development of self-regulation and how this underpins all the learning that takes place in school. Providing children with opportunities in the early years to explore, create, collaborate, empathise, etc., also became a significant talking point as it provided the foundations for how they not only approached their exams but managed all that is expected of them throughout their schooling/education. As Wendy considered the dilemmas and barriers for children, she began to consider how other countries approach the development of self-regulation, including the effective strategies educators use as well as the dilemmas and tensions schools and international teachers might face.

This chapter takes this discussion further and considers how children's self-regulation is developed in other countries and international schools, identifying similarities and differences as well as the importance of cultures and traditions. We consider how international schools have approached self-regulation, the strategies found to be effective and how embedding the principles and the ethos of self-regulation into the fabric of a school is key in influencing and shaping children's dispositions as they move into adulthood. These dispositions, which determine how children respond to others, are aspects of how they develop self-regulation – for example, approaching a problem with

DOI: 10.4324/9781003162346-3

enthusiasm and determination, developing skills related to resilience and creativity or growing in empathy. These are exemplified in Erin's story later in the chapter.

The more we researched self-regulation, the more it became clear that it is not an add-on or something that is done in settings and schools. It is actually intrinsic and permeates through the ethos – it is essentially what the school/setting is about. We also found that, in some international curricula, self-regulation is embedded within the content in terms of citizenship, support for children's emotional development and the dispositions and attitudes promoted. This chapter draws upon perspectives from international schools in Thailand and Taiwan, as well as other colleagues across Europe and Canada. This chapter does not claim to have considered all curricula in all countries but does recognise key strategies that can be used globally. It is important to note at this point the distinction between international schools and schools in other countries. International schools can select the curricula they wish to teach, whereas non-international schools will usually use the national curriculum relevant to their country unless they are privately financed schools and settings.

The chapter begins by providing an overview of some early childhood curricula and considers the expectations for children of this age group with a focus on how this relates to self-regulation. The various case studies highlight key features of early years practice and how challenges can be overcome.

Creating safe spaces – Hua Hin International School

For children to excel in the early years, they require space, time, challenging resources and quality interactions with adults. Our spacious environment offers natural, open-ended resources, allowing our children to 'free-flow' between the indoors and outdoors for much of the day and allowing them to choose where they want to play, what with and how. Children are free to utilise the space in the setting to just be themselves – for example, this child took a book and some cushions under a table and created an inviting and comfortable space.

Early Childhood Education and Care (ECEC)

When we first started to look at self-regulation and how this key area of child development is promoted, it quickly became apparent that the overriding factor in early years education is an understanding of the cultural expectations of the country where the school or setting is located. We know that replicating the practice or curriculum per se from one country into another does not produce the same outcomes due to the contrasting expectations of education systems, variations in how ECEC is funded and differences in cultures and national and local traditions. Some countries offer an integrated curriculum of care and educational standards, while other countries separate them. In addition, the age that children begin formal schooling and the type of provision offered prior to this differ from country to country.

In her book *School Readiness and the Characteristics of Effective Learning*, Tamsin compares school readiness to a lottery that involves a variety of factors, including where children are born, when they are born as well as their gender, home background and parental support, to name just a few (Grimmer, 2018). If we consider a sample of ECEC provision from around the world, these factors change depending on the culture, society and specific country viewed. One of the biggest differences is about when children begin formal schooling.

Based on statistics from the World Bank (2021) comparing 210 countries, it would appear that in 72% of countries children begin school at age 6 and in 17% children start at the older age of 7. In only 11% of countries children begin at age 5 or younger. It is worth noting that the official starting age listed for England and Wales is 5, however, the majority of children begin school in a reception class at age 4, which may or may not be formal depending on which school is attended. Children also begin compulsory education at age 4 in Northern Ireland, whereas in Scotland the official school starting age is 5. The discrepancy between official and unofficial starting age could apply in other countries, however, it appears that British children begin formal schooling at a much younger age than their peers around the world. The question remains whether British children fare better and gain more qualifications from their early start to school.

Sadly, research data shows that this is not true. If we look at the OECD (2019) data outlining student performance in reading, mathematics and science, we find the UK ranked 12th, 15th and 11th, respectively. All of the countries whose children outperformed the UK start formal education at the age of 6 or 7, with the exception of Ireland, which was ranked 6th in reading performance. Poland, Estonia and Finland were all ranked higher than the UK, and their children begin school at age 7; whilst China, Singapore, Korea and Canada were also ranked above the UK, and their children begin at age 6. Therefore, we can conclude the countries that do best in terms of academic success have an older school starting age of either 6 or 7.

Offical Primary School Starting Age

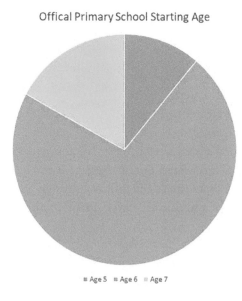

■ Age 5   ■ Age 6   ■ Age 7

(World Bank Data 2020-21)

Countries where children begin school later have ECEC provision, often in the form of kindergarten or preschool, each with their own curricula to prepare children for more formal schooling (OECD, 2013). For example, in Sweden they have a curriculum for preschool up until the age of 6, followed by an additional curriculum up to the age of 7. In Norway the framework prepares children up to the age of 6. In Finland the ECEC is in place until the age of 6, which is followed by a pre-school year until the age of 7, when children begin formal schooling. In Canada each province has its own curriculum covering from birth to 7 or 8 years. In Japan ECEC guidance is split between care from birth to 6 years and education from ages 3 to 6.

School readiness

In England the statutory Early Years Foundation Stage (EYFS) (DfE, 2021) outlines the development and learning expectations for children from birth to the end of the reception year, when children are 60 months or 5 years old. Children then move into Year 1 and are entitled to an education through the national curriculum (DfE, 2013), which adopts a formal educational approach towards learning. It must be noted that some children will have only just turned 5 years old the week before starting Year 1. The EYFS states, "It promotes teaching and learning to ensure children's 'school readiness' and gives children the broad range of knowledge and skills that provide the right foundation for good future progress through school and life" (DfE, 2021:5). However, the term *school readiness* is contested, and there are many perspectives on what it means. There is no nationally recognised definition, and some ECEC educators would understand it to be about moving into formal schooling in Year 1, whilst others would see it as a preparation for the transition into school itself at age 4 (Grimmer, 2018).

The development of self-regulation is now cited more explicitly, as the introduction outlined; however, we can't help but question the rationale for making such assessments at the age of 60 months, as it could be argued that self-regulation is not something that is continually assessed as a child progresses through the key stages in the national curriculum in England (DfE, 2013). Furthermore, many adults are often still developing their own self-regulation. That is not to say that children should not be assessed – many successful curricula worldwide have assessment points at this age, but it could be argued that assessing self-regulation and other aspects of the EYFS ought to be developed more and given higher priority or status with older children in the national curriculum.

Dispositions within ECEC

Within the English curriculum, the characteristics of effective teaching and learning are dispositions and attitudes which outline how children learn (see Chapter 4). These attributes are not unfamiliar to educators, as the development of dispositions has been intrinsically woven into the EYFS (DfE, 2021); however, children's dispositions have been fostered in a number of ways over the past decade or more, not always exclusively in the early years.

Through his work *Building Learning Power*, Guy Claxton (2002) considers the importance of developing dispositions for learning. He talks about how learning muscles need to be used and children need to develop a 'bounce back ability' when learning becomes hard. Resilience is one of the four 'Rs' in the Building Learning Power approach, recognising that when children are resilient they persevere and look for strategies to help them succeed (Claxton 2002). In the early years children develop resilience when they engage in their learning. When learning is directed by them and facilitated and supported by timely adult intervention, children's resilience becomes stronger. An example of this can be seen through sustained shared thinking when children are given the time and space to follow their own lines of enquiry, to extend their schemas or to work cooperatively with their peers and with an adult. Extended learning opportunities developed through a sustained shared thinking approach instinctively foster the development of the skills and behaviours in self-regulation, which are discussed in Chapter 6.

Emotional development and self-regulation in Canada – Sue Martin, author and researcher

There isn't a cohesive Canadian approach to education; there are some strands that are common elements in early childhood practice, although each province has different legislation (e.g., ratios, training requirements, etc.) and non-transferability of teacher preparation or early childhood educator credential recognition. Within early years documents, emphasis on resilience is a common theme, and both attachment and self-regulation are linked in most key documents. Shanker's work is often cited as a key source of their ideas about self-regulation (2021).

Ontario has a system-wide K–12 approach to 'behaviour' called 'Progressive Discipline', with each school board responsible for how it is actually rolled out. The idea is to make sure everyone feels safe, that there are positive relationships, a collaborative approach to creating a code of conduct, strategies to address potential bullying, and planned ways of addressing inappropriate behaviour. How this happens depends on the children's stage of development, nature, severity and impact of their behaviour. K–5 teachers tell me that, although the positive terminology works well for younger children, it carries shades of the old 'behaviour programs', where the word *behaviour* was understood to mean 'bad behaviour' with consequences and traditional methods of handling children with some punishment, whereas in early childhood their frame of thinking is different. The 'behaviour approach' is far less prevalent in childcare, where educators have been influenced by a different philosophy that is more respectful, developmental and consistent with research on emotional wellbeing.

Interestingly, early childhood educators and school boards seem to take different things from Shanker's work – for example, a longer-term perspective relating to improving social justice or simply children learning some degree of self-control, autonomy or ability to name and handle their emotions (Shanker, 2021). Somewhere between, educators see self-regulatory skills as being part of a repertoire of skills that might be called emotional intelligence, that in combination build resilience. Considered important to support self-regulatory work is Dweck's Mindset Theory (2012). The Ontario Kindergarten Curriculum (2016) has a lengthy section on self-regulation, offering teachers ways to support children through an inquiry-play-based approach, which links with attachment, a sense of sameness, predictability, ritual and rhythm and creates a sense of calm. Resilience may be strengthened when a young child discovers that they can manage a difficult situation, and is therefore not so daunted when they encounter a challenge again – but resilience involves a circle of strength building on emotional skills. We aim to help children become aware of their feelings, name them, manage them, talk about them, think of them positively and feel them without external controls or minimisation. Self-regulatory skills and executive functions are essential life skills enabling children to be successful in school and are all dependent on those early experiences.

Many curricula prioritise dispositions and attitudes, including children's self-regulation skills. The Te Whāriki curriculum (Ministry of Education, 2017) is recognised world-wide for its approach towards early years education with the image of the interwoven mat of principles and strands, which supports diversity, incorporates mastery, the learning of new skills, growth and the loose strands that denote a child's potential and their ongoing journey. The curriculum has at its heart a bicultural foundation with the initial foreword stating that, "All children grow up in New Zealand as competent and confident learners strong in their identity, language and culture." It goes on to note how it "encourages all children to learn in their own ways, supported by adults who know them well and have their best interests at heart" (Ministry of Education, 2017:2). What is key in this ECEC curriculum is how the five strands listed below are interconnected aspects of self-regulation:

■ Wellbeing.

■ Belonging.

■ Contribution.

■ Communication.

■ Exploration.

This curriculum promotes diversity whilst respecting tradition. In a similar way, the highly-regarded Reggio Emilia approach, in Northern Italy, socially constructs learning within the local cultural context, and children are seen as competent, collaborating with adults and their environment (Edwards et al., 2012). In addition, the Framework plan for ECEC in Norway holds values and traditions in high regard. It is adaptable to local needs, grounded in social pedagogy and has an emphasis on the dialogue between adult and child as well as creative experiences (Norwegian Directorate for Education and Training, 2017).

The Newfoundland and Labrador (2019) framework in Canada suggests that the two factors that strengthen children's resilience are attachment and self-regulation, and it outlines several dispositions and attitudes they seek to promote, including building resilience, expressing feelings, managing conflicts, problem-solving and playing cooperatively. In addition, the Scottish *Curriculum for Excellence* aims to foster children's knowledge, skills and attributes, which it hopes will equip children for the future, including relating to others and managing themselves (Education Scotland, undated).

It is also worth noting that around the world there are diverse pedagogical practices, and it is difficult to compare them. ECEC cannot escape the social, political and economic climate of each country, and education and childcare practices will reflect policies on issues like parental leave, working parents, the qualifications and pay conditions of educators and the view of the child by parents or educators. Singer and Wong examine infant daycare in several different countries and highlight how many practices and pedagogies are "embedded in the social-political context of their country" (2019:461).

However, even from this brief overview of different curricula, it is evident that the whole notion of self-regulation is not hugely different across the globe in terms of the dispositions, skills and behaviours that children develop and refine. What is different is how they are embraced within the educational beliefs and grounded in the country's traditions, customs and values. In addition, within each country these may be specific to particular areas and differ from region to region, as do the approaches adopted by schools and settings to embody local customs. For example, within schools and settings across England there are differences between urban and rural schools as well as in the composition of communities within a region. In the United States each state has its own curriculum documentation, which could be seen as fragmented, although it allows local areas to respond to the needs in that state (Melvin, Landsberg & Kagan, 2020). In China there are differences within the different provinces, rather than one national curriculum. A distinct feature is the emphasis placed on valuing and respecting the cultures and customs that children bring with them to school. For example, in Finland, Hong Kong and Singapore ECEC frameworks emphasise multilingualism to incorporate and reflect the diverse nature of their populations (Melvin, Landsberg & Kagan, 2020). We also found that in many international schools there is a resounding emphasis on celebrating diversity and valuing and respecting all the customs and traditions the children bring to the school.

Julie Way, headteacher, shares her ethos, hopes and aspirations for the children who make Hua Hin International School the vibrant school it is and how self-regulation is at the heart of this ethos.

Discussion with Headteacher Julie Way, Hua Hin International School

Self-regulation is what we are about; we invest in our children. We want our children to love learning and care for each other. We want children to have the dispositions to enjoy life and have opportunities to help them fulfil their aspirations. Our 'I values', as we call them, help to equip children with the skills, behaviours, dispositions and knowledge to be able to achieve this. Self-regulation is part of our belief in the education and curriculum we offer, as such it permeates through all we do in school.

Self-regulation is embedded in the ethos of our school and achieved through our 'I values':

- Inclusive.
- Intrepid.
- Inspired.
- Innovative.
- International.
- Individual.
- Imaginative.
- Inquisitive.

Communication and language development is central to supporting children's self-regulation, as this enables them to discuss how they are feeling when they have a disagreement with a friend or when learning becomes hard and children need to become more resilient and persevere. Providing opportunities to experience what it feels like when they 'get stuck' in their learning is important, as it enables them to develop strategies to be able to manage those feelings.

Communication and language development is also important, as the children bring many different cultures and languages with them as they develop friendships. The early years curriculum at Hua Hin school provides children with time and space to explore, discover and benefit from timely and quality interactions with adults. The resources promote challenge but, importantly, support children to make choices: they choose when they want to play, who they want to play with and what resources to play with – there is the option of going outside or staying indoors.

Our environment offers a place to learn and investigate in an atmosphere of calmness.

Adults observe the children closely – they notice what a child is doing, who they are playing with and how they interact with other children. They are able to

utilise this information to extend their learning, talk to the child and encourage them. The staff liaise with the parents and know the children well. They understand, respect and value all the child brings to the school community.

It is clear from listening to Julie talk that a child's self-regulation is developed intrinsically, and it is at the heart of all they do. It is also clear that being culturally aware and learning about the cultures of others helps children to empathise with each other. Countries such as New Zealand and Norway also stress the importance of valuing different cultures through their curriculum. The vision for the Te Whāriki curriculum is grounded in the statement *"Children are competent and confident learners and communicators, healthy in mind, body and spirit, secure in their sense of belonging and in the knowledge that they make a valued contribution to society"* (Ministry or Education, 2017:2; italics in original). The focus on play is also significant here and is something noted by a teacher in Sweden, who shared with us that child-initiated play is central to her setting. When children choose what they want to do, they are learning to respect others and develop empathy towards them.

Play and self-regulation

It is recognised worldwide that children learn through play: pretend play, small-world play, cooperative play, rough-and-tumble play, social play, etc. In a research paper, Whitebread et al. share how "play, particularly pretend or symbolic play, contributes to learning by supporting children's development of metacognitive or self-regulatory skills, which are in turn crucial in the development of problem solving and creativity" (2009:41). They see self-regulation as critically important. These types of play are the perfect way for adults to promote this development.

Children learn through play, and many countries ground their early years education and curricula in play pedagogy. Countries such as Portugal recognise that play is central to a child's development and advocate, like many others, that indoor and outdoor play should be available to all children. New Zealand provides exploration and uses play as a mechanism that combines learning and development. Sweden takes play a step further, seeing it as an 'omnipresent activity': "Play and enjoyment in learning in their various forms stimulate imagination, insight, communication and the ability to think symbolically, co-operate and solve problems" (OECD, 2013:33), all of which are key aspects of self-regulation. Scotland's curriculum talks about planned, purposeful play as being one of the key learning and teaching approaches to be adopted (Education Scotland, undated).

In play children learn through taking on different roles, interacting with others as well as playing independently. Chapter 5 links self-regulation with theory of mind, and Chapter 7 explores how role play and rough-and-tumble play can promote self-regulatory skills. The use of puppets in play is regularly seen across international settings as it depersonalises a situation for the child but still gives them the opportunity to explore the focus for the session and address the issues raised.

Using puppets – Jess Gosling, Taipei European School

I have often used puppets to model and show conflict scenarios. This was especially useful in the UK, where I worked in an area of high deprivation. I would observe conflict within my class and within the school environment and replay these conflicts with puppets. As these incidents often reflected what had happened in the class that week, we had clear guidelines never to name children in order to prevent a 'blame' culture. I also used 'adapted' stories from the Social and Emotional Aspects of Learning (SEAL) program (DfES, 2005) to raise concepts of conflict they may experience. However, instead of reading through long stories, which often used both language and scenarios which 'weren't quite right' for my class, I simplified them to clearly show the children an incident or problem. Following this, I would then model with the puppets several conflict-resolution (or otherwise) outcomes. The children would discuss with partners what they would do. Often, they would present other solutions which I had not thought about. We would then write up the problems and solutions we could use and refer to them when needed. The children were very engaged in this task and actually looked forward to watching the puppets. Sometimes the extreme reactions of the puppets would create a roar of laughter, which made the whole experience more light-hearted.

The value of play has been demonstrated through a wealth of research and yet, for some countries and cultures, questions still remain about whether play and learning are synonymous. Often there is tension within a country's beliefs about education between a more formal schooling approach and that of a play pedagogy. Supporting parents to understand the benefits of play is an important milestone for early years educators to overcome. This can be particularly noted in countries where there is a mismatch between the education provided by the state, which may be more formal, and that of private or international schools, which may want to adopt a play-based approach in ECEC. Educators in international schools cope with this by investing in their relationships with parents, getting to know the children and their lives outside of school and using this information to cater for the children's development steps.

Language learning

Earlier in this chapter headteacher Julie Way commented that an area key to children's development in self-regulation was language. Once children have developed their language they are in a stronger position to communicate their thoughts, feelings and emotions. Children enter our schools and settings having already begun to develop language and communication, and the role of the co-regulator is pivotal in supporting children to extend this as they grow.

Learning language depends upon children hearing language in order for them to develop their own communication methods and using language in order to develop their understanding. Children make connections through talk, and they use talk to extend, make explicit and reshape what they know. Talk also enables children to play and build relationships with others, which is vital for their social development.

Here are some ways that we can support early communication:

- Tune in to the child's signals and cues to engage in meaningful talk.

- Listen and respond to their language play.

- Copy the facial expressions, sounds and words made by young children.

- Share pictures and objects when you talk so that a child can link objects with words.

- Use labelling techniques and games – for example, show me your fingers, nose.

- Use clear speech and simple phrases, role-model appropriate and accurate language.

- Use strategies such as parentese (high-pitched voice and simple words/phrases), recasting (rephrase things), expanding (add to) and repetition to enable children to identify and decode meanings.

- Use non-verbal communication alongside talk – role-model facial expression, body language, gestures and intonation.

- Learn a few signs and use them every day and value all attempts at communication.

- Use expressive language, which includes rhythm and patterns.

- Maximise opportunities to develop children's problem-solving skills through talking whenever they arise.

- Model the 'rules' of language – e.g., turn taking, serve and return, listening.

- Introduce new vocabulary when appropriate.

- Ask open-ended questions to stretch the child.

- Have real, genuine and respectful conversations with children.

- Read stories every day.

- Set up role play and other environments that encourage talk.

Social interaction – Hua Hin International School

Children need to feel confident to talk to each other as well as talking with

adults. Playing with a partner in small world play can help a child become more confident and less anxious, whilst developing their language through play and interaction with peers.

When children collaborate and share

their ideas, they become more confident at tackling and solving their own problems because they are able to communicate their thoughts and ideas. Children are encouraged to do this throughout their time at our school.

Supporting children's self-regulation

In a discussion with Dr. Lynn Blakemore, an international teacher, about how self-regulation is promoted in her classroom, she shared her thoughts on the skills and characteristics of a self-regulated child, the international context, cultural considerations and strategies she adopts to support self-regulation. She highlighted the importance of being aware of culture and taking this into consideration when supporting children and working with parents.

Cultural considerations – Early years international teacher Dr. Lynn Blakemore

Self-regulation is the ability to control physical and emotional responses with attributes that include:

- Resilience.
- A willingness/motivation to try.
- Positive outlook/responses.
- Ability to adapt to change/new situations.
- Problem-solvers.
- Risk-takers.

It is important to understand the many cultural considerations within the international context when thinking about self-regulation. For example,

- Taking risks – sometimes this can be perceived as danger by some families, e.g., whilst at a school in Bangkok it was felt necessary to wrap the trunks of the trees in the Early Years garden to protect children from the bark. Whereas in rural areas there can be real dangers, e.g., children need to be aware of snakes and other wildlife whilst playing outside and going on bug hunts. In addition, during water-exploration sessions parents may express fears of their children catching colds if they play with water.
- Children with multiple carers – sometimes children may be looked after by a number of different people – for example, driver, nanny, nurse and parents. This could result in the children experiencing different responses and support in regards to developing their ability to self-regulate.
- Specialist teachers/sessions – in some schools children can be taught by up to five specialists in a day, e.g., Learning Resource Center teacher, Thai (language), PE, Swimming and Music. These multiple transitions could be unsettling for some young children and cause interruptions in a child's play.

- International teaching context – children regularly attend the same school where their parents teach, which can be challenging, e.g., if a nursery teacher has his/her own child in their class, then it can be difficult for the child to understand the different boundaries and expectations of their relationships within the school context.
- Making mistakes – Thai people believe strongly in the concept of 'saving face', i.e., avoiding confrontation and endeavouring not to embarrass themselves or other people, therefore making mistakes can be deemed to be negative. Within school we embrace the whole process of making mistakes as a tool for learning, and we model what we can do when things do not go to plan.
- High expectations with regard to the English language – sometimes parents of children with English as an Additional Language (EAL) feel that their children should be able to speak English within the first few months of starting at an international school, which may be beyond their capability.
- Seeing creativity as a process – internationally, this is not always such a familiar concept, and products or outcomes tend to be valued more than the process itself, e.g., a child may not be comfortable to paint/draw with no outcome but happy to draw a picture/painting of themselves with their family. The end result is then complimented and the 'product' cycle gets reinforced.
- General value of play – play may not always be valued as much as more structured learning.

We know that educators are very good at observing, and they know what children can or cannot achieve at a particular time. It is undeniable that adults play a significant role in developing a child's self-regulation. Future chapters discuss this further as they consider the role of the educator as co-regulator.

Understanding how children learn and helping children to understand how they learn are core tasks for any educator. This is something championed by the teacher in a school in Sweden who talked about the importance of motivation and developing resilience as part of the learning process. She noted how the process is often more important than the outcome. In her school children are encouraged to try and given the message that it is okay to make mistakes, similar to schools in England that also foster the approach of learning from mistakes. However, in some countries, making mistakes is not actively encouraged or even acceptable, as noted by Dr. Lynn Blakemore. Yet, if children do not know how it feels to make a mistake, how can they learn to recover from or manage the disappointment or frustration of getting something wrong. In some countries it is important to save face rather than make a mistake. Learning from our mistakes and overcoming difficulties is part and parcel of developing self-regulation.

Risky play

Risky play can also be viewed differently in international contexts or schools. In some cultures, children will not be encouraged to play outside for fear of hurting themselves. We need to show understanding and compassion to parents who feel anxious about their children taking risks. Sometimes this anxiety also stems from educators. For example, a teacher in Greece explained to us that children are generally not allowed to play outside in the rain because they could get cold and wet. In addition, recent research has shown that kindergarten educators in Greece do not tend to encourage perilous play or risk-taking games (Sakellariou & Banoum, 2020). This is in contrast to Scandinavian countries, where risky play is actively encouraged and children spend a vast amount of time playing outdoors. For example, one study in Norway found that children have a keen interest and strong urge to engage in risky play (Sandseter, 2007).

Risky play – Early years international teacher Dr. Lynn Blakemore

In our school there was a real debate around whether or not to remove a fireman's pole due to the perceived dangers and risk it posed to children's health and safety. As educators, we noticed when observing children that they generally know what they are capable of or comfortable with. We initially noticed children watching others slide down but not attempting it themselves. Then, when they did attempt it, they asked for some support until they were confident enough to do it on their own.

Risky play presents children with opportunities to develop their self-regulation in many ways. It offers opportunities to be creative and respond to difficulties, increasing their self-confidence and giving them a sense of achievement. Taking risks necessitates high levels of involvement and engagement as well as the use of higher-level thinking skills as children negotiate challenges, problem-solve and overcome obstacles. Our ultimate aim should be to help children master the skills they need to manage risk and danger for themselves. Children given the opportunity to experience this type of 'risky freedom' will grow in competence, confidence and self-regulation as they master a wide range of physical and social skills.

Modelling compassion

All early years educators are fully aware of how modelling facilitates learning, and this is no different for self-regulation when we model emotions. Having compassion is a pro-social behaviour and a strong attribute of a self-regulated child. It means they understand what it feels like to be kind to others and be in receipt of kindness from others. They are considerate, show concern and care for other people and the environment. Early years educators model what care looks like – they describe what they are doing and show a range of expressions of how they are feeling through their behaviours. They show kindness and gratitude. They smile and are welcoming. When considering others they are thoughtful and talk through how they and others might be feeling and the impact of their or others' actions. Talk is an important aspect of modelling compassion and, as such, it is important in the development of a child's self-regulation.

Modelling compassion and promoting self-regulation – Early years international teacher Dr. Lynn Blakemore

In our school we model compassion and promote self-regulation by:

- Staying calm and connecting with the child.
- Acknowledging feelings and use of language – e.g., "Sometimes I feel …"
- Raising awareness of body sensations, because we genuinely might not know this or have experienced it – e.g., "How does your body feel?" and then accepting children's responses, "Prickly!"
- Sharing yoga moments.
- Offering self-expression opportunities through dance, music and stories (narrated by teacher) then acting these out together.

Provision and the environment

Central to developing children's self-regulation is the provision of both the outdoor and indoor areas. What is provided for children in a child-centred ethos will change on a daily basis given that the needs of the child change, and so being able to adapt to those needs requires a flexible approach to the daily provision. Most early years settings – nationally and internationally – will have an area dedicated as a quiet area, which in many cases is a reading area; however, offering a space for children to be calm and reflective and to just 'be' is key. Involving children in the design and creation of the area encourages ownership, which not only empowers the children, but can also encourage them to go to this space when they feel the need, thus using the area for its intended purpose. Providing calming baskets with objects and equipment selected by children is a good example of how resources can support them.

Child-centred spaces – Hua Hin International School

These are examples of how the outdoor spaces change regularly to accommodate the children's ideas, schemas and interests.

Having resources that are interchangeable and able to be moved around by the children and adults is important because it can facilitate the children's interests and thinking depending on the themes the children are focusing on at that time.

In thinking about the environment, we believe that these designated areas are important, but they need to be utilised purposefully. We must ensure our spaces are meeting the needs of the children and are not being designed or driven by educational outcomes that may not consider individuals. In addition, children may not always use our self-regulation areas in the ways we expected or had in mind.

Provision – Early years international teacher Dr. Lynn Blakemore

We ensure our provision is child centred and will change our environment daily according to needs. We have a calm area in a space chosen by children, which contains calming baskets with objects/resources they have chosen. This helps some children who need additional support.

We adopt an 'in the moment planning' (ITMP) philosophy (Ephgrave, 2018), and the environment is set up to support this. For example, we take into account the stressful scenarios that children may have gone through just getting to school and have a soft start across all our Early Years provision each day. This ensures our children do not face immediate demands to leave their main carer or force themselves into a carpet time. It also reduces any unnecessary stress demands on children with regard to transitions. We have a rolling snack available, which promotes their independence and choice, and it doesn't interrupt the flow of their play. We are also encouraging children to pay attention to their body and how they feel.

The fact that we embrace ITMP (Ephgrave, 2018) supports the notion that children know their developmental capabilities, but these can be scaffolded in an appropriate way by educators. This makes activities achievable and within a child's zone of proximal development (Vygotsky, 1978).

Erin's story shows how a child's self-regulation was developed from the soft-start approach into school, which supported her through the transition from home to nursery, and shows how she is now in control of her own self-regulation. If we are promoting the development of self-regulation and want a collective approach towards it, we need to develop respectful relationships with parents. This helps them to feel listened to by educators and can reassure parents through regular communication. The case study of Erin's journey is a good example of how developing respectful relationships with parents helps a child to flourish and develop her self-regulation skills and dispositions.

Erin's story part 1 – International School

Erin joined nursery at an International School aged 3 years. Erin is Thai, and her parents have a strong command of English and they speak both Thai and English to her at home. On entry into nursery, it quickly became evident that Erin had a sound understanding of English, but as a student with English as an Additional language (EAL), she was naturally reluctant to speak English in an unfamiliar environment. As an only child, Erin was – and still is – very close to both parents, with dad often working from home.

Erin experienced a staggered transition into nursery, e.g., shorter initial hours, building up to half days; this was then extended to include lunch and then finally with children staying for the full day. This transition period was organised over a two-week period. The nursery also supported the concept of a 'soft start', which meant that parents could bring their children into the classroom and stay with them for up to a 15-minute period to help them to settle in.

Like many children, Erin found separating from her parents very stressful during the first month of starting nursery and would often become distressed and cry out for them at various points in the day. Mum and dad would always talk to Erin as they entered the nursery classroom with her and continually reassure her that they would return, but it remained a stressful situation for her.

The visual timetable displayed in the nursery became a focus for Erin, as she could see how the day would progress through the photographs, which ultimately led to the final image of 'Home time'.

She would often hold my arm and lead me over to the visual timetable and indicate to me through words, such as "Mummy, daddy, home," that she wanted me to 'talk her through' the day. Mum and dad also implemented various strategies to support Erin's transition, which included a family photograph that was attached to her dress via a key ring, followed by a voice recording (mum's voice) on a small device that was attached to her school bag. Erin would often ask to go out of the classroom to listen to this message and was clearly reassured, albeit temporarily.

The strategies used to support Erin's transition provide comfort and security through the recording of mum's voice and the family photograph on a key ring, whilst the visual timetable helps to give structure to her day and allows her to see what will be taking place, thus reducing anxiety generated through the unknown. In the moment planning (Ephgrave, 2018) is essentially about responding to the child appropriately at a particular time, and this requires observing and noticing what the child is doing so the adult is completely led by them. Ephgrave fully endorses the idea that starting with the child is

critical and … the adult finds ways to respond to the child so that the child will remain content and new learning is possible. Protecting the wellbeing of the child and responding to them in ways which respect and value their unique identity will maximise the progress children make.

(2018:3)

This distinctive child-centred philosophy embodies the early development of self-regulation, and it is clear to see why this has been noted as being a key strategy in developing children's self-regulation in this case study.

Enabling the educator to support the emotional development and wellbeing of the child is especially important because if a child has "low level well-being, they will not be able to engage, no matter how superb the setting is" (Ephgrave, 2018:19). All educators understand the value of trusting relationships and how this underpins the learning and development of the child. We expand on this in Chapter 8 when we explore the role of the adult. In the moment planning (Ephgrave, 2018) also ensures that there is a soft start to the day, so when children arrive at the setting or school there are no immediate demands placed on the child – they do not have to leave their carer or force themselves into a carpet activity. No educator is fully aware of the pressures and stressful scenarios a child may have already encountered that morning, but beginning the day with familiar adults and familiar routines allows the child to settle and eases the transition from home to school. Providing children with the opportunity to listen and understand their bodies' cues and respond to these feelings gives them choice and the ability to decide what to do, thus promoting independence.

Erin's story part 2 – International School

One of the strategies that Erin employed in the nursery classroom, possibly as a soothing or distraction strategy, was to go straight to the creative table (where there were mark-making resources) or to the painting easel and either draw or paint very detailed pictures of herself, always with her family.

These were admired and discussed in regards to the detail, and Erin would always react positively to the praise and acknowledgement of these drawings and paintings. This could have been a response to the affirmation of her family though, as opposed to the maturity and detail of her drawing. On reflection, what could initially be perceived as almost a 'repetitive or ritualistic drawing activity' could be acknowledged as a child's self-initiating strategy to support their own self-regulation. These behaviours and activities were noted by Erin's key worker and then informed the support strategies that were implemented.

Many children use spaces in the environment or specific activities as an emotional support or transitional object. We see this is Erin's story as she continues to return to the same area when she arrives in nursery every day. Her educators recognised the importance of her playing in this way as an emotional crutch, and they did not try to redirect her to other activities at this time. The role of the adult is to support children emotionally and promote their self-esteem, self-awareness and wellbeing, as Chapter 3 explores.

Erin's story part 3 – International School

Erin appeared to find reassurance and security in 'product-based' art activities, which created or achieved an end goal, but shied away from any 'process-based' art and messy-play opportunities that were on offer in the environment. We wanted to introduce her to the concept of process art and sensory/messy-play activities and for her to feel comfortable interacting with this type of play and enjoy the feeling of 'just doing and being involved'.

Initially, she continued to avoid these activities, but over time and with reassurance from both practitioner and her parents she relaxed a little and started to become curious and ultimately explore with fascination.

Throughout this transition period communication between parents and practitioner remained vital, as between us we could share our experiences of not just Erin's transition, but the whole family's transition into full-time education and develop relationships and ultimately strategies to support Erin's needs at that time. I recall talking to Erin's parents about a relevant story at the time called *A Beautiful Oops* (Saltzberg, 2010), which both parents took on board and used as a tool to support Erin's development in accepting her mistakes.

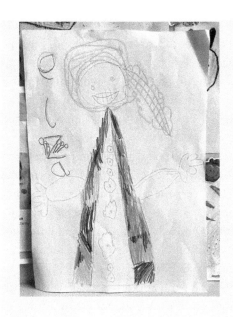

I recently had contact with Erin's Dad, who shared a photograph of a drawing that Erin had created where she had made a mistake in the orientation of her letter 's' but felt comfortable and confident enough to turn the error – or 'oops' – into a bunch of flowers, demonstrating self- regulation in action!

This case study embodies how an international school can support a child in developing different aspects of their self-regulation. It could be argued that some international schools have more flexibility in the curriculum they offer – for example, they can amend their curriculum to meet the different cultural needs of the children. They usually need a very good understanding of the customs and traditions that shape the children in order to ensure they can access the curriculum on offer. We have noted that there are key self-regulation qualities that are at the heart of these schools:

■ An agreed understanding of what self-regulation is about, which everyone in school believes.

■ An understanding that self-regulation is about promoting the whole child, their dispositions and their skills, not just self-control.

■ An ethos that sets children on the path to success by going beyond schooling and achievement and aiming for fulfilled adult lives.

Summary

Whilst our examination of other curricula is brief, it does identify some key similarities. The first is the importance of play – play is universal and not only central to child development but also significant in the development of children's self-regulation. Children learn a lot through play: how to interact with each other, have ownership of what they are doing, take control, follow their interests and extend their knowledge. Through play children can learn to collaborate, problem-solve and show empathy. The second key similarity is the importance of schools and settings having both a strong awareness of the cultural considerations that children bring with them as well as curricula grounded in local and national traditions and customs. The third is the importance of adult intervention and adults as co-regulators who model compassion, provide empathy and care, promote talk and vocabulary and, through a programme of carefully structured support, help the children to achieve.

We have also seen in this chapter how particular strategies and opportunities supported one little girl's self-regulation development. These strategies are not new, and we have seen them being used effectively in England. However, one of the advantages of international schools is that they appear to have more freedom to focus on educational philosophy. They can design or adopt a curriculum that embodies their ethos and embraces diversity. This is key when promoting creativity and problem-solving, as it requires an understanding of what is being asked of parents and children as well as flexibility in timetabling and resources. The integration of both care and education in a single framework provides a joined-up approach to the provision of early childhood education.

The key takeaway from this chapter is that those countries where schools and settings have self-regulation at the heart of their education are those that promote a culture of developing dispositions, learning, flexible thinking and reciprocal relationships. The next chapter further builds on the notion of the self by looking at the skills related to developing self-esteem, self-awareness and children's wellbeing.

Questions for reflection

1. What can we learn from different perspectives around the world?

2. To what extent is self-regulation at the heart of our practice?

3. How does our setting promote and celebrate cultural diversity?

References

Claxton, G. (2002) *Building Learning Power.* Bristol: TLO.

Department for Education (DfE) (2013) *National Curriculum in England for Key Stage 1 and 2 Framework.* Available at: https://assets.publishing.service.gov.uk/government/uploads/system/uploads/attachment_data/file/425601/PRIMARY_national_curriculum.pdf.

Department for Education (DfE) (2021) *Statutory Framework for the Early Years Foundation Stage.* Available at https://assets.publishing.service.gov.uk/government/uploads/system/uploads/attachment_data/file/974907/EYFS_framework_-_March_2021.pdf.

Department for Education and Skills (DfES) (2005) *Excellence and Enjoyment: Social and Emotional Aspects of Learning (SEAL): New Beginnings Foundation Stage.* Available at https://sealcommunity. org/sites/default/files/resources/pns_seal132305_newbeg_red_0.pdf.

Dweck, C. (2012) *Mindset: How You Can Fulfil Your Potential.* London: Constable & Robinson.

Education Scotland (undated) *Curriculum for Excellence.* Available at https://education.gov. scot/Documents/All-experiencesoutcomes18.pdf.

Edwards, C., Gandini, L., & Forman, G. (2012) *The Hundred Languages of Children: The Reggio Emilia Experience in Transformation,* 3rd ed. Santa Barbara, CA: Praeger.

Ephgrave, A. (2018) *Planning in the Moment with Young Children: A Practical Guide for Early Years Practitioners and Parents.* London: Routledge.

Grimmer, T. (2018) *School Readiness and the Characteristics of Effective Learning.* London: Jessica Kingsley.

Melvin, S., Landsberg, E., & Kagan, S. (2020) 'International Curriculum Frameworks', *Young Children, 75*(1), pp. 10–21.

Ministry of Education (2017) *Te Whāriki He whāriki mātauranga mō ngā mokopuna o Aotearoa Early childhood curriculum.* New Zealand Crown Copyright. Available at https://www.education.govt.nz/assets/Documents/Early-Childhood/ELS-Te-Whariki-Early-Childhood-Curriculum-ENG-Web.pdf.

Newfoundland Labrador (2019) *Navigating the Early Years: An Early Childhood Learning Framework.* Available at https://www.gov.nl.ca/education/files/Early-Learning-Framework.pdf.

Norwegian Directorate for Education and Training (2017) *Framework Plan for Kindergartens.* Available at https://www.udir.no/in-english/framework-plan-for-kindergartens.

OECD (2013) *Quality Matters in Early Childhood Education and Care: Sweden 2013.* Available at https:// www.oecd.org/education/school/SWEDEN%20policy%20profile%20-%20published%20 2005-02-2013.pdf.

OECD (2019) *PISA 2018 Results (Volume I): What Students Know and Can Do,* Paris: PISA, OECD Publishing. Available at https://www.oecd-ilibrary.org/education/pisa-2018-results-volume-i_5f07c754-en.

Ontario Kindergarten Program (2016) *The Kindergarten Program.* Ontario: Queen's Printer for Ontario. Available at https://files.ontario.ca/books/edu_the_kindergarten_program_english_aoda_web_oct7.pdf.

Sakellariou, M. & Banoum, M. (2020) 'Play within outdoor preschool learning environments of Greece: a comparative study on current and prospective Kindergarten Educators', *Early Child Development and Care, 190*(10), pp. 887–903. doi: 10.1080/03004430.2020.1813123.

Saltzberg, B. (2010) *A Beautiful Oops.* New York: Workman Publishing Company.

Sandseter, E. (2007) 'Risky Play Among Four and Five Year-Old Children in Preschool', in S. O'Brien, P. Cassidy, & H. Schonfeld, *Vision into Practice Conference Proceedings: Making Quality a Reality in the Lives of Young Children,* pp. 248–256. Dublin: Centre for Early Childhood Development and Education.

Shanker, S. (2021) *Self-Regulation: 5 Domains of Self-Reg.* Peterborough, ON: The MEHRIT Centre. Available at https://self-reg.ca/wp-content/uploads/2021/05/infosheet_5-Domains-of-Self-Reg.pdf.

Singer, E. & Wong, S. (2019) 'Emotional Security and Daycare for Babies and Toddlers in Socialpolitical Contexts: Reflections of Early Years Pioneers since the 1970s', *Early Child Development and Care, 191*(3), pp. 461–474.

Vygotsky, L. (1978). *Mind in society: The development of higher psychological processes.* Boston, MA: Harvard University.

Whitebread, D., Coltman, P., Jameson, H., & Lander, R. (2009) 'Play, cognition and self-regulation: What exactly are children learning when they learn through play?' *Educational & Child Psychology, 26*(2), pp. 40–52.

World Bank (2021) *Primary school starting age (years)*. Available at https://data.worldbank.org/indicator/SE.PRM.AGES.

3 Sense of self and wellbeing

Tamsin Grimmer

Introduction

Whilst teaching a reception class several years ago, Tamsin taught a delightful little girl, Olive, who refused to look in the mirror. On digging a little deeper, she said no one would want to be her friend because she was fat and ugly! This was extremely distressing to hear and comprehend. Usually in settings we avoid talking about appearance in anything other than a factual way, and we would never use terms like *fat* and *ugly*, instead choosing to focus on attributes and characteristics we can develop. Olive lived with her mum and three older sisters, all of whom were more than ten years older than her. Olive's mum explained to Tamsin that she and the older girls regularly dieted and found it difficult to maintain a healthy weight. Sadly and unknowingly, they were role-modelling unhealthy attitudes and poor body image to Olive, who was only four years old, and she had learned to use these derogatory terms to describe herself.

Tamsin and Olive's mum then set about the task of raising Olive's body image and self-esteem by working together and role-modelling alternative perspectives. Olive's sisters also actively tried not to talk about feeling fat or looking ugly at home. The school was a Christian school, and Tamsin recalls a circle time, later in the year, when the children were all passing around a magic box and peeping inside. They were told that inside the box they would see an amazing person that God loved very much. Stuck to the bottom of the box was a vanity mirror, so when they peeped inside they saw their reflection. It was a special moment when Olive peeped inside, saw herself and smiled a huge smile. This was the first time Tamsin had seen her look in a mirror.

Olive clearly had low self-esteem, and this had an impact on her whole wellbeing. This happens to all of us – we all have times when we feel worthless or unable to do anything right. Sometimes we may feel generally low or depressed, or perhaps feeling this way is the result of an accident or incident. A couple of years ago a friend of Tamsin's reversed his car over his laptop! He felt awful at the time and exclaimed that he never did anything right. Once he recovered, he realised it was just an accident and was able to

DOI: 10.4324/9781003162346-4

carry on with his day. How we respond to these moments is linked to our self-esteem, self-awareness, wellbeing and self-regulation. With poor self-esteem and a lower sense of wellbeing, it is harder to get up, brush ourselves down and try again. Self-regulation and our ability to be resilient, resourceful and have the resolve needed to cope with the various challenges life brings relies on our feeling OK in ourselves.

Just like Olive, our children have these moments too. Imagine Dexter, who is so busy helping his dad look after their dog that he forgets to hold on to the end of the dog's lead. Or Nazia, who was so keen to show her picture to her teacher that she knocked over the painting water and it spilled all over her picture. Or Katie, who has been told she is useless so many times she is starting to believe it. Some children cope with these knockbacks better than others. Helping children to have high levels of self-esteem, self-awareness and wellbeing provides them with a firm foundation and enables them to be ready to learn. This chapter explores how adults can promote children's sense of self through focusing on their self-esteem, self-awareness and emotional wellbeing.

Self-esteem and emotional wellbeing

Self-esteem could be described as how someone feels about themselves and having a positive feeling of self-worth (Chen et al., 2021). Research shows that children as early as five years old have a sense of self-esteem as prevalent as that of adults (Cvencek et al., 2016). Self-esteem remains fairly constant throughout our lives and can be aided or damaged by our relationships with other people, therefore it is vital that educators prioritise this aspect within the early years.

Children will experience a number of different stressors and challenging times throughout their childhood, as Chapter 1 explored. Changes in their home life or family circumstances may have an impact on their self-esteem, and transitions such as starting school or moving house could affect their confidence levels. With support from home and their educators, children will cope with these challenges. If we promote wellbeing, we will find our children are happier, feel more secure and will therefore learn more effectively. It is helpful if we measure wellbeing too, because as The Children's Society point out, "If schools [and settings] do not measure the well-being of their children, but do measure their intellectual development, the latter will always take precedence" (2015:11).

Porter asks the question, "What if schools valued wellbeing more than results?" in her article that links with the strategy in New Zealand, where the government has a wellbeing budget which clearly prioritises this within education (2019). She suggests we should invest in mental health and wellbeing services and improve child wellbeing by taking it seriously and putting support in place for vulnerable and disadvantaged groups.

Educators may choose to use the Leuven Scale for Wellbeing and Involvement (Laevers, 2005) to measure wellbeing in their schools and settings. The Leuven Scale has five points and considers wellbeing and involvement separately, however, the suggestion is to link to both scales for each child observed. It is freely available online and is really easy to use. Educators can use this information to put strategies in place if they identify a child is struggling with wellbeing.

Supporting wellbeing during transitions – Ruby Moxey

We noticed that a child's wellbeing was low during tidy-up time, and I identified that this transition was making him very anxious. Therefore, he was given a five-minute warning before tidy-up time when he collected a liquid oil timer, which helped him see the time passing. This made the transition a lot smoother and helped ease his anxiety.

There are many ways we can help children to increase their self-esteem and emotional wellbeing:

- Demonstrate how much we love and value them through developing a loving pedagogy.
- Build strong, authentic relationships and attachments and interact sensitively.
- Get to know the unique child and measure their wellbeing, seeking to increase it.
- Notice their interests and fascinations and tailor provision to meet them.
- Give them a voice and listen to what they say, acting upon it whenever possible.
- Acknowledge and respect their feelings.
- Create an emotionally literate environment.
- Use emotion coaching and problem-solving strategies.
- Value effort over attainment.
- Promote a 'can-do' attitude and encourage supported risk taking and challenge.
- Provide a predictable and secure environment.
- Role model and encourage positive behaviour.

When Moore and Smith (2018) studied self-esteem in relation to social and emotional wellbeing, they found that children who had higher self-esteem had fewer behavioural difficulties. This makes sense to us as, anecdotally, the children we have worked with in the past with lower self-esteem were often the children who needed the most support. It is also generally accepted that developing strong attachments in the early years has a very positive impact on relationships later in life.

Although there is a wealth of research into attachment, very few studies consider its links with self-esteem, however, research by Pintoa et al. (2015) confirmed Bowlby's hypothesis (1982) that children who have secure attachments with their parents go on to have a positive sense of self and self-worth, so higher self-esteem. In addition, Bavolek found that our experiences growing up have a large impact on our self-image, and adopting a nurturing approach has a positive influence on both self-image and self-worth (2000). Chapter 4 explores how we can use the principles of nurture in our practice.

Attachment and trauma awareness

With this in mind, early childhood educators must promote secure attachments in our settings and schools. We should become more aware of the impact that trauma can have on our children and families and how we can better support them. This understanding and ethos is part of a loving pedagogy and should impact every aspect of our provision (Grimmer, 2021). Seeing behaviour as communication is a good place to start trying to unpick why children might respond the way they do. In order to become co-regulators, children need to feel safe and secure with us, or, put another way, we need to become their secure base.

Research has shown the many positive benefits of secure attachments, including better self-regulatory skills (Bergin & Bergin, 2009), so investing in building these relationships is time well spent. Also having an awareness of Adverse Childhood Experiences (ACEs) helps educators to understand their children and respond more appropriately. There is an excellent resource which is freely available online and explains all about ACEs and how they can be managed and prevented: *The Little Book of Adverse Childhood Experiences* (Collingwood et al., 2018). It summarises what ACEs are:

Adverse Childhood Experiences (ACEs) describe a wide range of stressful or traumatic experiences that may occur as a child is growing up ... this can include:

- domestic violence.
- drugs and/or alcohol abuse.
- familial mental health issues.
- physical abuse.
- emotional abuse.
- sexual abuse.
- neglect.

- loss due to separation or divorce of parents.
- loss due to bereavement.
- incarceration of a family member.

(Collingwood et al., 2018:7)

Seeking connections – Lisa Gibbons, Denmead Infant School

George seeks connections wherever he goes. All adults are important to George. He needs to know who they are and the role they are going to play in his world and constantly looks to actively engage. George is a post-looked-after child and has been part of a very settled and loving family for virtually his whole life. So we can only assume something in those very early days, possibly even in utero, has impacted on George. George needs adults that give him lots of positive affection and love. He often misses his Mummy, so we get him through with a 'power hug' – a very tight squeeze to give him some of my love to get through until he can see Mummy again. Transition times are tough, and a special box to help him focus on something else whilst he waits for everyone to get ready for home time has really helped. A lanyard to wear with photos of all the adults in school that are important to him also helps him to know we are thinking about him even when we are not with him. For George, this is crucially the level of connection he needs. He needs you to show him you are thinking of him all the time and you are always going to be there for him. It can be intense. As he has become more secure with the adults around him, he relies on the strategies in place less and less. However, we know George, and we recognise when he is feeling wobbly, we pre-empt transition times that he may find difficult and we know exactly how to support him through these challenging times.

Research has shown that ACEs can have a very negative impact on children's lives, affecting physical health and wellbeing. They can even predict the likelihood of a child engaging in harmful activities or becoming violent themselves when they get older (Collingwood et al., 2018). According to Bellis et al. (2013), over 47% of people in the UK have experienced one or more ACEs in childhood, with over 12% of people having experienced four or more ACEs. Therefore, ACEs are quite common, which sounds disheartening; however, the good news is that there are many preventative measures and actions that can be taken that will lessen the impact of these ACEs (Collingwood et al., 2018). Some ways of managing and preventing ACEs are really simple and include ideas such as educators being aware of ACEs, providing stable and predictable routines and environments, building secure attachments with children and their families and actively teaching skills such as resilience and how to overcome difficulties.

Trauma awareness – Sue Martin, author and researcher in Canada

More is being understood about trauma in early childhood, and there are many additional situations that are being considered to be potentially traumatic for young children. Shifting perspective so that we see life from a child's point of view helps us understand how a child might experience things. That said, our understanding is that every child might make sense of what seems to be a similar situation in very different ways, so that makes it an extra challenge for caregivers. I am not confident that all teachers and early childhood educators in Canada are proficient in trauma-sensitive care and education, but awareness is much greater than only a few years ago. Many adults wanting to understand more about ACEs are attending a non-technical course called 'The Brain Story' by the Alberta Family Wellness Initiative (Palix Foundation, 2021). This offers five areas presented visually, including:

- Resilience – moving to positive outcomes.
- Brain architecture – how early experiences build brains.
- Toxic stress – disruption to brain architecture.
- Air traffic control – the executive function.
- Serve and return – positive interactions building brain architecture.

Concerns about ACEs are increasing, with educators using the term ACE as a buzzword but lacking skills to know what to do. "Despite progress in establishing a Canadian evidence base to prevent ACEs and to mitigate associated impairment, further research is needed to strengthen prevention and respond to ACEs" (Tonmyr et al., 2020:185).

In addition, the group of children most severely impacted by ACEs tends to be Indigenous. There are many reasons associated with colonization, mistreatment, life on reserves, loss of livelihoods such as fishing and hunting, ghastly experiences in residential schools resulting in intergenerational trauma, alcoholism, poverty, racism and social injustices. This paints a poor picture, and this isn't true of everyone, but there is much to be concerned about. In a very recent study of ACEs in a northern Ontario population of First Nations people, there is a clear pointing to the need for increased understanding of the ACEs and better understanding of how to support individuals. Indigenous 'ways of knowing' are an important part of the approach.

Jarvis (2019) shares that children who are continually stressed will struggle in schools and settings because they are in survival mode – they may have a shorter attention span; distrust adults or other children; have low confidence, self-belief and self-motivation; may be overdependent on others or may even find it hard to accept support. Therefore, we need to adopt an ethos and whole–setting/school approach where we stop seeing the child and their behaviour as the problem, but instead understand they may be highly stressed and their actions are a result of their past experiences. Expecting a 'difficult' child to focus and learn is unrealistic; instead, we need to offer understanding and support. Part of the response one school adopted included changing their language, so asking "What's happened to you?" rather than "What's wrong with you?" (Collingwood et al., 2018:19) helped them to encourage children to talk about their experiences to a caring and trusted educator.

A whole-school approach to Adverse Childhood Experiences (ACEs) – Gemma Rowlands

Collingwood et al. (2018) use the metaphor of a bank account to visualise the wellbeing of a child. Positive experiences and relationships, including those of the mother during pregnancy, add a penny to the child's wellbeing bank account. During the child's life, ACEs might make a withdrawal; however, with enough positive experiences, the balance will not be too adversely affected. The child can be resilient. However, for some children, their bank accounts may not have a strong bank balance to start with, and ACEs could even cause the child to become overdrawn. This visualisation has enabled me to really under-stand the impact that my practice could have on a child and their wellbeing. It is within our power as educators to create an environment and provide the relationships which make deposits into the child's wellbeing bank account.

For me, the most significant learning points were realising the important difference we can make and making a difference does not mean trying to change the children, but having unconditional positive regard, accepting and loving children where they are and providing the environment and relationships that they need to build their own resilience. Thinking about how this can be translated into practice, I can see that the difference we make can be on both a whole-school and an individual 1:1 basis.

Whole school

Ways that protective factors and resilience can be fostered at a whole-school level include:

■ Create a school culture which recognises and supports good mental health and wellbeing and puts relationships first. Use a trauma-informed lens which focuses on the causes of behaviour and trauma experienced rather than trying to address the behavioural symptoms.

- Provide training to support staff and raise awareness of ACEs and how to ensure promotion of protective factors and building resilience. For example, help staff to understand how common ACEs are and their impact on brain development and impact on their own practice.
- Consider how these ACEs impact the child through a proactive pastoral approach, rather than seeing behaviour that needs to be fixed.
- Have clear policies on behaviour and bullying.
- Support effective care-giving and parenting, building on family strengths and work with other professionals to help educate parents.

Individual class-level/1:1 interactions

Awareness of ACEs enables us to reflect and think about how to focus on appropriate protective factors and increase resilience. Some ideas include:

- Promote attachment through stable and nurturing relationships and positive interaction to minimise the impact of ACEs and become a secure base for the children.
- Serve-and-return interactions are essential to support the development of secure relationships, healthy brain development and good communication skills. This helps the child to feel involved and connected and builds self-esteem, as children are explicitly valued.
- Start with the child and what is good and positive and build on these attributes, rather than trying to fix or get them to catch up. This enables children to experience success and achievement, supports intrinsic motivation, self-esteem and self-efficacy.
- Promote positive friendships through interventions, circle time and group activities. This supports the feelings of inclusion and connectedness.
- Prevent bullying by teaching children how to respond to aggressive behaviour, recognise warning signs of bullying and how to take action. This could be done through role play, story-telling and puppets.
- Use emotion coaching to validate and accept feelings and promote a sense of belonging. This also serves to support emotional literacy and regulation skills.
- Model resilience, embrace mistakes, encourage problem-solving and demonstrate coping skills through using 'out loud thinking'. This helps children to think positively and feel that hardships can be overcome.
- Allow children to feel some discomfort and challenge so that they can learn to work through it. Understanding the child and what level of

discomfort and challenge is appropriate is key, and educators need to scaffold this.

■ Promote physical and emotional health and wellbeing through discussion. Incorporate physical activity across all areas of learning.

Seeing children through this lens gives an alternative way of viewing behaviour and enables greater compassion and empathy. This enables the start of a journey with the child through proactive pastoral care. Realise the power you have as an individual working with children to make a difference. We can all make deposits into a child's wellbeing bank account. There is value in each interaction, however small it may seem. Every penny counts.

We cannot become trauma and attachment aware overnight, but we can begin to reflect upon these issues and adopt an approach informed by this growing area of neuroscience. Here are a few ideas of how we can encourage our settings to grow in awareness:

■ Ensure all members of staff understand about ACEs, trauma and attachment through engaging in professional development.

■ Include being trauma and attachment aware in policies and procedures.

■ Adopt a loving pedagogy and prioritise wellbeing for staff and children.

■ Work in partnership with and get to know children and families and be aware of their backgrounds, whilst avoiding making assumptions about their upbringing or ACEs.

■ Reframe 'attention-seeking' children as 'attachment-seeking' children.

■ Use strategies like emotion coaching and problem-solving to resolve any conflicts.

■ Offer times throughout the day to check-in with children and hold them in mind.

■ Provide calming areas – e.g., a den or pop-up tent filled with cushions and blankets – and use calming strategies.

■ Allow children to use comforters or transitional objects if they are needed.

■ Provide a visual timetable or Now/Next boards to help children understand routines.

■ Be a role model by having a calm attitude and demeanour.

■ Create an emotionally literate environment in terms of resources, displays, books and underpinning ethos.

■ Actively teach positive dispositions, attitudes and skills, such as resilience, perseverance and a 'can-do' mindset.

■ Use labelled praise and encouragement, avoiding reward systems based on social compliance.

Avoiding reward-based systems that can damage children's self-esteem

Many schools and settings focus on 'managing' children's behaviour. This brings in an unhelpful power dynamic and implies that children and their behaviour need to be managed by adults, rather than seeing children as competent beings who may need support to develop self-regulation. If we use the term *supporting* rather than *managing*, and if we think about self-regulation rather than behaviour, it changes the focus and reminds educators of their role in co-regulating and teaching children coping strategies. Instead of a focus on sanctions and rewards, we can build relationships and enable children to develop independence.

Parents and educators need to be aware that, occasionally, in attempting to raise children's self-esteem by praising children too frequently, they may, in reality, be damaging children's self-esteem long term (Brummelman et al., 2017). Children can become reliant on this praise and link feelings of self-worth with the praise they receive, thus feeling bad or worthless if they are not praised. Some behaviour systems in schools and settings use methods that shame children in order to get them to conform – for example, when Charlie is talking in assembly, he is asked to stand up; or when Sonia is finding it difficult to sit still, she is publicly told to behave more like Nazma who is sitting beautifully.

There may be a specific place for rewards and incentives when they are used sparingly, when they tap into children's interests or intrinsic motivation and when they do not publicly shame children. However, whole-setting/class systems that link praise and sanctions with social shame or isolation are inappropriate and should be avoided. These types of systems are very damaging to children's self-esteem and undermine work around growth mindset (Dweck, 2012; Chapter 5). Research has shown the negative implications of praise (Lungu, 2018; Robins, 2012); and when trying to support children to develop self-regulation, it is vital that educators have a full awareness of the potential consequences of over-praise and reward-based systems, as these approaches can be preventing the very thing they seek to promote!

Public praise and reward systems work on the principle of rewarding children for positive behaviour and using sanctions for children when they do not follow the agreed code of conduct. We may regularly see a rain cloud and sunshine or a traffic light system used in the classroom; however, when we praise children, it's a bit like giving them a lovely sweet. They have a good feeling inside and want more, which, it could be argued, is a good thing because we want our children to behave. But, too many sweets and our teeth will rot and we'll become overweight. Too much praise and it can become meaningless – children may lose interest in our rewards, and we will have to think of bigger and better rewards in order to get them to conform! The incentive soon wears off. Children can become reliant on praise and dependent on our approval, leading them to judge themselves according to extrinsic criteria.

Praise linked to behaviour charts is based on the theory that children can be conditioned to behave in certain ways through positive reinforcement. Research into this area has mainly focused on animal behaviour and has shown that if we do A, the animal will do B. It relies on rewarding desirable behaviour so that this will be repeated, and sometimes it includes punishing undesirable behaviour so that this will not be repeated. It believes behaviour can be modified by offering extrinsic rewards or sanctions. However, although to a certain extent these systems work with children, this behaviourist approach ignores the world of emotions, the theory of self-worth and the power of intrinsic motivation. Just because the method can get results doesn't mean it is right or appropriate for us to use these methods for all children.

When using whole-class reward systems, children may feel pressured into behaving a certain way because they are scared of being publicly shamed or fearful that they will upset their teacher. So, there is a moral consideration here: Should we be making children feel bad, frightened even, in order to encourage them to behave a certain way? It seems inappropriate that, despite everything we know and understand about trauma and the effect that cortisol has on the brain, schools and settings still rely on these outdated systems. Instead, we should be basing our support systems on building relationships and attachment.

These reward and sanction systems will not work for all children, and for some they could be potentially damaging:

The invisible child – These children are in our setting and they never make a fuss. They are easy to look after – they are not particularly demanding of our attention because they are mostly compliant and submissive to the educators. For these children a behaviour chart is meaningless because they will never move up or down, and their behaviour is generally unnoticed. The chart gives the child the message that they are invisible.

The challenging child – We certainly know that this child exists. After five minutes in the room, this child's name will already be on our chart – and not for a good reason. For some children, getting their name on the 'rain cloud' will give them a bit of street cred! To begin with, they might want to comply, but very soon they realise that their best is not enough – they will never make it to the sunshine, so why bother. The chart gives the child the message that they are not good enough and never will be.

The high-achiever – This child works hard and always does well. Their name easily goes onto the sunshine, just by finishing their activities on time or helping tidy up. The chart gives the child the message that they don't need to work hard – they will always do well if they please the person in charge and are compliant. Robins (2012) shares a story about a child in assembly who, on seeing a disruptive child achieve a merit by managing to sit quietly for all of two minutes, asks her teacher for a merit only to be told, "No, you always sit quietly so you don't need a merit!"

The highly anxious child – Many children feel anxious during their time in our setting. Some children will live in fear that their name will go onto the chart. They may be worried or fearful about how their parents may respond, or simply be horrified about the possibility of the teacher telling them off. The reward chart will be adding to their already anxious day and unnecessarily filling their bodies with cortisol.

The child with low self-esteem – This child already feels like a failure. They try hard to please but somehow never manage to measure up. They feel unworthy, and if their name goes on the rain cloud this will reinforce this belief. The chart gives this child the message that they are worthless.

A more effective way to help children to understand the impact of their actions and behaviour, which can feel just as positive to a child as praise, is encouragement. This removes the judgement element that praise can often bring and focuses on effort and process rather than attainment and end-product. For example, praising saying "Good girl, Sammie, you've painted an amazing picture!" could imply that Sammie is only good because of her picture, and if her picture isn't amazing next time, she wouldn't be good. Instead, saying "Wow, Sammie, you should be so proud of yourself!" or "You spent a long time painting that. I love the colours you've chosen!" gives Sammie the message that her hard work and engagement are valued, not just the painting. Labelled praise or encouragement, when we reinforce what we are pleased with in the statements we say, is an effective strategy that also removes any judgement and reiterates the behaviour we want repeated. For example, "Great sitting, Freddie!" tells him that we like the way he is sitting down, or "What an amazing straight line!" tells the class I am pleased with the way they have lined up.

Lungu (2018:235) asks what sort of adult we want our children to become: "Do we want to form some obedient, humble, subservient person, dependent on the approval and appreciation of others or do we want autonomous, independent, responsible people with a good image and positive self-esteem?" The way we are using praise and rewards will determine the type of adults we grow. We want our children to know that, with enough hard work or effort, anything is possible, and we encourage them to become resilient, have a 'can-do' attitude and be happy to try new things. We also want our children to think for themselves, challenge authority if they need to and not be blindly compliant. Therefore, promoting self-regulation is a better stance to adopt than managing behaviour.

Self-confidence – Amy Skinner, St Andrew's Church School

I have recently been supporting a little girl, Kara, in my nursery class who has struggled with self-confidence. While purposeful praise is common in my practice, I had realised that Kara appeared to feel discomfort at being singled out when praised, so I needed to rewrite my response when praising to accommodate her. An example of how my normal practice changed to suit her needs was while junk modelling. I would usually praise, "Child A, I love the way you worked so hard to build this. I noticed this bit kept falling off and you kept thinking of ideas on how to fix it." Instead, I pointed to Kara's model and said, "Woah, this looks fantastic – someone has worked very hard on this!" Although this was difficult, and I had to take a few moments to think about and reword the praise in my head, Kara's big smile to herself demonstrated the benefits of my praise for this particular child.

At a later date, while teaching a group session, I asked the children if they wanted to share something they had done that day that they loved, worked hard at, found tricky or would like to do again. We listened to several children and spoke as a group about this. I then chose an area where I had seen Kara play in the hope I could give her a way to participate without feeling the pressure of the social group. "I noticed some children were playing hide-and-seek in the garden. Give me a great big smile if you enjoyed it!" Kara then gave me a big smile, and this subtle interaction supported her to feel included and a part of the group.

Amy skilfully notices that Kara needs support and is lacking in self-confidence. She had recognised that some children struggle with direct praise and found a way of showing Kara that she valued her contribution without putting pressure on her and praised her in a manner in which she could accept. It is this continued, natural and gentle interaction which probably gave Kara the confidence to then later participate in the group. This way of working necessitates educators who intervene sensitively and know their children really well.

The importance of our ethos

As educators, our ethos underpins everything we do and try to be. Therefore, if we want to develop children's self-esteem, self-awareness and promote their wellbeing, it relies on our ethos supporting this approach. This is about the atmosphere we foster, the attitudes we adopt and the environment we create – not only the physical environment, in terms of access to stimulating resources, but also the emotional environment. Tamsin would argue that we need to develop a loving pedagogy, because when children feel accepted and loved, they also feel valued, which contributes to their self-esteem and emotional wellbeing (Grimmer, 2021). Developing self-regulation would then follow.

Our loving pedagogy – Nancy Andrews, Milford Lodge, Australia

After reading a book questioning the value of group-care settings, a photo in our weekly news to families sprung to my mind, counteracting the opinion that children in group-care will not be loved as much as in home-based settings. The phrase "a picture can speak a thousand words" springs to mind. I had witnessed first-hand the care and attention all our staff put into forming attachments and settling new children into Milford Lodge at the beginning of the year. This photo for me captures the complete joy and delight we derive from our relationships with every child who attends our settings.

Love and *loving* are not always words that are used in relation to education, possibly due to the links with intimacy and sexuality; however, when we unpick what we mean when we refer to loving the children in our care, *love* is the obvious word choice. As educators, we want the best for our children. We hold them in mind when planning provision and try to keep them central in everything we do. We put rules and boundaries in place to keep children safe, and we enjoy spending time with them. A parent would probably come up with a similar list if asked how they demonstrate their love for their child. Describing a parent-child relationship as loving is totally appropriate, and Tamsin would argue it is the same for the educator-child relationship.

Adopting a loving pedagogy supports children to develop self-regulation because it:

■ Empowers children and offers them advocacy and a voice.

■ Helps children to feel safe, secure and ready to learn.

■ Gives children a sense of belonging and helps them to feel welcome.

- Takes into account trauma and attachment or any ACEs when considering the needs of children.

- Encourages an emotionally literate environment where we acknowledge and accept all emotions.

- Prioritises children's wellbeing over their attainment.

- Builds relationships, celebrates diversity and promotes inclusion so children see themselves and their families reflected in the environment.

- Seeks to support children to develop life skills for the future.

Demonstrating love to our children will also have a positive impact on their behaviour, because research shows that adopting a caring, nurturing, attachment-aware approach that encourages children to develop self-regulation reduces children's 'troublesome' behaviour (Aubrey & Ward, 2013). In addition, when we take time to observe and notice things about our children, we can attempt to unpick why they are reacting in this way. Our children will trust us and feel safe, secure and looked after. We believe that supporting children's self-regulation involves reflecting upon and redefining our ethos to make it underpin how we approach everyday situations.

Noticing the little things – Marlis Juerging-Coles, St John's Pre-School

One of the children at Pre-School was suddenly screaming and crying uncontrollably by the tuff tray. I rushed over and, after I checked she wasn't hurt, looked around for clues as to what had triggered her crying. This child speaks a different language at home and, whilst she is able to express basic needs and is very independent in her play, she can become selectively mute in times of distress. She also does not like physical contact and therefore can't be scooped up in a hug to calm her. I noticed her repeatedly looking at her trousers, which had gotten splashed with water whilst she was playing with the water in the tray.

I motioned for her to come with me and showed her the bag of clothes she has at Pre-School. Her crying slowed and almost stopped instantly. I signalled for her to go to the bathroom and get changed (again, I left her bag in the bathroom and stood outside because the child is very wary of her privacy). When she reappeared, she had changed her trousers but was still visibly upset, pointing at the wet trousers on the floor. I picked them up and showed her how I would place them on the radiator to dry.

When we came back into the Pre-School room, she still seemed reluctant to play again. I remembered this child really liked puzzles when she first started (she could do these independently and didn't have to ask for rules in a language she was still getting used to), so I got out the box of puzzles. She almost immediately engaged herself with a couple of them and spent about half an hour contently putting the puzzles together and then starting them again, before returning to more sociable play with some of her friends.

Self-awareness

Self-awareness could be described as being aware of yourself, your thoughts and your feelings as well as having an understanding of how other people perceive you. This ability is vital for children when developing self-regulation because they need to tune in to their emotions and be aware of others and the impact their behaviour may have on them. Self-awareness begins at about 18–24 months of age, when children first recognise their reflection in a mirror (Rochat, 2003). Prior to this, it is thought that children may not realise the image in the mirror is theirs, and this is an important milestone in terms of their developing identity and a sense of who they are as an individual.

Becoming self-aware will help children to learn from their mistakes, accept criticism and consider the world from the perspective of others. Anytime we want to get a better score or beat our personal best when playing games we are using our self-awareness. Therefore, we could describe self-awareness as a critical-thinking skill where children are able to adjust their behaviour and actions in the light of the circumstances around them. For example, if a parent were to ask a preschool-aged child to whisper because their younger sibling is asleep, a child with good self-awareness would be able to do this. Or, if a child wanted to build a taller tower than their friend's, they are using their self-awareness. This is difficult for young children and is only just beginning within the early years, with self-awareness growing with age.

Using a comforter – Laura Whitall, Charlton Nursery & Preschool

When Adrianna started nursery she brought a blanket from home as a comforter. She would carry the blanket all day and would refuse to engage in any activities. Educators used her attachment to the blanket to get Adrianna involved in different activities by using her comforter as the main 'attraction' in their activities. After a couple of weeks of Adrianna being in nursery, she began to interact with her educators without the need of the blanket. And, a few sessions after that, Adrianna started to drop the blanket during the middle of her play. Educators would use those moments to hide the blanket away, as seeing the blanket after not using it would sometimes make Adrianna upset. As the weeks passed, she would use her blanket less and less. When Adrianna became completely settled in the room, she would leave the blanket in her bag at the beginning of the day and ask her educators for it when it was time for her nap, showing a level of self-awareness.

Educators decided to let Adrianna keep the blanket during her settling process because they believed that allowing her to have her comforter gave her a sense of belonging and gave her confidence while in the room and dealing with new experiences.

Adrianna demonstrates self-awareness when she asks her educators for her comforter at nap time. She was aware of her feelings and knew that her blanket might comfort her. The ethos her educators have adopted allowed Adrianna's attachment needs to take priority and recognised the importance of transitional objects in helping her settle into nursery life.

Research links three and four year olds' growing self-awareness with their social and moral understanding and their ability to tell the truth (Bender et al., 2018), which is interesting when we consider the development of empathy, as discussed in Chapter 7. Being able to reflect upon their actions and behaviours, whilst also considering the experiences of others, is developmentally beyond many of the children we will work with in the early years; however, part of our role as educators is to role-model, interact with and support children as they begin to develop these skills.

We can help children to develop self-awareness by:

- Talking about feelings and emotions.

- Labelling our children's feelings and emotions in the moment.

- Encouraging children to make predictions and talk about whether or not they were right using "I wonder what would happen if" statements.

- Using thinking words and phrases, such as, "I think," "I agree/disagree," "I imagine," "I like/don't like " or "I wonder."

- Role-modelling by thinking out loud – for example, "I think I need to try a different way of building this tower, because last time it fell down quickly" or "I need to talk quietly because Freya said she has a headache."

- Using positive questioning that encourages children to think about the implications of behaviour or actions – for example, "What would happen if we did X?", "How might we do that without X happening?" or "What does Graeme need to do to help his Mummy?"

- Using mirrors and look at our reflections, celebrating that everyone is unique.

- Encouraging children to talk about their needs and role-model this – for example, "I am feeling really excited, I need to jump up and down!" or "You look a little sad, do you need a cuddle?"

- Building children's self-esteem and encouraging them to see themselves as amazing, strong and competent beings who have a growth mindset, believing anything is possible with hard work and help from others.

It is generally accepted that the early years are a vital time for children to develop the skills and attitudes necessary for future life, and early intervention with children and families really does work (Tickell, 2011; Allen, 2011). Sometimes our intervention includes supporting children to develop positive dispositions that will stand them in good stead for the future. The more we can help children to be self-aware and recognise their big feelings and emotions, the easier it will be for them to learn self-regulation. This relies on having supportive educators who can co-regulate and teach the children strategies they can use independently.

Supporting Isla – Marlis Juerging-Coles, St John's Pre-School

Isla is currently in the process of a CAMHS referral because, although she can be calm and wonderfully involved in her play, at times her behaviour is very erratic and even aggressive towards other children. With limited speech, she can struggle to express what is upsetting her, and triggers do not appear constant. I had noticed that Isla was most calm when being held, but in the setting this was impractical for long periods of time. I suggested trying a sling seat to enable educators to provide her with the physical close contact and reassurance

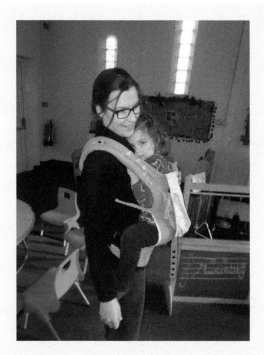

she needed whilst still having their hands free. So, after getting consent from Isla's parents, I tried her in the sling seat. After the first trial, I showed Isla where the sling was and, to my surprise and delight, over the next couple of weeks, she would frequently bring the sling to me, taking charge of her own needs. The frequency and length of time spent in the sling seat grew gradually less but was completely controlled by Isla. We haven't used the sling seat at all for a few weeks now because she hasn't chosen to use it and, overall, she has been a lot more settled at Pre-School.

Developing self-awareness also helps children to become more independent in their learning. It contributes to their academic skills as they learn to reflect upon their work, cope with classroom situations, empathise with others, explain their reasoning, draw conclusions and evaluate their own or others' work. Even very young children are able to take control of their circumstances and express their needs when they are self-aware, as the example about Isla shows. Despite her limited speech, she was aware that she needed to be held, and her educators empowered her by teaching her how to independently bring them the sling.

Summary

This chapter has thought about how children develop a sense of self-esteem and self-awareness as well as how this supports them when they develop self-regulation. We know the importance of building relationships and attachments with children and how adopting a loving pedagogy and being trauma and attachment aware can provide a good foundation for our practice. There are many ways we can support our children to become more self-aware and develop their self-esteem. The next chapter will build on this as it considers other skills related to control and inhibiting behaviour and explores various strategies we can use to support children.

Questions for reflection

1. In what ways do we build children's self-esteem and promote their emotional wellbeing?

2. To what extent is our practice trauma and attachment aware?

3. How might we further develop children's self-awareness and enable them to recognise their big feelings and emotions?

References

Allen, G. (2011) *Early Intervention: The Next Steps*. London: Her Majesty's Stationery Office.

Aubrey, C. & Ward, K. (2013) 'Early years practitioners' views on early personal, social and emotional development', *Emotional & Behavioural Difficulties, 18*(4), pp. 435–447.

Bavolek, S. (2000, November) 'The Nurturing Parenting Programs', *OJJDP: Juvenile Justice Bulletin* [NCJ 172747]. Available from https://ojjdp.ojp.gov/library/publications/nurturing-parenting-programs.

Bellis, M., Lowey, H., Leckenby, N., Hughes, K., & Harrison, D. (2013) 'Adverse childhood experiences: retrospective study to determine their impact on adult health behaviours and health outcomes in a UK population', *Journal of Public Health, 36*(1), pp. 81–91.

Bender, J., O'Connor, A., & Evans, A. (2018) 'Mirror, mirror on the wall: Increasing young children's honesty through inducing self-awareness', *Journal of Experimental Child Psychology, 167*, pp. 414–422.

Bergin, C. & Bergin, D. (2009) 'Attachment in the Classroom', *Educational Psychology Review, 21*, pp. 141–170.

Bowlby, J. (1982) *Attachment and Loss: Vol. 1 – Attachment*. New York: Basic Books.

Brummelman, E., Nelemans, S., Thomaes, S., & Orobio de Castro, B. (2017) 'When parents' praise inflates, children's self-esteem deflates', *Child Development, 88*(6), pp. 1799–1810.

Chen, X., Huang, Y., Xiao, M., Luo, Y., Liu, Y., Song, S., Gao, X., & Chen, H. (2021) 'Self and the brain: Self-concept mediates the effect of resting-state brain activity and connectivity on self-esteem in school-aged children', *Personality and Individual Differences, 168*. doi: 10.1016/j.paid.2020.110287.

Collingwood, S. Knox, A., Fowler, H., Harding, S., Irwin, S., & Quinney, S. (2018) *The Little Book of Adverse Childhood Experiences*. Lancaster, UK: Imagination Lancaster. Available at https://www.saferbradford.co.uk/media/4sff2jsx/little-book-of-aces.pdf.

Cvencek, D., Greenwald, A., & Meltzoff, A. (2016) 'Implicit measures for preschool children confirm self-esteem's role in maintaining a balanced identity', *Journal of Experimental Social Psychology, 62*, pp. 50–57.

Dweck, C.S. (2012) *Mindset: How You Can Fulfil Your Potential*. London: Constable & Robinson.

Grimmer, T. (2021) *Developing a Loving Pedagogy in the Early Years: How Love Fits with Professional Practice*. London: Routledge.

Jarvis, P. (2019) 'Why ACEs are Key to Behaviour Management', *The TES online*. Available at https://www.tes.com/news/why-aces-are-key-behaviour-management.

Laevers, F. (2005) *Well-being and Involvement in Care Settings. A Process-oriented Self-evaluation Instrument*. Leuven: Kind & Gezin and Research Centre for Experiential Education. Available at https://www.kindengezin.be/img/sics-ziko-manual.pdf.

Lungu, M. (2018) 'The Influence of Rewards Used in Child Education over the Development of Their Personality', *Journal Plus Education/Educatia Plus*, *19*(1), pp. 225–237.

Moore, J. & Smith, M. (2018) 'Children's levels of contingent self-esteem and social and emotional outcomes', *Educational Psychology in Practice*, *34*(2), pp. 113–130.

Palix Foundation (2021) *Brain Story Certification*. Available at https://www.albertafamilywellness.org/training.

Pintoa, A. Veríssimoa, M., Gatinhoa, A., Santosa, A., & Vaughn, B. (2015) 'Direct and indirect relations between parent–child attachments, peer acceptance, and self-esteem for preschool children', *Attachment and Human Development*, *17*(6), pp. 586–598.

Porter, T. (2019) 'What if schools valued wellbeing more than results?', *Times Educational Supplement*, 16 July. Available at https://www.tes.com/news/what-if-schools-valued-wellbeing-more-results?fbclid=IwAR1miFteJqxM1q0gP7O7Aeb9PPdluTEj8xWurFzQ_48pxGzQw1dvHU_uBxo.

Robins, G. (2012) *Praise, motivation, and the child*. London: Routledge.

Rochat, P. (2003) 'Five levels of self-awareness as they unfold early in life', *Consciousness and Cognition*, *12*(4), pp. 717–731.

The Children's Society (2015) *The Good Childhood Report*. Available at https://www.york.ac.uk/inst/spru/research/pdf/GCReport2015.pdf.

Tickell, C. (2011). *The Early Years: Foundations for Life, Health and Learning. An Independent Report on the Early Years Foundation Stage to Her Majesty's Government*. London: Department of Education. Available at https://assets.publishing.service.gov.uk/government/uploads/system/uploads/attachment_data/file/180919/DFE-00177-2011.pdf.

Tonmyr, L., Lacroix, J., & Herbert, M. (2020) 'The Public health issue of ACEs in Canada', in G. Asmundson & T. Afifi (Eds.), *Adverse Childhood Experiences: Using Evidence to Advance Research, Practice, Policy, and Prevention*, pp. 185–207. San Diego, CA: Academic Press.

4 Skills relating to regulating behaviour

Tamsin Grimmer

Introduction

During a visit to a school Tamsin observed a little boy who was clearly desperate to tell his teacher something and could hardly contain himself. He looked like he might burst and was literally jumping up and down with excitement. We can all imagine this child and have probably had a similar feeling ourselves – we really, really want to say something and know we have to wait until an appropriate moment. Or when we're in a meeting and we hear someone put a spin on a subject so much that we can hardly spot the truth and we feel like shouting out, "That's not quite true!" but have to hold back.

When Tamsin's children were little, the family didn't put Christmas presents under the tree until Christmas Eve. This was because it was too difficult for her children to hold back and not open any before the big day. Putting presents under the tree really early felt mean – a little like saying, "Here you are, but you can't have it yet ... wait!" Waiting is extremely difficult for young children, particularly for those who are on the autism spectrum.

These examples of inhibiting impulses and having to wait for things are linked with our self-control and self-discipline, which come under the umbrella of self-regulation. Many young children struggle with these skills, which is not surprising because many adults do too. For example, as adults we may find it difficult not to get angry if a driver goes through a red light, or we may feel frustrated when having to wait in a queue.

Emotional resilience

When we are able to cope with the various challenges life brings or overcome adversity, it is emotional resilience that enables us to do this. Emotional resilience is not something we are born with – some sort of innate ability – but, instead, it is a disposition we can foster and grow. Our role as educators is to help children to develop this skill. As Claxton

DOI: 10.4324/9781003162346-5

and Carr remind us, "It is the strength of these tendencies, we suggest, that changes over time, and which teachers influence, knowingly or not, through the kind of early years setting or classroom milieu which they create" (2004:89). Resilience is about bouncing back after difficulties or being able to adapt or overcome adversity.

Children might develop this skill naturally, perhaps through overcoming difficulties or through being determined and then successful, which positively reinforces their learning. They have found out through hard work that trying again and again will lead to success, and most children like the feeling when they have achieved or accomplished something. This is intrinsic motivation, wanting to overcome the difficulty because you know that perseverance will lead to success. Other children may need additional support from adults in order to learn this skill, but this doesn't make them any less resilient once they have learned it. There are many different factors that influence how easily a child learns to be resilient, including their personality and temperament, their health, the past experiences they have had in life, the way the adults around them have responded to them and also their home environment, including parenting style and modelled behaviour.

When children are emotionally resilient, they are better able to be independent, problem-solve, view situations positively and be more empathetic towards others. Very young children are still learning about their emotions and how to respond when feeling certain ways, and educators have a role to play in helping to develop resilience. Children need to learn they can ask others for help or assistance and this is a sensible way to seek comfort or support. We can help children to see beyond their immediate difficulties, towards the end goal or the resolution, or even towards a time when they will no longer feel this way. Sharing about our own experiences with children can help.

Defeating Evil Pea – Megan Bowkett, Mulberry Bush Pre-School

Villain and superhero role play is really popular with our little ones, and we find that they really respond to being given a task where they can help to save someone. With this in mind, we set up a scenario where Evil Pea trapped some vegetables and left the children

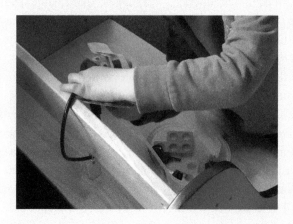

a note, which an educator read. The children needed to find the corresponding numbered lock and keys to save the vegetables, and we encouraged them to think about how they could solve the problem. There was lots of teamwork and excitement, especially when they spotted the note when they arrived in the morning.

Ways that adults can help grow resilience in children include:

- Talk about our emotions and share about times when we have been resilient.

- Be available to help and support when needed, avoiding jumping in too soon.

- Role-model being resilient throughout the day.

- Teach children how to recognise when they need time or space and the importance of having breaks.

- Talk about the future and end goal to help children see beyond their current challenges.

- Share stories of others who have been in a similar position and have overcome difficulties, to help put things in perspective.

- Remain positive and encourage a positive outlook.

- Use visual cues or timetables to help children manage transitions and talk openly about changes or uncertainty.

- Encourage and praise when a child overcomes a difficulty saying, "You should be proud of yourself!" or "You did it!" Reiterate it was their ability to persevere that led to success.

- Foster a growth mindset.

Emotional Resilience – Chloe Webster, Pebbles Childminding

Pre-lockdown, our cohort of children at the time all turned two within months of each other and, as any practitioner knows, emotions and tensions can run high during play with a group of just two-year olds all finding their own way and developing their personalities whilst trying to navigate social scenarios and collaborative play.

Our previous experiences taught us that each child needs different degrees of support as well as different methods to begin to develop emotional resilience and intelligence, and what has worked for one previously may not always work for others at the same age/stage of development.

For us, the most important and beneficial 'work' we have done with our children in relation to emotional resilience is role-modelling. Our children learn so much from us, whether it be communication, kindness or how to process our emotions. So, by not only modelling and naming our feelings and emotions during high-pressured or emotive scenarios, this enables the children to witness first-hand that all emotions and feelings are acceptable, but there are ways in which we can process and respond to them, whether that be time, space or verbalising to our peers how their actions have made us feel.

As practitioners, our role in supporting children's emotional resilience is not to 'tell' them how to feel or what to feel, but rather to support them in understanding their emotions and the best way for them to process and overcome these strong feelings.

Some children prefer to be alone and take themselves away from a scenario, some will seek adult support and comfort, whilst some may choose to engage in a discussion and talk themselves calm – whatever works for the individual child we support and facilitate as best we can. Always on hand to support and guide children as they navigate these complex and confusing emotions, we see our 'work' and role in developing children's emotional resilience as a supportive one until children have developed the skills and knowledge to then manage these scenarios and emotions themselves, knowing what works best for them.

We now have children who remove themselves from situations and take time to chill out or read a book when feeling angry or upset, children who approach adults and say "I'm feeling sad, will you cuddle me?" as well as children who can discuss with their peers their own thoughts and feelings about a scenario and navigate these conflicts and find solutions themselves, managing their emotions maturely and with very little support or input from us.

Our children's return to the setting from our closure due to lockdown is testament to their emotional intelligence and resilience. As they returned to us seamlessly after over three months away from the setting and settled back into the routine and their prior relationships and friendships as if they'd never left.

Dispositions and attitudes

There are many different dispositions and attitudes we would like to foster within early childhood – for example, independence, resilience, creativity, 'can-do' attitude and motivation, to name a few. The Statutory Framework for the Early Years Foundation Stage in England (DfE, 2021) identifies three characteristics of effective teaching and learning that consider how children learn rather than what they learn. The three characteristics are: (1) Playing and Exploring, which is often described as motivation; (2) Active Learning, described as engagement and (3) Creating and Thinking Critically, which is all about children's thinking skills. These are a helpful way to think about the process of learning and the sorts of attitudes we want to promote.

When planning, it is sometimes better to consider how our enabling environment and the positive relationships we build might foster these dispositions, rather than thinking about topics, themes or specific subjects of learning.

Ways we can grow and promote positive dispositions and attitudes in our settings include:

- Building secure attachments and developing effective relationships with significant adults and peers.

- Tuning in to children and identifying interests, fascinations and schemas.

- Providing a stimulating learning environment with access to open-ended resources and loose-parts play.

- Focusing on wellbeing of adults and children.

- Responding sensitively to children – this will reinforce the growth of their dispositions.

- Role-modelling how to do something.

- Co-constructing learning with educators and children working together.

- Scaffolding and extending children's play.

- Supporting the child in the moment.

- Simplifying language or simplifying the task.

- Highlighting the main features of the task.

- Asking questions to encourage further learning.

We really love this quote from Fisher, "A key role of the early childhood educator is to sustain children's thinking and follow the momentum of their learning" (Fisher, 2016: 108). Using the term *momentum* is helpful in explaining the way that learning continues and adults just need to remain attuned to the children and be ready to support if needed or appropriate.

Inhibiting impulses

It is natural for young children to have impulses, and not all impulses should be inhibited – for example, if something is too bright, we close our eyes or turn our heads away from the light source. However, one of the skills that forms part of self-regulation is our ability to inhibit impulses. Sometimes we want to act or react in a certain way, almost as a reflex or immediate response; however, it may not always be appropriate or acceptable to behave in that way. For example, when we feel angry with someone, we may feel like lashing out, but this is not an acceptable way to act. We need to control this impulse and stop ourselves from doing it. This is difficult for young children to do. It relies on their understanding that there are acceptable and unacceptable ways of behaving in the first place. They need to know what is right and wrong and why and then be able to respond appropriately.

Children also need to navigate the subtle differences in expectations throughout their day or routine. It's OK to cheer our friends during our 'All about me' time first thing in the morning, but when we are in assembly a little later, we have to stay quiet and still. Or, when we feel like jumping up and down in excitement on our birthday, that's OK, but when we feel like jumping on the bed when our parent is asleep, it's not. Adults can help children by explaining the whys and wherefores of a situation and communicating the expectations before and during an event. Communication is a key way of supporting our children.

Inhibiting impulses is about willpower and our ability to control ourselves when we feel a certain way. Genes play a role in shaping this, as it relies partly on our temperament and personality, but we are also able to foster and develop our willpower and gain more control over our actions by learning and practising these skills. Our ability to inhibit our impulses can be linked with executive-function skills, which Chapter 5 discusses. It is also important to consider the age and stage of development of the children in our care. Generally speaking, the older the child, the more self-control and self-discipline they will display. Educators are able to help children by understanding that they will find this area difficult, having realistic expectations and removing them from a situation if we can see it is causing a problem. We see the bigger picture, whereas children do not. So, if we know a child will get upset if they see their friend playing with a certain toy, can we arrange it so that they do not see it in the first place? Or, if we know they will find it difficult not to take a second biscuit, can we put the plate of biscuits away after they have had one?

Inhibiting impulses through risky play and adventure – Childminder

As a childminder, I am in the fortunate position of being able to use our local area to incorporate risky play and adventurous activities. On one occasion, when visiting a local animal park, the children were invited to hold snakes,

lizards and tarantulas. The children were really brave, sometimes more so than the adults! They overcame their fears as they held these creatures, and it became a talking point for a long time afterward. My first impulse would have been to run away, but with encouragement from the children, and after seeing how brave they were, even I managed to hold a snake!

There are many other ways we can help children to inhibit their impulses, such as:

- Teaching them other ways of acting – for example, showing them how to jump up and down when excited, stamp their feet instead of hitting or kicking when angry, etc.

- Role-modelling alternative ways of responding – for example, taking a break or deep breath.

- Role-playing or sharing stories about situations where someone had to stop themselves doing something.

- Playing stop-start, traffic-light games or Simon Says, where children practise stopping and following instructions.

- Supporting children to withstand temptation – for example, removing temptation from their sight or teaching them strategies for how to delay gratification, such as looking away, singing to yourself or distracting yourself.

- Teaching children to use words and talk about their feelings and their impulses – saying "I really want to hit you right now!" is better than hitting.

- Reminding children of the rules or what they are supposed to be doing.

- Labelling praise and encouraging children when they inhibit their impulses.

- Offering children breaks and freedom to recharge their batteries.

- Providing calm spaces where children can escape.

An inviting calming space – Laura Gee, Hillocks Primary Academy

We use lovely stories, pictures and colour to talk about how we are feeling. This is our calm space in my nursery room. Children are free to access it at any time.

Another issue that we may come across in our settings is about our motivation. Children may not be cooperative with adults because they don't want to do the tasks or activities the adults want them to do, therefore we need to try to make the activities so exciting and engaging that they will want to participate. One way to do this is to follow the children's lead and fine-tune our provision to meet their interests and fascinations. So, we need to pay close attention to our children and observe them in order to tap into their intrinsic motivation.

Controlling our emotions

Part and parcel of inhibiting our impulses is controlling our emotions. When we feel overwhelmed with emotion, it is usually when we have the impulse to react a certain way, and sometimes this may not be appropriate. So, any strategies we can teach children about how to manage their big emotions will really help. The best place to start is labelling and acknowledging children's feelings and emotions. This not only helps children to know what they are feeling and put a name to it, it also validates those feelings. This is the first part of emotion coaching and is an effective strategy when helping children. This fits with Siegel's idea of 'Name It to Tame It' (Siegel & Bryson, 2012:27), which is a great phrase that reminds us of the importance of naming children's emotions.

'Name It to Tame It' – Holyrood Nursery Swinton, Thrive Childcare and Education

We were struggling with some of the children demonstrating challenging behaviours as they were unable to regulate their feelings and wanted a way in which we could support that effectively. So, we created a self-regulation space in the room with the children and explained to them how it could be used. They could share ideas about things they could add which would calm them down. We added breathing stars and fidget boxes, real-life emotion pictures and some comforters. Staff began to consistently use 'Name It to Tame It' strategies as they could see children displaying different emotions.

One child who was really struggling responded well to the new space and the strategies we were using. Over time he began to take himself to the space to calm down rather than act on his feelings by biting or lashing out, as he had used to. When staff approached the child, the first thing they would do is acknowledge his feelings, rather than reprimanding or arguing with him. Once he had returned to a state of calm and it was appropriate, we could then gently explore what happened with him and discuss better ways to deal with his anger.

We found out that children are much more capable of self-regulating than we first thought! We realised it's often our responses that make the situation worse. With a consistent approach from all staff, children have been using the self-regulation spaces as a place to be calm and process their thoughts and feelings. Children are now much more confident explaining how they feel, and staff are aware of naming these feelings with the children.

The biggest change we have made would be the staff's awareness of labelling feelings for the children, e.g., saying, "I know you're angry/sad/frustrated" instead of "You're ok/fine". This has been a real learning moment for us. We have been sharing this with parents too.

Part of the 'Name It to Tame It' strategy is about telling and retelling stories to support children with their emotions (Siegel & Bryson, 2012). This is particularly helpful when the emotions involved are uncomfortable in some way. For example, if a child feels frightened or very worried about something, retelling the story about the time when that happened can help. So, if someone who is really frightened of dogs is out walking and a big dog runs toward them, it can actually help to retell the encounter as a story, "Do you remember the time when that big dog ran toward you and you felt worried?" It might sound like reliving the traumatic experience, but talking about things we are frightened of or anxious about can be very therapeutic. Talking about the situation helps to desensitise us, which allows us to gradually get used to the thing we are frightened of or anxious about.

Lieberman et al. (2011:468) call the process of putting feelings into words 'affect labeling' and note how it dampens or lowers the distress people feel. Therefore, it is important for children and adults to feel able to talk about their emotions and help make sense of the feelings involved. Over time, through telling their own stories and through adults naming emotions, children will become more emotionally literate and feel better able to deal with these big feelings.

Emotion coaching

Emotion coaching is an evidence- and research-based approach to supporting children (Gilbert, Gus & Rose, 2021) that uses emotion labeling as part of the first step in the process. This strategy was initially recognised by Gottman, who studied parents' response styles when their children were behaving in challenging ways (Gottman et al., 1996). He noticed that they mostly responded in one of four ways: disapproving, dismissive, laissez-faire or emotion coaching. For example, if a child was upset over a spilled drink, the parent might disapprove by saying, "I told you to be careful!", they might dismiss the feelings involved by saying, "Don't cry, it's only a spilled drink!" or they might respond in a very laissez-faire manner by saying, "You'll be alright, I'm sure you'll manage to clean it up!" None of these responses is very helpful to the child in the moment, and none of them are supportive in helping the child to learn from the situation. Gottman suggests that an emotion-coaching response is both high in empathy and also supportive in terms of offering guidance for the child. So, saying, "I'm sorry you spilled your drink. You must feel sad. Let's clean it up together" would be a better way of responding. This acknowledges the feelings involved and offers a way forward for the child.

Key to this concept is the idea that all emotions are acceptable, but not necessarily all behaviours – there are no positive or negative emotions, no good or bad feelings, just emotions and feelings. However, how we act when we feel that way might be positive or negative, good or bad. Some feelings may make us uncomfortable, while others may make us feel lovely, but having all of these feelings is very natural and they should all be validated and accepted. So, when we are feeling sad, we need to explain to our children that we are sad and why; or, when we feel excited about something, we need to share that excitement with them.

Emotion Coaching – Jenna Jefferies, Charlton Nursery & Preschool

Yosef (3 years old) was born premature, and as SENCo [Special Educational Needs Coordinator] I had been working closely with the child's family and identified a developmental delay of around 12 months. Consequently, Yosef was struggling to express himself, and the easiest way he could make himself heard in nursery was to cry, fall to the floor and occasionally bite or spit. We recognised this as real frustration on his part and created opportunities for Yosef to learn how to express himself appropriately.

Following training, I introduced 'emotion coaching' techniques to the staff team, and we found modelling and labelling helped children to identify their own emotions. For example, adults said, "I can see you are so happy when you play with the trains. Trains make you happy" and "You are very angry, you want the bike now. I can see you don't want to wait." We paired this labelling language with an emotional-regulation register with visual cues prompting children to move their photograph to the emotion they are feeling. This was also shared at home. Furthermore, we introduced simple games, such as emotion matching, where Yosef was encouraged to sort photos of emotions into feeling happy or unhappy. Following these interventions, Yosef is beginning to use language to express himself and is able to identify complex emotions, such as 'angry' and 'scared'. Moreover, he is using these expressions within his play. Recently, when we explored light using torches in a darkened room, Yosef entered reluctantly and stated, "I'm scared!" We were so proud of him using his words to share his feelings and were able to better support him because of this.

Emotion coaching helps us to co-regulate our children's emotions by responding in the moment and supporting children through their big feelings towards a resolution. There are three main steps involved:

1.   Acknowledging feelings, naming and labelling emotions and practising acceptance of them.

2.   Exploring the issue further, sometimes setting limits on the behaviour (if needed).

3.   Problem-solving and resolving the issue.

Step one is the most important step because it is often through acknowledging and validating a child's feelings that the situation de-escalates and begins to calm down. Children want to be understood and labelling a child's emotions and offering authentic empathy helps them to feel better.

We will usually try to find out what happened and explore the issue with the child or group of children. At this point it is important that we remain non-judgemental and impartial. We are fact-finding here and being the behaviour detective we mentioned in Chapter 1. Children may need reminding if any behaviours displayed are unacceptable – for example, "It's not OK to poke your friend with a stick when you are excited" – to set limits on their behaviour. We could follow this with choices, if we feel it is appropriate – "You can either take the stick outside into a space or choose to play with something else."

The third step of problem-solving may not always be needed, but some situations will necessitate it – for example, if there is an argument over a toy or resource, using a problem-solving approach turns the situation into an opportunity to learn how to resolve conflicts. In this scenario we could use the six steps from the HighScope approach (HighScope Educational Research Foundation, 2020). This strategy fits nicely within an emotion-coaching approach and turns arguments or conflicts into problems to solve, which makes them a positive learning experience for all.

The HighScope six steps are:

1. Approach calmly, getting down to the children's level – we need to remain calm or we run the risk of escalating the situation.

2. Acknowledge and label feelings – this fits with the first stage in emotion coaching.

3. Gather information – remember, we are behaviour detectives on a fact-finding mission and should remain impartial in our responses.

4. Restate the issue as a problem to be solved – we need to use language the children will understand and see it as an opportunity for everyone to learn.

5. Ask for ideas for solutions and choose one together – by now we usually have an audience, so we can involve all the children in thinking of solutions.

6. Be prepared to give follow-up support – we might be needed to support the children as they work through their solution.

(HighScope Educational Research Foundation, 2020)

Problem-solving with the children – Childminder

When children need to resolve arguments, I use the High/Scope six steps to turn the issue into a problem to be solved. This makes it a positive learning experience for all the children in my care. I have created a display showing the different ideas of how we can solve problems together. Children refer to these ideas throughout the day as and when they need them. Sometimes, if they are struggling to resolve a problem, I will need to intervene, and I always begin by getting down to their level, then acknowledging the feelings of all children involved. After talking about the issue, we turn it into a problem – for example, by saying, "Oh no, we have a problem: two children want to go ride on the balance bike and we only have one. How can we solve this?" If they cannot think of any ideas, we return to our board and choose a solution we think will work together.

The wonderful consequence of using this method is that children learn to resolve conflicts and difficulties themselves. Once, when Tamsin was teaching in a Reception class, the first time she realised that two children had a problem was when they fetched the sand timer and, when quizzed about it, they explained that they were taking it in turns on the computer. It's at that moment that we can breathe a sigh of relief and think, "Yes, they've got it!" After all, part of our role is to help children gain independence and prepare them for the time when we won't be there to support them. This problem-solving wheel is a similar idea to the display board and is a method of sharing solutions with the children of how we can resolve issues independently.

There are a few essential ingredients that need to be in place before we can use emotion coaching as a technique. We must tune into our children's feelings and pay attention to our own emotions. Emotions are a natural and valuable part of life, so we need to observe, listen and learn how our children express their different emotions, watching for changes in facial expressions, body language, posture and tone of voice. We can use these emotional moments as opportunities to connect with our children and teach them about our feelings and how we act and react when we feel a certain way. Ideally, we will show our children that we understand what they are feeling, we take their emotions seriously and we will not dismiss them. When using this approach, we need to remain non-judgemental and impartial and avoid taking sides, making judgements or criticising how they feel.

Emotion coaching – Gemma Rowlands, Moorlands Infant School

A group of children were shown the playground where they would be playing the next day after lunch. As the children were being brought back to the classroom, one child appeared to struggle with the idea of leaving the playground. He started to walk away from the group and said, "I'm cross, I wanted to be at the front [of the queue]." First, I had to ensure his safety by limiting his behaviour, "I can't let you walk away. I have to keep you safe".

He stopped and stayed at the edge of the playground whilst I asked a colleague to take the other children back to the classroom. Once the other children were safe in the classroom, I sat with him:

Adult: "Are you sad because you were not at the front of the queue?"

Child: "I'm sad because I really want to play on the playground."

Adult: "You really wanted to play on the playground now, it looks like lots of fun! You will definitely get to play on it tomorrow. Could we do something else until then?"

[Short Pause]

Child: "Playing with the sand also looks fun."

We returned to the classroom to play in the sand pit.

By enlisting my emotion-coaching knowledge, I was able to acknowledge and validate his disappointment, limit his behaviour and support him to find an acceptable solution. After being validated and given time to process his feelings, he was happy to join the class. This involved attunement with the child: listening sensitively and meeting his emotions with empathy and acceptance. This helped to contain his feelings and demonstrates co-regulation. He quickly calmed himself after an initial angry outburst and was empowered to find a solution. This experience also highlighted the importance of understanding what his behaviour was communicating. His initial reaction indicated anger at not being at the front of the queue. By giving him the opportunity to fully explore and express his emotions, he was able to specify more clearly the disappointment he felt, and we found a way forward which he was happy with.

When we're using an emotion-coaching response, it can also be helpful to learn a script or have some particular phrases up our sleeves to use at certain times. This helps us to respond quickly without having to think about how to phrase things and can also help with consistency within our team. We can also share these ideas with parents and carers, which helps to build consistency with home and role-models how we respond in our setting.

Ideas of key words or phrases to use include:

- It's OK to feel cross, but it's not OK to hit your friend when you are cross!

- You look really excited – when I get excited I like to jump up and down like this.

- Let's find some things to do together that you love to do.

- I sometimes feel like crying too.

- I'm here for you.

- I understand.

- I can see you're feeling sad/angry/jealous.

- I wonder if you're missing your mummy/daddy.

- How can I help you?

- What happened?

Resolving conflicts – Jess Gosling, Taipei European School

In my setting we have used several strategies to solve conflicts. Often these conflicts include sharing, and the children always want to explain that they had an item first or put it down momentarily and another child picked it up. I listen to their dispute, which we talk through calmly. I then ask them what they can do to solve the problem. Over the course of the year, we have modelled ways of solving an issue with sharing: using a timer to time a popular toy use, using Stone Paper Scissors or moving away for a while to try something different. Whenever a child approaches with a disagreement, I always ask, "Have you talked to them? What did you say?"

This comment gives them time to reflect, then return and try to use their words. As we have modelled and provided this language, they are (mostly) able to calmly talk through the situation, and it is quickly resolved.

Using the six principles of nurture

When we nurture something or someone, we care and act in an encouraging or nourishing way. An example would be when we nurture a seedling and place it in an environment where it can grow, whilst feeding and watering it and making sure it has enough light or sunshine. If we think about how we might nurture children, we need to consider the environment around them as well as making sure they feel safe secure and their basic needs are met.

Writing about adopting a nurturing parenting approach, Bavolek (2000:2) shared how "Nurturing parenting processes employ nurturing touch, empathy, empowerment, and unconditional love to promote the overall health of the child." We do this too when we adopt a loving pedagogy and empower children, teaching them how to be empathetic as they build relationships with each other. The principles mentioned below help us to apply nurture within an educational context.

The six principles of nurture should underpin our practice and will help children to achieve more in our schools and settings:

1. Children's learning is understood developmentally.

2. The classroom/setting offers a safe base.

3. The importance of nurture for the development of wellbeing.

4. Language is a vital means of communication.

5. All behaviour is communication.

6. The importance of transition in children's lives.

(Lucas, Buckland & Insley, 2006)

Using the principles of nurture in school – Headteacher Rachel Tomlinson, Barrowford Primary School

Our Nurture room, which we call 'the nest', is designed with a home-like feel to be a bridge between school and home: a warm and friendly environment where children feel emotionally safe and secure, and therefore develop their individual needs further. A place where we give children the opportunity to grow in confidence and be engaged in a small-group environment to become more successful learners in their classrooms and the school community.

Within the nest we have a small kitchen area, where the children can enjoy cookery, baking and a place to prepare snacks for us to share at the table. There are comfortable sofas on which to share our news, thoughts and games with one another during daily circle time. In addition, there is a sensory room filled with lights, sounds and many other sensory materials. We also have our own outdoor play and garden area.

The nest is a targeted intervention based on a carefully routined session where there is a balance of learning and teaching, affection and structure within a home-like atmosphere. Children follow a structure and routine that is clear to both staff and children, which includes group listening and speaking, learning and games, individual and shared playing and social skills. The group runs on consistency, positive reinforcement and praise. We endeavour to immerse our young people in an accepting and warm environment. This helps to develop positive relationships with both teachers and peers by providing a variety of experiences, opportunities, approaches and resources to address children's needs within a culture of trust while incorporating the six principles of nurture.

These principles remind us to keep the child central to our planning and to consider their stage of development, not just their age. We know the importance of attachment theory, so ensure our settings provide the secure base and nurturing relationships needed for children to have a positive sense of wellbeing. We work closely with parents and carers to support children, keeping their emotional needs at the forefront of our thinking. When educators explain to children what is happening and why, they better understand their circumstances and why they might need to behave a certain way. These principles also remind us that children are communicating with us through their behaviour, and transition can have a big impact on them and how they act and react. We need to build children's sense of self-esteem and self-awareness and promote skills such as resilience so that they will be prepared to face the joys, changes and challenges that everyday life brings.

We want to enable our youngest children to achieve their full potential, and the World Health Organisation has developed its own guidelines that offer recommendations for caregivers to follow to promote early childhood development. They have labelled these 'Nurturing Care' and suggest that they cover five domains: good health, adequate nutrition, safety and security, responsive caregiving and opportunities for learning (World Health Organization, 2018). All children have the right to develop and learn (UNICEF, 1989), and all caregivers should nurture them as they grow.

Summary

Developing self-regulation leads to emotional resilience and the ability to maintain a sense of calm when faced with challenges or difficult situations. When we feel this way, we may need to stop ourselves from acting in the way that feels most natural, for example, lashing out or running away. This relies on a developing the ability to inhibit our impulses as well as control our emotions. This chapter has explored these skills and thought about various strategies that help us and our children to develop them, for example, the 'Name It to Tame It' approach, emotion coaching and problem-solving. As educators, we need to have several strategies up our sleeves to equip us as we respond mindfully to children.

As educators, we need to nurture and support our children as they build these skills and help them to become more emotionally literate, able to talk about their feelings, more emotionally resilient and able to remain calm in stressful situations. It is our job to role-model, teach children to use words to describe their emotions and be alongside the children ready to interact in the moment as and when we are needed. The next chapter considers the development of self-regulation in relation to executive function and metacognition.

Questions for reflection

1. How can we help children to grow positive dispositions, such as resilience and a 'can do' attitude?

2. When might it be appropriate to use emotion-coaching and problem-solving techniques within our routine?

3. How can we adapt our practice in the light of the six principles of nurture?

References

Bavolek, S. (2000, November) 'The Nurturing Parenting Programs', *OJJDP: Juvenile Justice Bulletin* [NCJ 172747]. Available from https://ojjdp.ojp.gov/library/publications/nurturing-parenting-programs.

Claxton, G. & Carr, M. (2004) 'A framework for teaching learning: the dynamics of disposition', *Early Years, 24*(1), pp. 87–97.

Department for Education (DfE) (2021) *Statutory framework for the Early Years Foundation Stage.* Available at https://assets.publishing.service.gov.uk/government/uploads/system/uploads/attachment_data/file/974907/EYFS_framework_-_March_2021.pdf.

Fisher, J. (2016) *Interacting or Interfering?: Improving Interactions in the Early Years.* Maidenhead: Open University Press.

Gilbert, L., Gus, L., & Rose, J. (2021) *Emotion Coaching with Children and Young People in Schools: Promoting Positive Behavior, Wellbeing and Resilience.* London: Jessica Kingsley.

Gottman, J., Katz, L., & Hooven, C. (1996) 'Parental meta-emotion philosophy and the emotional life of families: Theoretical models and preliminary data', *Journal of Family Psychology*, *10*(3), pp. 243–268.

HighScope Educational Research Foundation (2020) *How Does High/Scope Help Children Learn How to Resolve Conflicts?* Available at https://highscope.org/faq.

Lieberman, M., Inagaki, T., Tabibnia, G., & Crockett, M. (2011) 'Subjective Responses to Emotional Stimuli During Labeling, Reappraisal, and Distraction', *Emotion 11*(3), pp. 468–480.

Lucas, S., Buckland, G., & Insley, K. (2006) *Nurture group principles and curriculum guidelines: Helping children to achieve.* London: Nurture Group Network.

Siegel, D., & Bryson, T. (2012) *The Whole-Brain Child: 12 Proven Strategies to Nurture your Child's Developing Mind.* London: Robinson.

UNICEF (1989) *United Nations Convention on the Rights of the Child.* Available at www.unicef. org.uk/Documents/Publication-pdfs/UNCRC_PRESS200910web.pdf.

World Health Organization (2018) *Nurturing Care for Early Childhood Development: A Framework for Helping Children Survive and Thrive to Transform Health and Human Potential.* Available at https://apps.who.int/iris/bitstream/handle/10665/272603/9789241514064-eng.pdf.

5 Skills relating to executive function

Wendy Geens

Introduction

Imagine that your headteacher or senior manager calls you into the office and says, "The education inspectors are on their way – we've just had the call!" You immediately enter superhero mode and begin to make mental and physical lists of all the things you need to do. Then the phone rings and it's a parent who needs to talk about their child's special educational needs assessment. After supporting the parent as best you can, you answer the door to one of your apprentice's supervisors, who needs to do a joint observation of his practice with a member of staff. You quickly delegate this and begin sorting out paperwork, then finish the resource labelling you'd put off for weeks. Your executive functioning skills have really come into their own as you plan, prioritise, organise, delegate and execute the many tasks you have to complete – all while attempting to keep your stress levels down and maintain a calm demeanour for the sake of your colleagues.

   In this chapter we consider the role of executive function in supporting children's self-regulation and its connections with Theory of Mind (ToM). We do not claim to be experts in this area and have drawn upon the research and work of others to contextualise what is meant by the term *executive functions* as well as the specifics of the skill sets for each area within them and how the skills develop through age phases and activities that promote the development of executive functions. We have tried to illustrate this by including case studies from settings to give examples of how executive functions are promoted. The recent revisions of the Personal, Social and Emotional Development Early Learning Goals in England (DfE, 2021) have raised the profile of executive functions and the role they play in developing children's self-regulation. With this in mind, this chapter aims to contextualise the theory as well as suggest pragmatic approaches towards supporting children's development in executive functions.

DOI: 10.4324/9781003162346-6

Executive functions

Earlier chapters noted that self-regulation is not simply about children managing their emotions and behaviours (Conkbayir, 2017; Shanker, 2021). It involves a series of complex brain responses, specifically between the limbic and the prefrontal cortex areas. In its simplest form, executive functions are the skills developed in the prefrontal cortex (cognitive) area, and they are used in conjunction with and in response to the limbic (behaviour and emotional) area. They begin to develop early in a child's life and are built on gradually, becoming more complex as the child grows to adulthood. The Center on the Developing Child at Harvard University refers to executive function as the "air traffic control system" in the brain:

> Being able to focus, hold, and work with information in mind, filter distractions and switch gears is like having an air traffic control system at a busy airport to manage the arrivals and departures of dozens of planes on multiple runways.
>
> (2011:1)

Put simply, executive functions are our brain's way of managing our busy lives, and they involve us using our working memory, processing information, remaining on task and being able to complete tasks, just like in our inspection example above.

Historically, the term *executive function* is not new. In fact, it has been an area of study in adults for some years now, while research into executive function in the early years has grown more extensively over the past two decades (Garon et al., 2014). It is generally accepted that the first five years of life play a fundamental role in the development of executive functions, and most children learn to control their impulses and demonstrate cognitive flexibility, follow instructions and achieve self-directed goals (Garon et al., 2014). The *Encyclopedia on Early Childhood Development* (CEECD, 2021) notes that executive functions are the "cognitive abilities needed to control our thoughts, emotions and actions" and, as such, have an "impact on a person's social, emotional and intellectual life, from childhood to adulthood." These skills are sometimes referred to as 'soft skills', which could imply they are not important; however, it is our view that they are vital for children to develop and for society to function peacefully and efficiently.

Wendy recently met with a wonderful group of colleagues in a nursery setting to discuss the term *executive function* and what they think it means or implies. The initial responses included, "Higher expectation process", "Something that is within the expectations of a senior manager or leader" or "Something that is of higher importance". The term actually relates to the everyday skills we need and use habitually as we go about our lives – for instance, listening to a child telling us about their day at school whilst jotting an appointment on the calendar and thinking about what everyone will be having for dinner. These skills include transferring rules or information from one context to another, making plans, being able to focus, regulating our emotions and prioritising. With this in mind, we can see the magnitude of these skills and agree they are of immense importance, as indicated by the colleagues in the nursery setting.

Executive functions are the skills we take for granted that allow us to perform habitual tasks in our daily lives, therefore opportunities to develop these skills in early childhood are critical because, as they grow and develop, children continue to build upon their earlier, simpler skills through their primary and secondary education. They are the skills that help children to write paragraphs, remember what was asked of them and the order of instructions given or remember the steps in a calculation problem. They also impact our social relationships and therefore help us to sustain friendships. The Center on the Developing Child explains, "Just as an air traffic control system requires the interaction of multiple people – pilots, navigators, controllers, weather forecasters – our human executive functioning system requires that each type of skill utilize elements of the others" (2011:9). So, these skills overlap and are interrelated with each other.

The development of a child's executive functions is dependent upon the adult support they receive and the opportunities and experiences they have. Educators use scaffolding to support children in their learning and help them expand their executive functions. For example, a two year old is not expected to know and remember when they have to stop playing for lunch or the subsequent steps of putting the toys away, going to the bathroom to wash and dry their hands, collecting their packed lunch, taking it to the blue table and eating their lunch. Instead, the role of the adult is to break this down into smaller, achievable steps to ensure children are successful in their everyday tasks.

Adults in settings scaffold the opportunities they put in place and establish consistent routines to help children remember what is expected of them and the order in which they complete tasks. First, the adult will ask the children to stop playing, then they will help put the toys away and show them where the toys go. Next, they may take them to the bathroom and role-model how to wash their hands. Whilst it is not expected that young children can do this at the age of two, over time and through consistent daily repetition of these actions and the gradual removal of the scaffolding, as children grow older they will know what is meant by an instruction to stop what they are doing, clear the toys and get ready for lunch. Scaffolding is about breaking down tasks into smaller tasks and knowing what to do for those smaller tasks.

For example, a teacher reminding children to fasten their coats when they go out to play actually involves a number of steps that need to be completed in the following order:

Step 1 Listen to the instruction.

Step 2 Collect their coat.

Step 3 Put the coat on.

Step 4 Fasten the coat.

Step 5 Walk out to the play area.

Asquith (2020:21) explains how executive functions are "needed for everyday tasks, such as getting dressed, and whilst attempting a difficult or new task." Examples of such tasks in schools and settings include children remembering to hang coats on their pegs before they go into the classroom or sitting in the correct place and being ready to learn. By thinking about everyday, routine tasks, we can see how important it is for young children to have executive functions. Developing the skills and behaviours associated with them in the early years is key for future development and success. It is important to note, however, that children are not born with these skills, but it is likely they will develop them. As all children develop at different rates, the development of the skills will also be at different rates. In addition, their development will be dependent on the different experiences they encounter as they grow. Whilst children have the capacity to develop these skills through positive early experiences and relationships at home and within settings, more negative experiences can limit the development of the skills. Factors such as stress can have an adverse impact on a child's executive function; this itself means that early years educators are an important cog in the lives of young children.

Chapter 1 introduced Shanker's self-reg model (2021), which highlights the importance of stress and how understanding stressors is key to children developing self-regulation. For this to be effective, it is important that educators and parents alike consider how to reduce stress if they are to promote and develop executive functions. For example, a child who is sensitive to light and walks into a setting that has bright fluorescent lighting is likely to be immediately stressed. It would then become more difficult – some might say impossible – to help the child develop their working-memory skills if the child is in a state of stress. The Shanker self-reg model (2021) considers how stressors can affect the development of cognitive functioning, draws upon five domains of self-regulation (biological, cognitive, emotional, social and prosocial) and argues that heightened stress in any of these domains can lead to problems in behaviour, mood, learning and development. These experiences can have a negative impact on developing executive functions, as mentioned earlier in this chapter. Here is a reminder of Shanker's (2021) five-step approach for supporting children to develop the skills they need to understand their emotions and bring them back to a state of calm:

1. Read the signs of stress and reframe the behaviour.

2. Recognize the stressors.

3. Reduce the stress.

4. Reflect: enhance stress awareness.

5. Respond and restore energy.

Anyone who has worked in settings and schools will be familiar with children who may not be ready to learn, listen and be focused. Bringing children back to a calm state is necessary if they are to access opportunities for learning. When adults take on the role of co-regulator they are able to support children to develop self-regulation.

Consistent expectations – Reception teacher Melanie Ellis, Chewton Mendip Primary School

We have a child who will hit other children who enter his space. He has broken equipment when an adult or child has asked him to tidy up at the end of a session or to stop doing something. His behaviour can change very quickly – for example, during the first half-term at school, he was using a gardening trowel, digging in the plant pots and moving the soil around in the large tubs. When the session ended, he ran across the outside learning area with the trowel and charged towards a large dome mirror, which he cracked.

We now have one adult to support him during transitions explaining what is going to happen beforehand, giving him notice so there are no surprises. We talk through our expectations during 'tidy up time' and have an increased focus on positive praise for each small step he makes towards helping. We invited his parents in for a meeting to discuss his feelings and responses to situations at home and discussed a consistent approach to managing his feelings and behaviour during activities he didn't enjoy. The consistent expectations have made a positive impact on his behaviour both at home and at school, and his parents have commented on his improved, calmer attitude at home. It is still very much an ongoing working progress.

Exploring the three types of brain function

Executive functions are sets of cognitive skills with goal-directed behaviours – that is, they are skills that are inextricably connected and enable us to do things whilst also being needed for managing behaviours.

They have been categorised into three types of brain function:

- Working memory.

- Mental/cognitive flexibility.

- Self-control/inhibitory control.

Let us now look at each skill set in turn, determining and identifying their purpose, the opportunities to support the development of the skill set and the behaviours they may display. The examples of activities provided also show how the three areas are interconnected with activities promoting the development of several functions.

Working memory

Our working memory is a cognitive process whereby a temporary storage area in the brain holds facts or information in the short-term, meaning we can work with information without losing track of what we are doing. Doing mental mathematical calculations, following instructions and recalling facts are good examples of this. Working memory is hugely important in learning; it enables children to remember songs, the shapes of letters and their friends' names. As such, skills associated with working memory are listening and concentration as well as good visual processing. Asquith (2020:25) notes how we can support younger children to develop these skills: "Consistent routines provide opportunities for babies and young children to develop their working memory. Repeated experiences strengthen their brain connections and praise encourages them to join in and feel good about themselves." As an early years educator, Wendy regularly used visual timetables to help children to understand or know what would be taking place next. For some children this took away the unknown of what would happen and allowed them to feel safe and secure in the class – this is further exemplified by Erin's story in Chapter 2. Additionally, providing particular children with opportunities to develop their attention and concentration through a range of different games and interests was a successful approach to adopt.

Observation of free play – Wendy Geens

Wendy recalls working with a child who was just five years old as he started in year one. He had a fascination with numbers and loved talking about numbers. He would regularly be observed counting using the 100-square grid, moving objects and counting how many were in a set. He would often look for patterns in games. During a free-play afternoon he decided he wanted to do more and use the reverse side of the 100-square grid, which was a blank 100-square grid. He said, "We can make a game with this and then another person can play" and promptly fetched the box of different-sized bears. As he took the bears out of the box, he said, "This bear is a big bear, and he can go at the back." All the large bears were placed together, four in a row, and the medium bears were placed next to the big bears, with the small bears placed on the row in front. He then began to make up rules about how the bears could move around the grid. "The small bears can go anywhere, the big bears can only go forward, but the medium-sized bears can go forwards and backwards but not sideways." As he explained through his ideas and the rules of his game, it was clear to see that the game was not that dissimilar to chess. The object of his game was to move all the bears to the opposite side of the board. The boy then went on to invite another child to play his game and, as he explained the rules to another child, it was clear the other child was struggling to remember them and said, "Dinosaurs would help him." They then swapped the bears for the dinosaurs and generated a new game together with even more rules, as there was a wider range of different dinosaurs. What is interesting in this is that both the children were developing a number of self-regulation skills and were able to sustain their concentration for a period of time. The mathematics they were engaged in related to counting, space and positional language. This was a wonderful example of two children developing self-regulation skills – attention, concentration, empathy and problem-solving – through play.

The example above highlights how focusing on a child's interests – in this case dinosaurs – means a child is likely to sustain their attention for longer. Furthermore, if an adult provides an object based on the interests of a child, they may name the object they are holding and look and focus on the object to help to develop the child's attention. This works equally well when a child has chosen the object that has captured their interest and is one way to develop their attention.

Many of us have difficulty with our working memory at times; however, when it impacts on our ability to complete tasks or manage our day, it may become an issue. According to the International Dyslexia Association (2021), 10% of people have weak working memory; however, when we consider children with specific learning disorders – for example ADHD or dyslexia – this can be as high as 50%. Examples of problems with working memory are not being able to follow examples or being unable to complete mental calculations, such as 17 add 24 subtract 9.

There are many ways we can support children to develop their working memory:

- Play movement games and copy actions or dance moves.

- Sing songs and rhymes, which become increasingly complex as our children grow and develop.

- Read stories with repeated refrains and encourage children to join in with the words.

- Play word games that encourage an extension to the previous set of information, like "I went to market and I bought an apple … I went to market and I bought an apple and a banana … I went to market and I bought an apple, a banana and a cherry".

- Play games such as 'Kim's game', which requires children to remember the objects on a tray, then when they are covered, one is removed and the children have to guess what is missing.

- Encourage children to create obstacle courses and challenges that require them to remember different ways of moving, balancing or adjusting their weight.

- Play traditional board or card games, such as 'Happy Families' or 'Snap'.

- Create patterns out of construction materials or other resources.

- Copy repeating patterns of objects, words, sounds, movements or claps.

- Break down instructions into smaller steps, gradually adding more information as children are able to follow them.

- Provide photos of activities, memory books and use visual timetables as aides-memoires.

Planning what to play with – Ursula Krystek-Walton, Thrive Childcare and Education

In our Salford Royal setting, Reuben in our 2–3 room has been struggling with emotions and went through a period when he was finding it hard in the mornings coming into nursery. We developed a picture lanyard of Reuben's favourite activities and play areas to help him plan where to play. When he was dropped off, he could look at the lanyard of pictures and decide what he wanted to do that day. This worked well to support this transition.

Cognitive/mental flexibility

Mental flexibility – or cognitive flexibility, as it is sometimes known – is about thinking multiple things at the same time or being able to switch from one mental task to another. Being able to change our attention from one situation to another is a skill we regularly employ as adults without knowing or thinking we are doing it. Providing children with a variety of early problem-solving opportunities helps them to develop cognitive and mental flexibility. One such activity for developing these skills is trying to find the right shapes to fit into the spaces in a jigsaw. Wendy can recall several occasions as a reception teacher where children would spend time initially trying to push a cylindrical shape into a square space, watching them as they rotated the shape, turned it upside down and eventually looked for another space and went through the same process until the shape slotted into the correct space. During these observations some children may seek support or show frustration, and with the adult questioning and providing specific language and vocabulary, children make sense of what they are doing and try alternative methods. It is these kinds of early learning experiences that help children to develop their mental and cognitive flexibility.

Behaviours children display when they are struggling in this area can include:

- Frustration when small things go wrong.

- Repeating the same mistakes.

- Becoming anxious when plans or routines change.

- Not wanting to follow a new schedule.

- Repeating the same actions over and over again without success.

We often see these behaviours in classrooms and settings where children have not yet developed their cognitive and mental flexibility. As educators, we need to help children to develop resilience and provide an ethos which enables them to develop their skills and overcome difficulties in a supportive environment.

There are many ways we can support children and promote cognitive and mental flexibility:

- Playing sorting and matching games.

- Providing shape-sorters and post boxes.

- Building puzzles and jigsaws.

- Engaging in problem-solving activities.

- Providing opportunities for loose-parts play.

- Engaging in logic games and puzzles.

- Providing construction materials.

- Playing opposite games, like Simon Says where children sometimes obey what Simon says and sometimes do not.

- Following a recipe and cooking activities.

- Providing a 'surprise' or 'challenge' holder on a visual timetable to account for changes in the daily routine.

- Playing guessing games, like 'I spy' or 'Who am I?', which require children to remember previous ideas.

- Encouraging children to persevere when they meet challenges and praising them when they overcome them.

Loose-parts play – Ursula Krystek-Walton, Thrive Childcare and Education

At our Salford Royal setting there is a real focus on Physical Development as we know that promoting physical activity and physical literacy helps to support

children's emotional wellbeing and self-regulation. Loose parts are used both indoors and outdoors to encourage children to create and problem-solve, using their bodies in different ways. We have noticed that children will engage for a long time with this, persevering, practising, evaluating, enhancing as they develop in confidence.

On one occasion, Tanwen and Omar were experimenting with water cascading using a large tyre, some guttering and the top of a cable drum to make a table. We deliberately positioned this next to a tap so that we provided access to materials and water for the children to freely explore.

Children are constantly using their brains and bodies when engaging with loose parts, and adults are on hand to assist and scaffold as necessary. We often find children will challenge themselves – for example, through creating an obstacle course to commando-crawl under.

Self-control/inhibitory control

Self-control is about being able to manage frustrations or feelings and regulate the emotions. It is not self-regulation. Self-control is about being able to resist doing or saying something, however tempting it is, in order to keep our upstairs brain engaged (Siegel & Bryson, 2012). Being able to manage this helps us to be less impulsive, pay attention and stay focused on what we are doing. This is the same for children and adults alike – for example, if a child wants a toy but the toy is already being played with by another child, they have to manage the emotion of not being able to have what they want and learn not to simply take the toy from the other child. As such, the ability to resist acting impulsively and know the impact one's own words or actions can have on others is an important and complex skill to develop. This requires the child to have developed a certain amount of theory of mind and an understanding of the causes and consequences of emotions (Asquith, 2020).

There are many ways we can support children and promote self-control and inhibitory control:

■ Encourage children to notice their own emotions and remember what to do when they feel that way.

■ Engage in role play and perspective taking activities.

■ Read stories that involve children having to wait or not getting what they want immediately.

■ Encourage turn-taking activities.

■ Play start-stop games or games that involve changing direction, such as 'North, South, East, West', the 'Bean game' or the 'Traffic Lights' game.

■ Encourage children to focus and maintain attention by tapping into their interests and fascinations.

■ Help children to resist responding when full of emotion by role-modelling pausing and reflecting before acting.

■ Adopt an emotion-coaching approach which accepts all emotions but sets limits on behaviours when appropriate.

■ Role-model how to act when we feel a certain way and talk about feelings and emotions.

Ethan's space – Sarah Dunn, Holyrood Nursery Salford Royal, Thrive Childcare and Education

Ethan in our Toddler room attends nursery one day a week. We have been supporting him with his feelings and settling into nursery. Ethan now knows that the self-regulation tepee in his toddler room is a space to use when he feels upset or tired. When he comes into nursery he now says, "I go lie down". He will initially go to lie down, and when he is ready for his breakfast he will go over to the breakfast table. Having this space available for him has been invaluable in helping him settle and allowed him to join the group in his own time.

Problem-solving

Children engage in problem-solving all the time. They are figuring out what needs to be solved, how to go about it and, in seeking solutions, they persevere and try things out – for example, eventually reasoning why the cube will not fit into the round hole. They may invite support from an adult, and in doing this they are learning to ask for help and sharing their frustrations. As a co-regulator, the adult can reassure and talk through what it feels like to be frustrated; equally, when the children select the right shape for the space, the adult can support the child by smiling and sharing in their success, and the child learns that through perseverance they can achieve. Problem-solving is about finding creative methods and requires persistence from the child, but it also requires educators to allow time for children to think through the problem, make sense of it and consider different ways of resolving it as well as teaching children how to seek support if needed. Therefore, a child needs to know when to seek support, how to ask for it and how to explain the problem. Jigsaw puzzles are wonderful resources for promoting both the development of problem-solving strategies but also for working collaboratively and cooperatively with others.

Boaler (2015) highlights that although children begin school as competent learners, this can change during the course of more formal education:

> Children begin school as natural problem solvers and many studies have shown that students are better at solving problems *before* they attend maths classes. They think and reason their way through problems, using methods in creative ways, but after a few hundred hours of passive maths learning students have their problem solving abilities knocked out of them.
>
> (Boaler, 2015:53–54)

Whilst it is worrying to read quotes such as this, it is also a wake-up call for us to review our educational provision. As educators, knowing how to solve a problem and distinguishing the information we need from the information not needed are all skills that require children to develop flexible thinking, a 'can-do' attitude and motivation, and they form part of our executive functions. Problem-solving offers children opportunities to collaborate and talk to each other as well, which links with the social side of self-regulation (see Chapter 7). Problem-solving is not just about solving the problem, it is about developing the skills and dispositions for solving it. In addition, actively promoting opportunities to solve a puzzle and find a solution to a problem is an embedded approach in many international early years curriculums, as discussed in Chapter 2.

Metacognition

Promoting children's executive-functioning skills also promotes metacognition – that is, children's ability to think about thinking or be aware of their own thought processes. We can help children to set themselves goals, monitor their progress, reflect upon whether or not they have met their goals and develop critical-thinking skills. If we take loose-parts play as an example, it demonstrates how we can incorporate these ideas into everyday life. When playing with loose parts children need to think, plan what they want to do and how they intend to do it and then consider how successful they were. These are all executive-functioning skills.

Many settings adopt 'Plan, Do, Review' or a similar approach, which encourages children to think about what they intend to do and how they might go about doing it. "The process of children engaging daily in planning, carrying out plans, and then recalling what they did often drives more complex play and learning over time" (Maier, 2016:18). Children can use their executive-functioning skills as they plan, make decisions, problem-solve, accomplish tasks and reflect on their learning with educators and peers.

Planning and review time – Jenna Jefferies, Charlton Nursery & Preschool

A colleague and I created some actions following training around executive functioning. We introduced planning and review time for children in the preschool room. This began with modelling simple language around planning, i.e., teachers stated openly and loudly for children to hear statements like, "My plan for this afternoon is to … (make some nice smelling playdough/create an interesting model/play doctors in the home corner)". Adults began to present children with a question about their day, and we quickly noticed children responded with well-thought-out and considered plans. A younger child, new to the classroom, responded, "My plan is to make a fire engine using all these boxes!"

Review time was introduced shortly afterwards, which enabled children with an opportunity to reflect on their day using concrete objects/toys/photographs to trigger their memory. We then began to notice children hosting their own 'review' times within their role play. One child announced, "I'm doing review time" as she gathered some resources. We have found planning and review time has been a very simple way to enable children to really think about their own learning. Introducing the narrative and language is powerful enough alone to generate discussion and help give the child's day more meaning.

Metacognition is also linked to children's self-awareness and developing an understanding that they can achieve and be successful when they try hard, learn and practice their skills. This is a growth mindset in action. A growth mindset is typified by a belief that intelligence, talents and our personality can be developed with enough time, hard work and education, and our true potential, which is yet unknown, can be cultivated through experience and learning (Dweck, 2012).

We can cultivate a growth mindset in our children by:

- Promoting a 'can do' attitude.

- Teaching children how to be resilient and persevere through challenges.

- Scaffolding when children find situations or activities difficult.

- Using emotion-coaching techniques.

- Seeing incidents that arise as opportunities to problem-solve.

- Viewing challenges as an opportunity to develop skills and grow.

- Praising resilience, hard work and thinking rather than ability or intelligence.

- Sharing mantras, such as "Everyone makes mistakes".

- Valuing the process of learning not the end product.

- Actively encouraging children to try new things.

When children start having an awareness of themselves, they are also developing an awareness of others. Knowing that people have different likes and dislikes relates to Theory of Mind, which we will briefly discuss next.

The connection with Theory of Mind

Although Theory of Mind (ToM) came to light in the 1970s, it has evolved through research and neurological studies, with new information about it emerging over the last 18 years. ToM is defined as the "ability to infer and represent the intentions, beliefs and desires of others" (Coulacoglou & Saklofske, 2018:105). It has also been referred to as "'commonsense psychology', 'naive psychology', 'folk psychology', 'mind reading' and 'mentalizing'" (Coulacoglou & Saklofske, 2018:105). ToM is not only about understanding that other people have thoughts and feelings that are different to their own, it is also about understanding that this will have an impact on the actions of those people. Therefore, it is linked with perspective-taking and empathy. If an adult or child finds seeing things from someone else's perspective difficult, it will have a knock-on effect on their ability to function socially (Coulacoglou & Saklofske, 2018).

For a very young child, this may be as simple as thinking about and responding to questions about their own perspective or the perspective of their educators and peers. So, if we think about what this looks like in a setting, it could be, "I have the yellow ball, you have the green ball" or "Who is holding the teddy?" We can support children to develop ToM by talking about our intentions and why we do what we do or sharing our feelings or speculating aloud with children – for example, "I think she is wearing her wellies so that she can jump in muddy puddles!"

When working out if a child has ToM, researchers tend to use a false-belief task, which attempts to ascertain if a child can see the perspective of another person. One such task is called the 'Sally-Anne task' (Baron-Cohen et al., 1985) and tells the story of Sally, who puts a marble in her basket. When she has left the room, Anne moves the marble into her box. Sally returns and the child is asked where Sally will look for her marble. If the child says "In the basket", they are able to take on Sally's perspective and realise she didn't know Anne had moved the marble. If the child says "In the box", the suggestion is that the child is unable to see Sally's perspective. Typically, in these tasks three year olds are not able to recognise the false belief and therefore have not yet developed this aspect of ToM, and research has shown that children do not begin to pass these tasks until they are at least four. This research has been replicated and challenged, with some authors claiming that the false-belief task does not adequately assess ToM because ToM is actually more complex than this (Bloom & German, 2000), whilst others have found that children have more success in these tasks when supported by adults who talk through the scenario using simple questioning (Psouni et al., 2019).

There are undoubtedly links between executive functions and ToM, as a number of studies have highlighted. One early study suggested that ToM enhances executive function, whilst another suggested that executive function is a requirement for the development of understanding ToM. Children attempt to make sense of others' behaviours by taking into account their mental and emotional states – for example, if they see another child crying, they may say, "He is sad". We can encourage children to do this by confirming what they say and perhaps elaborating, "Yes, he is sad because he is missing his daddy. His daddy will come back soon." Carlson et al. (2004: 1105) recognise the links between ToM and executive functions, explaining: "When pre-schoolers have great difficulty taking someone else's perspective, as in false belief tasks, they also have obvious shortcomings in self-control. They have a very hard time resisting temptation, controlling attention, and keeping their actions and utterances in check."

There are other groups of people who can have difficulty with certain aspects of both executive function and ToM – for example, autistic people; those with major depressive disorder, mesial temporal lobe epilepsy, some forms of dementia, lower competence in language, social communication difficulties, schizophrenia, or damage to specific areas of the brain or deaf people and those with hearing loss. All children under five tend to fit into this group. Limited ToM makes it difficult to understand why people do and say the things they do, understand true intentions and take on different perspectives and therefore has implications for a child's ability to make friends, engage in pretend play and tell stories.

Carlson et al. (2004) go on to note how executive-function deficits limit a child's ability to express their ToM competence. This is continuing to be a field which is to a degree organic as new studies are bringing about new information, but what are clear are the connections between ToM and inhibition control, cognitive flexibility and working memory. In Chapter 6 we will make further links to executive functions and ToM when we discuss listening, maintaining focus and attention.

It is worth noting that ToM is undoubtedly complex, although at its core it is the ability to understand other's intentions – that is, we have the capacity to understand that others have thoughts and feelings that are different from our own (Amodio & Frith, 2006; Apperly, 2012; Baron-Cohen, Leslie, & Frith, 1985). As humans, we can try to determine what others are thinking or feeling at certain times through our interactions with them; however, the reality is, the only person who truly knows what he or she is thinking or feeling is the person themselves.

We can help children to develop Theory of Mind by:

- Using language associated with feelings and behaviour.

- Engaging in role play and pretence and taking on different roles in play.

- Role-modelling different perspectives to young children.

- Speculating aloud about what people are doing and why.

- Sharing books and stories that talk about a character's thoughts and feelings.

- Developing children's emotional intelligence.

Promoting executive functions through play

Having considered some of the theory behind executive functions and the links with Theory of Mind, it is worth now considering how we support children to develop their skills in our settings. As co-regulators, we develop warm, caring and trusting relationships with children; we talk through our thinking and say why we are doing something and we role-model this. An established way to support children's development in executive functions is through promoting play and thinking out loud. Vygotsky famously reminds us of the importance of children's play as he says, "In play a child always behaves beyond his average age, above his daily behaviour; in play it is as though he were a head taller than himself" (1978:102).

Here is a list of activities that promote executive functions in the early years:

- Copying actions and finger rhymes.

- Repeating songs and rhymes.

- Number and pattern play.

- Songs with actions.

- Hiding objects or hide-and-seek.

- Role-play games.

- Imaginary play.

- Small-world play.

- Physical games, obstacle courses, throwing, rolling a ball.

- Playing musical statues.

- Taking it in turns.

- Telling stories.

- Matching and sorting games.

- Board games.

- Cooking.

- 'I spy' games.

All the above can be extended through increasing the challenges in some way – for example, by making the actions progressively difficult to copy or more complicated, or by providing obstacles for children to move around and in different directions. Number rhymes can become harder by counting backwards as well as forwards, and matching games can be extended by changing the rules – for example, first fit all the red shapes into the space, then change to green shapes, etc. We can also encourage children to engage in role play, pretence and imaginative play as good opportunities to help develop inhibitory control and working memory. We explore this further in Chapter 7.

Creating a den – Hua Hin International School

This photo demonstrates how children make good use of loose parts and use the outdoor space to create their own den and space. The children have risky freedom and are given permission to use the materials – such as large crates – independently.

Summary

When we consider the many skills involved with executive functions and ToM, supporting children's development in this area is complex. The very nature and interconnectedness of executive functions helps us to understand the processes that children are engaging in and, whilst we may be promoting one skill set, such as working memory, we are also developing inhibitory or self-control skills and, at times, cognitive thinking. The development of executive functions begins very early in life, and they are grown through positive experiences and relationships, so that when children reach adulthood they can go about their daily lives completing tasks, multi-tasking, ordering their schedules, planning ahead, organising their families and understanding and interacting with others. At the beginning of this chapter, we highlighted that the term *executive function* tends to be associated with something of greater importance or something more senior and of higher importance. It is without doubt that these skills are profoundly important given the very nature of how we utilise them to perform simple tasks in our daily lives.

Sometimes children may appear to not be listening, however often a lack of executive-functioning skills is hindering their ability to do so. In the next chapter we will further build upon our understanding of executive functions when we look at the skills relating to listening, maintaining focus and paying attention in more detail.

Questions for reflection

1. Reflect on the executive functions skill set of working memory, cognitive flexibility and inhibitory control. Make a list of the activities you have used to promote each in the last few days. Are there gaps?

2. What activities could you include in the future to promote executive functions and consider how the children in your setting will benefit?

3. Is there any additional training that might be needed for educators to fully understand how to promote executive-functioning skills?

References

Amodio, D. & Frith, C. (2006) 'Meeting of minds: The medial frontal cortex and social cognition', *Nature Reviews Neuroscience*, (7), pp. 268–277.

Apperly, I. (2012) 'What is "theory of mind"?: Concepts, cognitive processes and individual differences', *Quarterly Journal of Experimental Psychology*, 65(5), pp. 825–839.

Asquith, S. (2020) *Self-regulation Skills in Young Children: Activities and Strategies for Practitioners and Parents*. London: Jessica Kingsley

Baron-Cohen, S., Leslie, A., & Frith, U. (1985). 'Does the autistic child have a "theory of mind"?', *Cognition*, 21(1), pp. 37–46.

Bloom, P., & German, T. (2000) 'Two reasons to abandon the false belief task as a test of theory of mind', *Cognition*, 77(1), pp. B25–B31.

Boaler, J. (2015) *The elephant in the classroom*. London: Souvenir Press.

Carlson, S., & Mandell, D., & Williams, J. (2004) 'Executive Function and Theory of Mind: Stability and Prediction From Ages 2 to 3', *Developmental Psychology*, 40(6), pp. 1105–1122.

Center on the Developing Child at Harvard University (2011) *Building the Brain's "Air Traffic Control" System: How Early Experiences Shape the Development of Executive Function: Working Paper No. 11*. Available at https://46y5eh11fhgw3ve3ytpwxt9r-wpengine.netdna-ssl.com/wp-content/uploads/2011/05/How-Early-Experiences-Shape-the-Development-of-Executive-Function.pdf.

Conkbayir, M. (2017) *Early Childhood and Neuroscience: Theory, Research and Implications for Practice*. London: Bloomsbury.

Coulacoglou, C., & Saklofske, H. (2018) *Psychometrics and Psychological Assessment: Principles and Applications*. London: Elsevier.

Department for Education (DfE) (2021) *Statutory framework for the Early Years Foundation Stage*. Available at https://assets.publishing.service.gov.uk/government/uploads/system/uploads/attachment_data/file/974907/EYFS_framework_-_March_2021.pdf.

Dweck, C.S. (2012) *Mindset: How You Can Fulfil Your Potential*. London: Constable & Robinson.

CEECD (2021) 'Executive Functions', *The Encyclopedia on Early Childhood Development*. Available at https://www.child-encyclopedia.com/executive-functions.

Garon, N., Smith, I.M., & Bryson, S. (2014) 'A novel executive function battery for preschoolers: Sensitivity to age differences', *Child Neuropsychology: A journal on normal and abnormal development in childhood and adolescence*, 20(6), pp. 713–736.

International Dyslexia Association (2021) *Working Memory: The Engine for Learning*. Available at https://dyslexiaida.org/working-memory-the-engine-for-learning.

Maier, C. (2016) 'Supporting Dual Language Learners: Teacher Plan-Do-Review in the Preschool Classroom', *ReSource,* Fall 2016. Available at https://highscope.org/wp-content/uploads/2018/08/Supporting-Dual-Language-Learners.pdf.

Psouni, E., Falck, A., Boström, L., Persson, M., Sidén, L., & Wallin, M. (2019) 'Together I can!: Joint attention boosts 3- to 4-year-olds' performance in a verbal false-belief test', *Child Development*, *90*(1), pp. 35–50.

Shanker, S. (2021) *Self-Regulation: 5 Domains of Self-Reg*. Peterborough, ON: The MEHRIT Centre. Available at https://self-reg.ca/wp-content/uploads/2021/05/infosheet_5-Domains-of-Self-Reg.pdf.

Siegel, D. & Bryson, T. (2012) *The Whole-Brain Child: 12 Proven Strategies to Nurture your Child's Developing Mind*. London: Robinson.

Vygotsky, L. (1978) *Mind in Society: The Development of Higher Mental Processes*. Cambridge, MA: Harvard University Press.

6 Skills relating to listening, maintaining focus and attention

Tamsin Grimmer

Introduction

Tamsin's mum recently witnessed a lovely exchange between a little boy of around two years old and his parent. They were in a shop and choosing a pen from the display. The mum said, "We'll give this to Grandad" and the little boy replied, "No, for Daddy" to which his mum replied, "Not Daddy, Grandad. It's going to be Grandad's birthday!" The little boy took this in for a moment and then said, "My Grandad?" His mother replied, "Yes!" He reiterated, "My Grandad?" and his mum affirmed, "Yes!" On hearing this news, he was so excited, he just had to tell someone. So, at this revelation, the little boy walked over to Tamsin's mum, a complete stranger, and said, "It's going to be my Grandad's birthday!"

This was a lovely moment to witness, but it also demonstrates the difference between hearing and listening. We can sometimes hear something without really taking in what it means, without really listening. We have all done this at times and then thought, "I have no idea what that person just said", and we realise we weren't truly listening. This little boy needed to hear the words a few times to take in the exciting news that his Grandad was having a birthday. I wonder if he'd recently had a birthday, or whether he didn't realise that grownups still have birthdays, but whatever he was thinking, it was of enormous importance when the meaning sank in.

Encouraging children to listen

Listening is not as simple a skill as one might first think. True listening is not just hearing the words spoken, but also responding to them. Children develop listening skills in stages. Initially, they have their sense of hearing, which is their ability to hear sounds by sensing the vibrations in the ear, that begins developing in the womb when babies can hear their mothers' heartbeat and digestive system and, eventually, noises outside the womb after about 23 weeks of gestation. This is why most children are able to distinguish their

DOI: 10.4324/9781003162346-7

mother's voice at birth. Although a baby's ears are fully formed by around 35 weeks, their hearing continues to develop, or fine-tune, until several months after birth.

Soon the baby learns to react or respond to sounds or speech and will begin to look for the source of a sound. They will make eye contact with familiar adults and will be able to move their body in response to these sounds – for example, looking towards the dog if it barks or crying and crawling to their parent after hearing a loud unexpected noise. Babies tend to be very distractible, only focusing their attention for a few moments at a time. They are learning to distinguish between sounds, which is a skill that will help them learn to read and write in the future.

Initially, young children will pay attention to one thing but be easily distracted by other noises, sights or sensory stimulation. This is called single-channelled attention – at first their attention span may be short and it will grow over time. They will then begin to share attention with an adult and may be able to move their attention from one activity to another or listen to an adult talking to them whilst also paying attention to an activity. This is two-channelled attention, which usually develops when a child is about four or five years old.

By about five years old a child can usually focus attention, ignore distractions and maintain attention when listening for a sustained period of time. Although younger children have the ability to listen, maintaining attention involves them wanting to be distracted by the speaker and necessitates children having enough self-regulation and self-awareness that they need to stop playing in order to listen. Sometimes it will appear that a child hasn't heard an adult talking to them at all – they may not respond or may be so deeply engrossed in an activity that they are not easily distracted from it. This is typical and not something to cause concern.

There are many ways we can encourage children to listen:

- Role-model active listening with them.

- Use the child's name before speaking to them.

- Move closer to the child before addressing them.

- Get down on the child's level or lower.

- Encourage eye contact (but do not force this).

- Use gestures or sign language to reinforce words.

- Use voice to encourage listening – for example, tone and pitch.

- Share pictures or objects of reference to help aid understanding.

- Keep activities short and storytimes brief.

- Instructions should also be short, clear and brief.

- If space allows, use a smaller, quieter area for focused group times.

- Face the child and avoid covering our mouths when we speak.

- Avoid seating children near potential distractions, such as resource boxes or books.

Whole body listening

- Use your ears to listen
- Use your eyes to look at the speaker
- Use your head to try to understand
- Use your memory to try and remember what the speaker has said
- Keep your hands and feet still
- Only talk when the speaker has finished

The Social and Emotional Aspects and Learning (SEAL) materials share a useful idea for talking to children about the skills they use when listening and concentrating. Sharing these skills in a song or using actions and pointing to the parts of the body can help:

"eyes (to see)
ears (to hear)
mouth (to speak)
head (to think)
hands in lap (to concentrate)."

(DfES, 2005)

Many settings use posters, symbols or visual supports to help the children to remember. When Tamsin was teaching, she used a bear called Po, who had labels for "eyes looking", "ears listening" and "sitting down with feet still". She would introduce him at the start of carpet time. Using signs and gestures to reinforce her words, she would run through the carpet-time rules together, and Po joined in, acting as an aide-memoire during the session. The children would sometimes take him to their table if they were trying to concentrate to help them focus independently.

Some children will find it more difficult than others to focus attention and listen. These children may need extra support, and we can bear in mind these questions when supporting them:

- Why should they listen right now?

- Do they *want* to participate in the session?

- Do they *have* to participate in the session? Does it matter if they don't?

- Is our practice developmentally appropriate for this child?

- How might we engage them or better tap into their interests?

- Are they able to stand or move around during this session?

- How can we make the space more comfortable?

- Are fiddle toys easily accessible?

- Can the child be positioned nearer the adult leading (e.g., at the front, next to another adult, somewhere with a clear view of the story or activity)?

■ Can we keep instructions or information shared clear and brief?

■ Would the child be able to join the group for the last couple of minutes so that they successfully join in focused group times until the end? (Over time, introduce them to the group earlier to increase their focus.)

■ Can we use a kitchen timer to focus for a set amount of time? (Even if the timer rings whilst we are still focusing, finish the activity before focus is lost.)

■ Can we reduce the session time by building in breaks and remaining flexible in our delivery?

■ Can we involve the child to play a more active part in the session?

■ To what extent have we given feedback or labelled praise to the child for participating?

Using 'Ting' listening – Reception teacher

I came across the concept of 'Ting' (traditional Chinese listening) when I was a young teacher, and it transformed my thinking about listening. It shows that listening is not just about hearing with our ears, but it is also about being present, using our eyes to see, giving undivided attention and focus, thinking and feeling.

In the past, I had sometimes dismissed children's feelings when they shared something with me by not fully listening – for example, a child may have said, "I'm not playing anymore", and I may have replied, "Yes you are, come on, just five more minutes." I thought I was jollying the child along, but actually I wasn't listening to them. They needed their viewpoint and feelings to be acknowledged. Similarly, in the classroom I mistook compliance with listening – if a child was sitting still and looking at me, I assumed they were listening; however, they may not have been thinking about what I was saying at all. Sometimes this was highlighted to me when I would ask a child a question and they responded with something random and totally off topic like, "My Granny is buying me some sweets!"

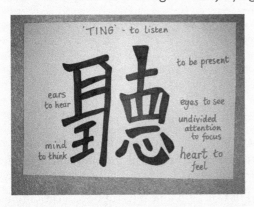

I now see listening as a reciprocal process. In order to listen to others, children need to be listened to.

Sustained Shared Thinking

Sustained Shared Thinking (SST) is a concept that evolved from the Effective Provision of Preschool Education (EPPE) research (Silva et al., 2010) which noted that in the most effective settings, educators were interacting to sustain children's learning and enable them to think. It is now widely recognised as part of the role of an effective educator. It involves being attuned to children, playing alongside them and engaging sensitively to move their learning forward. We may do this through interactions, such as asking open questions, role-modelling, speculating, problem-solving or evaluating how an activity is going. This closely matches other theories, most notably Vygotsky's (1978) idea of the zone of proximal development, when a child moves forward in their learning through interacting with a more knowledgeable adult or child, and Bruner's (1996) ideas about scaffolding children's learning.

Fisher (2016) builds on this by considering how the adult can *maintain the learning momentum*, and she suggests the following methods:

- Commenting.

- Pondering.

- Imagining.

- Connecting.

- Thinking aloud.

- Talking about feelings.

- Reflecting back to children.

- Supporting the child to make choices and decisions.

- Explaining and informing.

- Posing problems.

- Staying quiet.

All of these interactions rely on the relationship the educators have built with their children, and their availability to interact or react to them in the moment. Breaking down the phrase SST can help us to understand this concept a little more: *Sustained* means continuing for an extended period of time, without interruption; *Shared* implies something that we do together and *Thinking* is the process that we use to consider, problem-solve and reason about things. So, when we share in thinking about something for a sustained time, we are participating in SST. All parties need to contribute to the process, and the thinking needs to develop or extend in some way. It's what we do with the children when real learning takes place. This could be with a child of any age, from birth upwards. It's that sustained period of time when we engage in a reciprocal experi-ence, taking learning forward – for example, when we play peep-o with a very young baby and they begin to anticipate that you will reappear. We are sharing a moment – a moment of sustained learning and interaction. It's also when we are about to explore a wood with a three year old and they say, "We might see elephants there!" What follows is a discussion about the woods, elephants, several different animals and their habitats that we would never have anticipated discussing with such a young child. Again, we are sharing a moment – a moment of sustained learning and interaction.

It is our role to provide a context within which these interactions can take place. In this environment, the children will be encouraged to develop their own thinking, problem-solve, and grow the positive dispositions that will help them as they learn to self-regulate. Observing our children is at the heart of this practice, so that we can get to know them really well and understand how to move their play forward, engage in SST, scaffold activities and enhance the experience for the child. We need to remember that different children will require different levels of support, and all children develop at different rates, so we must treat them according to their individual needs. Part of this role is to provide an enabling environment where children can explore, investigate, experiment and generally be themselves, which Chapter 8 will explore.

'Looking into the pond' observation – Preschool

Abdul and Charlie are crouched at the side of the pond with their key person, Bev. They are looking at and talking about the tadpoles in the pond:

Charlie: "There's a big one there!"

Abdul: "That's my one. It is the leader because it has a long tail"

Charlie: "But my one has a shorter tail and it's growing legs!"

Abdul: "Mine is the oldest because it has the longest tail!"

Bev: "Can you remember the book we looked at yesterday about tadpoles and frogs? What did it say?"

Abdul: "Tadpoles are baby frogs!"

Charlie: "Yeah, and my one is getting legs like a frog too!"

Bev: "Let's try to think about what happens to the tadpole to turn into a frog. First we have the eggs, the frogspawn … "

Charlie: "Like jelly!"

Bev: "Yes, it did look a lot like jelly didn't it! Then we have tiny tadpoles … "

Abdul: "Then they get big like my one!"

Bev: "Yes, Abdul they do! Then what happens next?"

Charlie: "They get legs like my one! So, my one is nearly a frog!"

Abdul: "But what about the tail?"

Charlie: "They don't need a tail when they have legs!"

Abdul: "Coz we don't have tails, do we!"

Charlie: "I do!"

Both boys run off holding their hands behind their bottoms, wagging imaginary tails!

As educators, we often share SST moments like this one with Abdul and Charlie, when the children are engaged and really think about something. The role of the educator is to support and extend children's learning, engage in the process with the child and use our knowledge of prior learning and understanding and the children's interests to assist us. SST involves the adult and child developing an idea or skill together. It's not about giving children answers or even about correcting misconceptions, although we may sometimes need to do this; instead, it is about listening to children's ideas, valuing them and sharing our own ideas. It's about having a genuine desire to find out and having a natural conversation together.

Here are a few ideas of how to encourage SST. Children should have opportunities to:

■ Become involved in things that interest and intrigue them.

■ Access a rich and stimulating learning environment and continuous provision, which includes risk and challenge.

■ Engage in activities inside and outside and have space to move freely.

- Become deeply involved, explore and investigate – this requires time.

- Link learning with home experiences and their cultural background.

- Make their thinking visible, i.e., recording ideas in words and images.

- Ask and answer open-ended questions.

- Problem-solve and resolve conflicts.

- Reflect upon and review what they are doing or how they are accomplishing something.

- Engage in different-sized groupings and have adult-child 1:1 time.

Waiting and delaying gratification

Young children will often find waiting difficult. As adults we can find waiting hard too – we are often impatient when at the traffic lights, or when we are about to go on leave, our last day at work feels like the longest ever! Mischel, Ebbesen, and Zeiss (1972) conducted some research that has become known as the marshmallow test. The experimenter offered children a choice of two treats (marshmallow and pretzel) and then said if the child could wait 15 minutes for the experimenter to come back, the child would be allowed to eat their favourite treat; however, if the child asked the experimenter to come back earlier, they would get the other treat. Their research linked a child's ability to delay gratification with ways of overcoming frustration and inhibiting impulses. Other research studies also linked a child's ability to delay gratification and wait for something they really want with increased academic achievement in later years. The implication of this was that some educators believed waiting and delaying gratification were skills we should foster; however, more recent research has cast a shadow on these original findings. Watts, Duncan and Quan (2018) repeated this famous research test but found different results. Their research suggests that once other factors are taken into account – such as socio-economic status, home environment, gender and ethnicity – the correlation between delaying gratification and higher academic achievement is perhaps not statistically significant, or at least it is much weaker.

Educators need to limit times when children are waiting, or sedentary times. Many settings and schools have routines that require children to wait at various times – for example, when washing hands for lunch, when lining up for assembly or when waiting for parents to arrive. Effective educators will keep these times active by singing action rhymes, playing following-the-leader games or moving around. It is also a good idea to have a selection of sensory toys or fidget toys available to help keep little hands busy.

Peter's story – Nicola Abreu, Widcombe Infant School

Peter is 56 months old and a popular member of the reception class with a selection of close friends who seem happy to play with him. He joins in with class discussions but finds it hard to wait his turn. Unfortunately, when Peter's emotions overwhelm him, he throws whatever he may have in his hand at the time or grabs whatever is closest to him and throws this. Peter becomes angry very quickly, then his face turns red, he stamps his feet and shouts and screams loudly to demonstrate his anger. He sometimes destroys his own work by smashing up a model or tearing up a piece of art or writing. This will often then exacerbate his emotions.

He will also run away from adults and appears to enjoy the control that this gives him. He will smile and taunt the adult by suggesting that he cannot be caught. If he is angry at another child, he will physically hit, push and kick the other child. Until recently, he has refused to accept responsibility for his actions or freely offer an apology. He appears to disassociate himself from the situation and will often blame others.

We have noticed a range of triggers for his behaviour:

- Making transitions – generally from his chosen activity to an adult-directed task.
- Sharing toys and resources.
- Feeling unable to complete a task, even if he can do it.
- Having to wait his turn.
- Not being able to do exactly what he wants when he wants.
- Being engaged in exuberant, excitable play. He finds it hard to control his excitement and will start lashing out at children.
- Being looked at by other children.

We have put a variety of strategies in place to support Peter:

- Sand timer – to give him a visual warning of when a play session is coming to an end and help to prepare him. We discuss what will happen next and give him options to save his work or model for later.
- Visual timetable – used in conjunction with the sand timer to illustrate what will come next and show him when he will be able to return to his chosen activity.
- Air-filled seating wedge – the wedged cushion aids his concentration and helps him to stay still for a longer period of time.
- *The Colour Monster* – we shared this story (Llenas, 2015) with Peter and he enjoyed categorising emotions with a variety of colours. This has supported us to discuss how he is feeling in child-friendly terms and is helping him to start to label his own emotions.
- Breathing – Peter finds it helpful to take deep breaths. This enables him to gain some control and gives us time to talk him through his options.
- A basket of calming toys that he can independently come and select from when he feels overwhelmed – this basket contains an expanding ball to open and shut as he takes a breath, sealed bottles that contain various little balls that float up and down, stretching coils, squishy creatures and playdough. Most of the items are sensory.

We will want to use a range of strategies to support children and not just rely on one. Part of our response will be looking at the ethos of our setting to try and avoid waiting or sedentary times and also considering if we need to interrupt the child's play if this triggers them to become upset. In addition, we will want to consider teaching children specific strategies they can adopt if they need to wait or find it difficult to sit still – for example, how to distract themselves, how to think about something else or how to shift their attention elsewhere by looking away or moving away from the thing that is frustrating them. We can also include strategies aimed at individual children we identify who may find this difficult – for example, Peter has a basket of sensory items available to support him, including bubble wrap to pop, which helps him to concentrate and distracts him when he is feeling overwhelmed or angry.

Sitting still and sedentary behaviour

As we have discussed, it is a good idea to limit sedentary times, not least because children find waiting difficult and frustrating. However, there are noted health benefits for avoiding sedentary behaviour, such as reduced obesity and increased posture and spinal health, and research has shown the importance of limiting these times (Dugan, 2018; Ellis et al., 2018; Cardon et al., 2014). Despite this, many educators see children sitting still as the optimal conditions for learning, particularly in school. There is a misconception that a still child is a learning child. This is not true, with the opposite actually being the case (Connell & McCarthy, 2014). A report by the Institute of Medicine in the US found that "Children who are more active show greater attention, have faster cognitive processing speed, and perform better on standardized academic tests than children who are less active" (2013:2).

There may be many reasons why a child is not yet able to sit still and pay attention in the way many educators expect. In addition to the five traditionally thought about senses – touch, taste, sight, hearing and smell – we also have vestibular, proprioceptive and interoceptive senses. These lesser-known senses can have a large impact on our bodies. Our vestibular system is in charge of our balance and coordination, proprioception is our awareness of where our bodies are in the space around us, while interoception is our internal bodily awareness, which tells us when we feel full after a meal or need to go to the toilet (see Chapter 1). Young children are still developing these senses. When sitting still, our vestibular system is asking us to move; our proprioceptive sense is seeking sensory input and pressure, which we mostly get through movement; and our interoceptive sense is deciding if we need to leave the room for the toilet! Simply put, our bodies are not designed to sit still for any length of time.

In addition, some children may have additional needs that make sitting still more difficult, such as, Attention Deficit and Hyperactivity Disorder (ADHD), Autistic Spectrum Condition (ASC) or Sensory Processing Disorder (SPD). These children will find it harder to maintain focus and attention, and their bodies may require more sensory input or experience sensory input differently. An inability to sit still and maintain attention, however, is not necessarily an indication of needs. Most young children – in fact, most people in general – find it hard to stay in one position for a while, and sitting comfortably is not as simple as it may sound. It requires our bodies to be in tip-top physical condition to be able to sit without any complications.

Versfeld (undated), a physiotherapist in South Africa, outlined the abilities that a child needs in order to sit comfortably and work at a table:

Children who fidget, move around and slump when sitting often lack the necessary muscle strength, flexibility and endurance for maintaining an erect posture: they may find sitting erect causes discomfort in the back and legs. In order to sit comfortably and work at a table children need:

- Hip flexibility to allow the thighs to rest parallel to each other on the seat of the chair with the pelvis vertical.
- Trunk flexibility and muscle endurance to keep the trunk erect with ease and comfort.
- Neck flexibility and muscle strength to keep the head erect and steady when moving the arms.
- Trunk stability: the ability to keep the trunk and head steady when moving the arms.

Research has also demonstrated that children spend a vast amount of time whilst in child-care settings being sedentary – more than educators realise (Ellis et al., 2018; Määttä et al. 2016). Therefore, as educators, we need to encourage our children to be more physically active and lead by example. We also need to be aware of the amount of time children are being active or sedentary during our watch. In order to find out, we could spend time observing children and measuring their time spent being sedentary or active during a typical session. Sedentary behaviour includes sitting down on the floor, sitting on a chair, lying down, standing still or fairly still at a table or workstation, and kneeling down – anything that involves very little physical activity. Whereas active behaviour includes movement play, running, climbing, jumping, chasing, crawling or standing at a table or workstation if moving around – anything that involves physical activity and movement. A time-sample observation is a useful tool to use for this, as shared in the case study.

Time sample looking at sedentary behaviour – Preschool

We sometimes use time samples as an observation technique, and after attending training which looked at physical movement, we decided to complete some with a focus on sedentary behaviour. The results were surprising. We found that the majority of our children, even children like Nikita who we thought of as active, spent longer being sedentary during our session than we had realised.

SEDENTARY TIME SAMPLE

CHILD: Nikita   DATE: 8th January   TIME: 9:30am – 11:am

SEDENTARY:

Includes sitting down on the floor, sitting on a chair, lying down, standing still, or fairly still at a table or workstation, kneeling down. Involving very little physical activity.

ACTIVE:

Includes movement play, running, climbing, jumping, chasing, crawling, standing at a table or workstation if moving around. Involving physical activity and movement.

TIME	9:30	9:40	9:50	10:00	10:10	10:20	10:30	10:40	10:50
SEDENTARY (S) or ACTIVE (A)	S	S	S	A	A	S	S	A	S

NOTES

Nikita went into the construction area and found the miniature red sports car, then he lay on his right hand side on the edge of the car-mat and moved the car along the road. He stayed at the car mat for a while, watching Harry and Moses who were building with blocks. Later he stood up and joined Harry and Moses and helped them gather more blocks – this was the most active he had been all morning. He then went over to the rolling snack bar and sat eating snack for a while. After snack he chased Noah outside, running for about 5 minutes before he was called in to sit for a story.

This led to us reflecting upon our daily routine and looking at the learning environment. We offered children more opportunities to stand at activities rather than sit and kept an eye on the children who we noticed would choose to be less active, overtly encouraging them to join in with active games or more physical play.

Here are some ideas of how we can make our sessions more physically active for our children:

- Audit provision in terms of opportunities to develop fine and gross motor skills.

- Integrate movement and manipulative skills into all areas of learning and development.

- Provide sufficient indoor and outdoor space for movement.

- Allocate time for children to fully engage in and explore, develop and master the use of a wide range of small and large equipment.

- Offer opportunities to engage with open-ended resources and loose-parts play.

- Encourage the children to access their own equipment and make up their own games and activities.

- Role-model ways to move and how to engage with resources physically.

- Encourage physical experiences (bouncing, rolling, rocking, splashing).

- Value all attempts to move and encourage and support children's efforts.

- Support children's natural ability to assess risk for themselves.

- Join children in movement play.

- Limit sedentary times and incorporate movement breaks into the day.

- Invest in some specific resources, such as wiggle cushions, exercise balls to be used as chairs, and rocker boards.

- Incorporate sensory breaks into our daily routine, e.g., yoga, breathing and mindfulness activities.

- Work with parents and carers to encourage children to be active at home.

In the UK, the government has published Physical Activity Guidelines, which recommend the type and amount of physical activity children should engage in (DHSC, 2019). Recent statistics from Sport England (2021) show that between 2019 and 2020 less than 45% of children met these guidelines. Although sad, this is perhaps not surprising, as children spend a vast amount of time inside using technology or generally being inactive compared to past generations, when children would have played outside more. A recent Ofcom survey (2018) found that children aged between three and four spend an average of 14 hours per week watching television and a further nine hours per week online. On top of this, the 2016 National Statistics Health Survey for England found that 83% of children aged between two and four spend less than an hour being physically active in a typical day (NHS Digital, 2016).

Age	Activity
Infants (less than 1 year)	Physically active several times a day in a variety of ways. For non-mobile infants, this includes 30 minutes of tummy time spread over the day while awake.
Toddlers (1–2 years)	180 minutes (3 hours) per day in a variety of physical activities at any intensity, including active and outdoor play, spread throughout the day.
Pre-schoolers (3–4 years)	180 minutes (3 hours) per day in a variety of physical activities spread throughout the day, including active and outdoor play. Including at least 60 minutes of moderate-to-vigorous-intensity physical activity.
Children and Young People (5–18 years)	At least 60 minutes per day of moderate-to-vigorous-intensity physical activity across the week. Engage in a variety of types and intensities of physical activity across the week to develop movement skills, muscular fitness and bone strength. Minimise the amount of time spent being sedentary and, when physically possible, break up long periods of not moving with at least light physical activity.

Adapted from Department of Health and Social Care (2019) *UK Chief Medical Officers' Physical Activity Guidelines*

Tamsin was recently told about a city toddler who, growing up in London, had not seen an apple tree before – let alone an orchard. His mum took him to visit an orchard, and he saw apples growing on a tree for the first time. He remarked, "Mummy, why did someone stick all those apples in the trees?" This may make us laugh or smile at his innocent naivety, however, it highlights a more serious issue that modern society is being faced with: the disconnect between children and nature. The National Trust acknowledged this concern in their *Natural Childhood* report, where they noted that "one in three [children] could not identify a magpie; half could not tell the difference between a bee and a wasp; yet nine out of ten could recognise a Dalek" (National Trust, 2012:5).

The term *Nature-Deficit Disorder* was coined by Richard Louv in his controversial book, *Last Child in the Woods* (2010). Despite its name, this is not a medical diagnosis; rather, he uses this term as a metaphor to describe the children of this generation who are, quite literally, deprived of nature and the freedom to play outdoors. He suggests that these children are more likely to have physical and emotional illnesses as a direct result of not playing outside or being connected with nature. With the decline in children playing outside, it is easy to see why Louv is concerned and, in fact, why we all should be. This has implications for children and their ability to maintain focus and attention, and we believe that if children are more physically active and spend more time outside, they will be better able to focus when the situation requires this.

Maintaining focus and attention

Many young children find concentrating difficult. This is typical for a young child, and as educators we shouldn't chastise children; instead, we should acknowledge they will find it hard and amend our provision accordingly whilst offering lots of opportunities for sustained engagement, outdoor play and movement activity. Tapping into children's interests and fascinations and encouraging SST will also help with this.

The key is to know our children really well and build up strong, positive relationships that will allow us to better judge how to increase their focus and attention and when to intervene successfully. If we use what we know about children's interests and fascinations as a starting point, then we can plan interesting, exciting activities that will intrigue and motivate them to participate. Successful engagement of children involves being attuned to them; empathising with their needs, wants and desires and offering them nurturing opportunities that empower and inspire them.

Many settings and schools use the Leuven scale of involvement and wellbeing as a way of measuring children's engagement in what they provide (Laevers, 2005).

"A child who is involved is completely 'absorbed' by the activity" (Laevers, 2005:10) – for example, they will be motivated and driven to be engaged with the activity and show intense mental activity and satisfaction in what they are achieving. Laevers shares that, "Involvement is only possible when an activity challenges you, when it is not too easy and not too difficult. Children with a high level of involvement operate at the very limits of their capabilities" (2005:10).

When children demonstrate high levels of involvement, we know that what we are providing for them is fully engaging and challenging them. There will be less time for poor behaviour, as when children are engrossed in activities, they will be focused and concentrating. Being fully involved necessitates high levels of self-regulation as children maintain their attention, are less easily distracted and inhibit their impulses to play elsewhere.

Some children will find it difficult to maintain focus and attention because they have additional needs of some kind. There are specialist programmes of support aimed at specific groups that we can also draw upon to support all our children – for example, using strategies like 'attention buckets' from the *Attention Autism* training materials (Davies, 2020). Many settings use visual timetables, picture cues, props, objects of reference and sign language to help children maintain attention and focus during whole-group sessions. If you feel a child needs additional support or is struggling beyond that of their peers, it is important to seek advice and guidance from a SENDCo (Special Educational Needs and Disabilities Coordinator) or another specialist.

Ways in which we can support children to maintain focus and attention include:

- Aim to increase levels of involvement and wellbeing.

- Limit waiting times and keep them as active as possible.

- Minimise sedentary times.

- Remain attuned to the children and notice when they are getting restless. Respond to these signals and move the activity on.

- Provide fidget toys for children to use during high-focus times.

- Allow children to access sensory and fidget toys for use at other times.

- Minimise distractions.

- Plan ahead. If you know a particular child will struggle to concentrate, find an alternative activity for them, then bring them in for the last few minutes so that they can be included and experience success.

- Over time, slowly increase the length of time children are expected to focus.

Encouraging attention – Jenna Jefferies, Charlton Nursery & Preschool

Leo attends our 2–3 year room and was struggling to access activities within our continuous provision for more than a few seconds at a time. He demonstrated fleeting attention, bounding from one activity to the next. We worked with his parents to create targets on a support plan, and we made an application to the local council for top-up funding. We were then able to create a specific plan tailored to Leo's needs. This included creating a Workstation space for Leo with small, manageable tasks which he could complete within his attention span. The rationale behind this was that Leo would then see similar tasks set out in the classroom and would be able to transfer and apply his new knowledge to the task.

Additionally, we implemented the following to support children's listening and attention skills in general:

■ Attention buckets – Attention Autism.
■ Visual timelines of routine with warnings for transition for all children – for example, using a sand timer or rain stick.
■ ALWAYS using a child's name before giving any instructions.
■ Using stripped-back language – "now wash hands, then outside".
■ Playing listening and attention games, such as body percussion, run and touch, or sounds lotto, and using 'Beat Baby' (a soft toy used to support maintaining a steady beat and emotional development with the children).

More recently we have been reading literature which links working memory with focus and attention. Therefore, we are providing memory-strengthening games for Leo, such as 'Kim's game', matching card games and recall games or stories. Consequently, Leo is able to concentrate for longer periods of time and is able to generalise knowledge he has learned in workstations to the classroom.

Many children will fiddle with things and will need to keep their hands active, and no amount of asking them to stop touching things will work. If we move them away from the shelves, they fiddle with the child in front. If we move them away from other children, they fiddle with their own shoes! Despite what many educators may think, fiddling with things does not mean they are not listening. Jarrett (2017) shares that asking young people to stop fidgeting may backfire, as research shows that fidgeting can help us calm down and keep us alert when we are bored. Fidget toys could be described as self-regulation tools that help children to maintain focus and attention as well as provide calming sensory feedback (Hinck, 2017). In addition to the attention benefits of fidget and fiddle toys, they can also help children to develop fine motor control and hand-eye coordination and dexterity. Using manipulable materials such as play dough or plasticine can also help to strengthen the muscles in children's hands, which will help them with future literacy skills.

Research with adults in Higher Education also found that fidgeting can help soothe, calm and self-regulate our minds during listening tasks (Karlesky & Isbister, 2016). As Hinck explains, "Fidgeting is our body's way of releasing restless energy" (Hinck, 2017) and can help to improve focus and even reduce anxiety and stress. Some resources are specifically designed to keep hands and fingers active, such as fidget spinners, poppets or click-toys, whilst others are designed to relieve anxiety and stress, such as soft stress balls or squishies.

Summary

When considering the skills involved in supporting children's self-regulation, we need to consider their ability to listen, maintain focus and attention. Young children will find this difficult, so the key message is that we need to accept this and plan our provision bearing it in mind. In this way our activities and expectations will be developmentally appropriate as we limit sedentary behaviour and minimise waiting times. Expecting children to sit still is not only unrealistic but also can be counter-productive, as a "moving child is a learning child" (Connell & McCarthy, 2014).

This chapter has outlined ways in which we can engage in Sustained Shared Thinking, encourage children to listen, make our sessions more physically active for them and help them to maintain focus and attention. The main way to do this is to be attuned to children, tap into their interests and fascinations and offer plenty of opportunities for movement. The next chapter considers self-regulation in the context of social development and how children develop social confidence and empathy.

Questions for reflection

1. How can we ensure our expectations for children are developmentally appropriate with regard to listening, maintaining focus and attention?

2. How active or sedentary are our children during a typical session? How do we know?

3. To what extent are children engaged and fully involved during a typical session? How do we know?

References

Bruner, J. (1996) *The Culture of Education*. Cambridge, MA: Harvard University Press.

Cardon, G., De Craemer, M., De Bourdeaudhuij, I., & Verloigne, M. (2014). 'More physical activity and less sitting in children: Why and how?', *Science & Sports, 29* (Supplement), pp. S3–S5.

Connell, G. & McCarthy, C. (2014) *A Moving Child is a Learning Child: How the Body Teaches the Brain to Think*. Minneapolis, MN: Free Spirit Publishing.

Davies, G. (2020) *Practical Help with Autism* (Attention Autism). Available at https://ginadavies.co.uk.

Department of Health and Social Care (DHSC) (2019) *UK Chief Medical Officers' Physical Activity Guidelines*. Available at https://assets.publishing.service.gov.uk/government/uploads/system/uploads/attachment_data/file/832868/uk-chief-medical-officers-physical-activity-guidelines.pdf.

DfES (2005) *Excellence and Enjoyment: Social and emotional aspects of learning (SEAL): New beginnings Foundation Stage*. Available at https://sealcommunity.org/sites/default/files/resources/pns_seal132305_newbeg_red_0.pdf.

Dugan, J. E. (2018). 'Teaching the body: a systematic review of posture interventions in primary schools', *Educational Review, 70*(5), pp. 643–661.

Ellis, Y. G., Cliff, D. P., & Okely, A. D. (2018) 'Childcare Educators' Perceptions of and Solutions to Reducing Sitting Time in Young Children: A Qualitative Study', *Early Childhood Education Journal, 46*(4), pp. 377–385.

Fisher, J. (2016) *Interacting or Interfering?: Improving interactions in the early years*. London: Open University Press.

Hinck, M. (2017) 'Can Fidget Toys Help Your Child's Ability To Focus?', *Flushing Hospital Medical Center: Health Beat*, April 13. Available at: https://www.flushinghospital.org/newsletter/can-fidget-toys-help-your-childs-ability-to-focus.

Institute of Medicine (2013) *Educating the Student Body: Taking Physical Activity and Physical Education to School* (Report Brief). Retrieved from https://www.nap.edu/resource/18314/EducatingTheStudentBody_rb.pdf.

Jarrett, C. (2017) 'State of unrest', *New Scientist, 236*(3151), pp. 33–35.

Karlesky, M. & Isbister, K. (2016) 'Understanding Fidget Widgets: Exploring the Design Space of Embodied Self-Regulation', *Proceedings of the 9th Nordic Conference on Human-Computer Interaction* (NordiCHI '16), 38, pp. 1–10. doi: 10.1145/2971485.2971557.

Laevers, F. (2005) *Well-being and Involvement in Care Settings: A Process-oriented Self-evaluation Instrument.* Leuven: Kind & Gezin and Research Centre for Experiential Education. Available at https://www.kindengezin.be/img/sics-ziko-manual.pdf.

Llenas, A. (2015) *The Colour Monster.* London: Templar Publishing.

Louv, R. (2010) *Last Child in the Woods: Saving our Children from Nature-Deficit Disorder.* New York: Atlantic Books.

Määttä, S., Ray, C., Roos, G., & Roos, E. (2016) 'Applying a socioecological model to understand preschool children's sedentary behaviors from the viewpoints of parents and preschool personnel', *Early Childhood Education Journal, 44,* pp. 491–502.

Mischel, W., Ebbesen, E., & Zeiss, A. (1972) 'Cognitive and attentional mechanisms in delay of gratification', *Journal of Personality and Social Psychology, 21*(2), pp. 204–218.

National Trust (2012) *Natural Childhood Report.* Available at https://nt.global.ssl.fastly.net/documents/read-our-natural-childhood-report.pdf.

NHS Digital (2016) *Health Survey for England 2015 Physical activity in children.* Available at http://healthsurvey.hscic.gov.uk/media/37752/hse2015-child-phy-act.pdf.

Ofcom (2018) *Ofcom Media Literacy Tracker 2018 – Parents of Children Aged 3–4 – 25th April to 18th June 2018.* Available at https://www.ofcom.org.uk/__data/assets/pdf_file/0023/116258/parents-children-3-4-data-tables.pdf.

Silva, K., Melhuish, E., Sammons, P., Siraj-Blatchford, I., & Taggart, B. (Eds.) (2010) *Early childhood matters evidence from the Effective Pre-school and Primary Education project.* Abingdon, UK: Routledge.

Sport England (2021) *Active Lives Children and Young People Survey: Academic Year 2019/20.* Available at https://sportengland-production-files.s3.eu-west-2.amazonaws.com/s3fs-public/2021-01/Active%20Lives%20Children%20Survey%20Academic%20Year%2019-20%20report.pdf?4Ti_0V0m9sYy5HwQjSiJN7Xj.VInpjV6.

Versfeld, P. (undated) *What abilities are needed for sitting erect with ease and comfort when working at a table?* Available at https://skillsforaction.com/training-for-sitting.

Vygotsky, L. (1978) *Mind in society: The development of higher psychological processes.* Boston, USA: Harvard University

Watts, T. W., Duncan, G. J., & Quan, H. (2018) 'Revisiting the marshmallow test: A conceptual replication investigating links between early delay of gratification and later outcomes,' *Psychological Science, 29*(7), pp. 1159–1177.

7 Social development

Tamsin Grimmer and Wendy Geens

In all their discussions in collating this book, Tamsin and Wendy recognised that self-regulation is developed through learning alongside others. After all, how can we ask children to empathise and understand how it feels to be someone else if they have had no encounters with others. We know the attachments children make in their very early stages are fundamental to all aspects of a child's development, but this is especially so for developing self-regulation. Initially parents are co-regulating and supporting their children, then gradually, as children grow, the people they connect with widens away from just their immediate family to close members within their community, settings and school, and friendships with peers. As children develop they learn how to respond, care and show empathy for others as well as interact in social situations. It is clear that developing self-regulation is not something a child can navigate their way through on their own – they need the security of the people that care for and love them.

In this chapter we explore how learning in a social context offers natural opportunities to develop self-regulation. We consider the work of Vygotsky and Bronfenbrenner through the lens of social constructivism and sociocultural theory. As we explore how children interact with others, we begin to see how this shapes the dispositions they need for social participation. A significant pedagogical approach in this development is the child learning through role play, perspective-taking and adopting the roles of others, as this helps them to consider how they would behave and function in certain situations in society. We explore the skills and attitudes this promotes as children develop self-regulation.

Considering the 'self' in self-regulation

In the introduction to this book, we explained that the 'self' part of self-regulation is slightly misleading, implying that it is something children do alone or for themselves, whereas in reality, self-regulation is inextricably linked with others and it would be

DOI: 10.4324/9781003162346-8

impossible to develop in complete isolation. There is also an element of self-awareness involved, as Chapter 3 discussed. Children are growing up in a social world and their lives are intertwined with others, therefore it would be impossible for children to self-regulate without learning alongside others.

Children are rarely alone or apart from others in our settings and schools; therefore, they need to learn how to interact socially with one another and develop self-regulation alongside their peers. Other children can be very distracting – they may make noises or want to direct play in the child's direction. In addition, we as adults can take children's focus away from their goals by inviting them to join us at snack-time or helping by tidying up.

Thoutenhoofd and Pirrie (2015) noted that research and theory around self-regulation has often ignored the social origins and nature of it, thus discussing behaviour and cognitive self-regulation to the detriment of social aspects. "There is an evident failure to account for the stratification of learning in ways that reflect social systems more generally" (Thoutenhoofd & Pirrie, 2015:75). There are many opportunities for children to develop self-regulation in a social situation – for example, when:

- Imitating others.

- Playing with friends.

- Ignoring distractions and noise in a busy setting.

- Accepting the viewpoint of another child.

- Following the rules of play, regardless of who created the rules.

- Talking in a group or having a conversation; knowing when to talk and when to listen.

- Needing to share resources or equipment.

- Discussing a problem.

- Planning where we will play and with whom.

Confidence and the social connection

It is worth considering the dispositions that a socially confident child demonstrates; however, before we examine what they may look like, let's consider a scenario: Imagine you have just taken on a dream job. It's the one you have been waiting for, but it's 150 miles away. You make the decision to move house. You know this is a big decision, but you have made an objective and rational choice to do this. You not only have to build relationships with colleagues in a new job but also build friendships with people you have never met before. You have to get to know your neighbours, establish new routines and find out where different places are. You plan, organise and persevere during this period of change. Now imagine that you are four years old. You won't be seeing your friends again. You won't see the familiar face that greeted you each morning when you arrived at the setting. You don't know where anything is in the new setting. In short, everything you knew and understood has changed. It's daunting, and the uncertainty and unfamiliarity can be frightening. It leaves us feeling vulnerable and insecure.

Practitioners and teachers are regularly faced with the task of welcoming and supporting a child new to the setting, and often one of the strategies they use to help the child is the support of another child. This child is often the one who will welcome and greet visitors to the setting or classroom. It's the child who smiles and enjoys guiding and helping other children. It's the child who has learnt the value of listening and knows when to speak and how to react or behave. This is the child who will show the new child where the fruit snack is kept and where the toilets are. They will invite the new child to play a game, encourage them to meet other children and ask them what they would like to do. This child will sit next to them and regularly ask them if they are okay. It could be argued that this child is socially confident.

These are the attributes of a socially confident child:

- Happy to make friends with others.

- Smiles frequently.

- Does not need to be the centre of attention.

- Can listen to others and knows how to respond, which shows they are listening.

- Knows how to share with other children.

- Understands the importance of taking their turn.

- Is kind to others and can show empathy.

- Is considerate and thinks about others.

- Recognises when to wait.

- Knows that they have a voice that is valued.

The attributes above are all part of their disposition and enable them to behave and respond in a manner that is acceptable to others. Young children start developing these attributes early, and their interactions with other children are key because this is where they learn. Sometimes a child who likes being the centre of attention may find it difficult to accept the views of others. They may find it harder to make friends because they find listening difficult. Children need to be taught how to respond to others, let others speak and learn to take their turn. Adults are in the ideal position to model these skills and attributes. They can help children to ask questions, model kindness by smiling and showing genuine interest, acknowledging what children say or do, valuing their culture and diversity, and giving them the time and space to think and to be. Educators can also show that they believe in them and tell children they can achieve by encouraging them to be successful.

Being socially confident is more than developing skills – it's about having an understanding of who they are and being happy with who they are (see Chapter 3). When others invite them to join their games, they feel included and part of the group. Social confidence can be learnt, and we can support children using stories. We recommend *Shine* by Sarah Asuquo (2020), a wonderful story about a little boy who loses his confidence and gradually regains it. However, the most effective way for children to achieve social confidence is through being with other children – for example, interacting at school/setting, playing at a friend's house, going to parties or playing at the park. Experiences such as travelling on a bus, greeting people in shops and knowing when to speak with a shopkeeper or when to hand over the money are all experiences that help children to learn about how to respond and communicate with others. They begin to read the signs and respond to others' behaviours – for example, if the shopkeeper smiles, they are more likely to smile back. If they say "thank you" to the bus driver, the driver will respond with a smile. These may look like small interactions, yet they are fundamental in building those early experiences that shape children's social confidence. Imagine if the first time a child travelled by bus at the age of three or four the bus driver wasn't having a good day and was unfriendly or shouted, grumbled, complained or showed a frown or cross expression with their eyes tightly squinted. How would this make that child feel? Would it put them off getting on a bus again? Would they be hesitant or wary – unsure of what to expect or expecting unpleasantness on future bus journeys?

Glazzard and Trussler (2020) talk about the importance of social confidence and note how children with "poor social confidence find it more challenging to develop social interactions and social connectivity" (2020:105). When we consider the impact social confidence can have on mental health, we begin to realise the importance of supporting children to develop this in early childhood. Whilst it would be appropriate to discuss mental health in more depth, it is so complex that we would not do it justice here. It is, however, important to note that every aspect of developing a child's self-regulation will impact on their mental health and wellbeing, and developing social confidence is maybe more important than initially imagined. As Glazzard and Trussler note, "if all children feel included and valued, and their differences are respected, this will help to develop children's social confidence" (2020:108).

Social constructivism

When we consider how children learn socially, it is helpful to think about different perspectives, such as social constructivism and sociocultural theory. As children develop, they build on what they know and can do and learn from others around them. We see this in our schools and settings as children learn through talk, interacting in groups, role-playing and collaborating with others. Vygotsky (1978) built upon constructivist theory and suggested that the social elements of learning cannot be ignored. He believed that children learn through interactions with others, the environment around them and cooperation with peers.

Learning through talk – Nursery Teacher Kate Bate, Cinnamon Brow CE Primary School Nursery

We believe that early communication and social skills are pivotal and intentionally bring Communication and Language and Personal, Social and Emotional Development into everything we do. Research shows that the more nursery rhymes a child knows in the early years, the better communicators and readers they will become. We have embedded this into our progressive curriculum and have nursery rhymes and focused texts that children will learn off by heart by the end of each year. We always introduce a new topic or text using an exciting hook which will capture children's interests and imagination in a multisensory way. We begin exploring each text intentionally picking out key words and phrases, thus expanding our children's language and vocabulary. For example, whilst reading *Walter's Wonderful Web* (Hopgood, 2015), we encountered the word *determined*, which was new to many children. We explained this word using role play and physical examples, incorporating it into our everyday language. We would use this word in context throughout the day, praising the children they were being determined like Walter. Before we knew it, we heard the children using this word in their everyday speech and had parents saying the children were using this word at home too.

We find acting out stories an effective way to teach new vocabulary and will regularly recap and revisit stories and rhymes previously learnt to encourage sticky learning. We will re-enact *We're Going on a Bear Hunt* (Rosen, 1993) whilst walking to forest school or enjoy re-telling the story of *Monkey and Me* (Gravett, 2018) with actions. We have found that teaching a text in such a multisensory way really enables cognition and learning, whilst also introducing children to new vocabulary and high-quality language at the same time.

As a school, we follow the *Word Aware* programme (Parsons & Branagan, 2021), introduce new language, and choose the same base word across the whole of our EYFS provision. We would teach this very intentionally following the multisensory *Word Aware Rap*, choosing the words using our speech-and-language baseline assessment, ensuring gaps in the children's learning are addressed. For example, our two-year-old and rising-three provision might teach the word BIG over two weeks, using a physical prop and photograph on the wall (at child level) to support this. In our pre-school setting, we would spend one week covering BIG and then move to the word BIGGER using props and a photo display, building on the children's knowledge of BIG as a foundation to learning. Our reception classes would recap both BIG and BIGGER during the first week, then introduce the new word/concept BIGGEST using props and photos. We ensure these words are used regularly within our teaching and learning and, before you know it, the whole cohort will be singing the *Word Aware Rap* to each other!

Helicopter Stories (Lee, 2015) also play an important role in our Early Years language development and provide the children an opportunity to have their voice heard. We ensure each child has the opportunity to express themselves and have enjoyed watching confidence fly, attention and listening skills improve and children regularly acting out their own stories within continuous provision, not just during our practitioner-led sessions. They also use new vocabulary within their play, such as 'stage', 'characters' and 'script'. We are beginning to introduce talk partners too, which is a strategy used in Reception and older-year groups when children share their ideas with each other, often during carpet time. This helps them to voice their thinking and discuss their ideas with a peer.

Developmentally, there are several different social milestones we would expect children to meet as they grow. It is worth remembering that all children develop at different rates, so although we may match an age range to a milestone, we must take into account individual differences and the circumstances surrounding a child. As the table suggests, these social milestones involve interactions with others.

Age	Social developmental milestone
Newborn	Distinguishes mother's voice from another. Can imitate simple movement of the face, head and hand modelled by an adult.
2–3 days	Discriminates between mother's face and stranger.
6–8 weeks	Begins to self-soothe – for example, sucking fist when tired or upset. Visual scanning tends to concentrate in eye region.
10 weeks	Social behaviour changes appropriately as baby can respond to facial expressions without simply imitating caregiver. Joint attention, joint emotion.
2–3 months	Turn-taking face-to-face interaction. Social smiles produced in response to another person's smile.

(Continued)

Age	Social developmental milestone
4–5 months	Discriminates between emotional expressions (facial and vocal in combination before vocal or facial alone).
6 months	Loves to play and interact with main carers. Likes to look in a mirror.
7–8 months	Recognises emotional expressions happy and angry. Will respond to request to show an adult a toy.
9–10 months	Able to coordinate interacting with objects and people at the same time. Social referencing.
1 year	Attaches emotional meaning to a particular object in the environment.
18 months	Starts to pretend. Relationships and friendships outside the family begin to develop. Recognises self in mirror.
2–3 years	Able to think about things that are absent or hypothetical. Desires and beliefs projected onto dolls/toys; explains and predicts people's behaviour. Understands the connection between desires and actions.
3–4 years	Begins to grasp that their deceptive actions will bring about false belief in another. Will predict character actions even when beliefs contrast with their own.
4–10 years	Begins to understand the conditions under which pride, shame and guilt are experienced. Theory of Mind develops.

Social Milestones adapted from Mathieson (2007:53)

Vygotsky talks about teaching children within the Zone of Proximal Development (ZPD), which describes when a child in a social situation can achieve or understand more than they would have been able to on their own. Usually a child would be working with a 'More Knowledgeable Other' (MKO), an adult or peer who acts a little like an expert in the situation and enables the child to learn (Vygotsky, 1978). We see this when children are playing together and they bounce ideas off each other or one child shares their knowledge about a particular theme. An example of this is when a group of young children started talking about what the beach is like. One child, who had obviously been to a beach, began to share his lived experiences about building a sandcastle and jumping over the waves. He acted as an MKO for the other children.

In relation to learning self-regulation, children will often be working within their ZPD as they take risks, need to problem-solve and maintain mental flexibility. Children may find it difficult to inhibit their emotional responses and find it challenging when socially interacting with others. We can help children by acting as an MKO, role-modelling how to interact with others, labelling our emotions and explaining how we can respond when we feel certain ways.

Encouraging positive interactions – Reception teacher Melanie Ellis, Chewton Mendip Primary School

Two children were using the 3D wooden shapes to construct a dinosaur land with buildings of various heights. A third child arrived and stomped through the area, knocking down the buildings and kicking the blocks across the carpet. When we talked to the third child about why he had done so, he had simply wanted to play with them. We discussed and modelled how he might join them appropriately. Similar incidents occurred for the first few weeks of the term. We began to shadow the child during independent learning time and play alongside him and whomever he had chosen to interact with. We would build towers and ask each other to knock them down and talk about how we felt. We had competitions to build different structures and highlighted examples of good independent learning from other children, re-enacting and role-playing and providing good examples for him to learn from. After several weeks his behaviour settled and he built positive relationships with his peers, and then they began inviting him to join them. He is beginning to independently access the provision more appropriately and is now forming friendships, which is lovely to witness.

Bronfenbrenner's ecological systems theory

Building on a social constructivist approach, Vygotsky also considered how culture and wider society might impact our children's development (1978). However, Bronfenbrenner exemplifies this within what has been described as sociocultural theory. This theory takes into account that our children are not growing up in isolation, they are part of a family, community and wider society. As they grow, their network of connections expands as mentioned above. Bronfenbrenner developed an ecological systems theory, which is often depicted by concentric rings around a child in the centre, as he attempted to explain the many influences on that child (Bronfenbrenner, 1979). His theory is grounded in the understanding that the relationships the child encounters are central to their development. It is not simply the immediate family that he sees as significant, but also others whom the child encounters in different situations. Bronfenbrenner's theory also considers the many layers of society and environments, how they interact with each other and how this will impact or influence the child.

Bronfenbrenner organised a person's environment into five different systems: microsystem, mesosystem, exosystem, macrosystem and chronosystem, which are sometimes described as layers of an onion or likened to Russian dolls in the way they are nested within each other.

Ecological Systems Theory
(Bronfenbrenner, 1979)

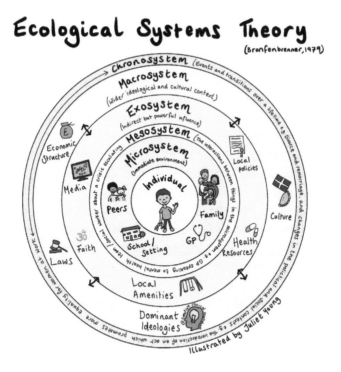

Chronosystem (Events and transitions over a lifetime e.g. Divorce and remarriage, and changes in the policies which affect us)

Macrosystem (Wider ideological and cultural context)

Exosystem (Indirect but powerful influence)

Mesosystem (The interactions between things in the microsystem)

Microsystem (Immediate environment)

Individual

Economic Structure
Media
Peers
School/Setting
Faith
Laws
Local Amenities
Dominant Ideologies
GP
Family
Health Resources
Local policies
Culture

Illustrated by Juliet Young

We can see from Juliet's image how the child is at the centre and those closest to the child – for example, their family – form the microsystem. This is arguably the most important and influential system as it involves the people with the greatest influence on the child. Working outwards from the centre, the mesosystem considers interactions between people in the child's microsystem, e.g., the way the family interacts with the school or setting. The exosystem, although indirectly influencing the child, still has a powerful impact as it includes the local environment, media and the parents' friends or workplace. For example, if a parent's working hours or employment status changes, this could mean the child's sessions in nursery reduce and thus would have a big impact on the child. The macrosystem indirectly influences the child and refers to the larger societal perspective, such as economic structures, laws, cultural values, the socio-economic status of the family and the way society views their ethnicity or race. Bronfenbrenner includes the chronosystem as the part of his system which relates to the impact that events or transitions may have on the child as well as the time the child is born into. For example, if a child experiences loss at a young age or their parents separate, this will impact their development. In addition, children born in the 2020s will have very different experiences from those born in the 1920s. Therefore, time and transitions are significant when considering child development.

Bronfenbrenner's theory – Juliet Young, trainee clinical psychologist and illustrator

Bronfenbrenner's ecological systems theory provides a useful framework to understand the influence of context on a child. My illustration is an attempt to capture the multiple systems Bronfenbrenner proposed. The child's imme- diate (micro) system has a strong and direct influence on their life – e.g., family rules. The exosystem is likely to be having an indirect influence too – e.g., what a child watches on TV can shape their values. The macrosystem – e.g., culture and economic structure – will also form the wider context in which they live. Bronfenbrenner also emphasised the influence of changes over time – e.g., the introduction of free school meals or extra funding for nursery places – and called this the chronosystem. Finally, the mesosystem highlights the interactions between different systems – e.g., conversations about the child between nur- sery and parent. As a trainee clinical psychologist, this framework is etched into my mind when I consider the difficulties, strengths and development of a child.

Bronfenbrenner's ecological systems theory reminds us as educators that we cannot study a child and think about their development without taking account of the many different cultural and social influences on them. This is about considering them holistic- ally and as part of a much wider culture and society. Some educators bear in mind this theory when observing the children in their care.

Using the ecological systems theory as an assessment tool

Chronosystem
When Jade was born 18 months ago this gave
Isla the additional identity of "big sister".
Jade's mum changed jobs and now works at
the vets on Green lane. Isla talks about
this a lot.

Wendy and Tamsin invite their Early Years Initial Teacher Training PGCE trainees at Bath Spa University to use Bronfenbrenner's theory to unpick a child in context and draw a rough out- line of these concentric rings, putting a child at the centre and then filling in the many influences around them in each system. This helps them to have a wider window and view the child more holistically.

Role play and imaginative play

In role play children take on the role of others and begin to think about what it is like to be someone else – for example, a family relative, a firefighter, a shopkeeper, a bus driver or a character from a familiar book. In these roles they are thinking about what typical behaviour might be for that character or what people in these roles might say and do, then mirroring this in their play. They can then begin to develop their understanding that others have feelings and thoughts which are different to their own and begin to empathise.

Children begin to adopt different roles in their play as young as 8 to 18 months of age, when they may enjoy copying their main carer. We can support children by allowing them to help us complete tasks, such as using a dustpan and brush or sorting the washing. Completing activities together will encourage them to use their working memory, have cognitive flexibility and inhibitory control as they focus on helping us and try to ignore distractions or choose to ignore their desire to do other things.

'Helping' to clean the house

Harry always wanted to help his dad from a very young age. If he was cleaning the house or sorting the washing, Harry would want to help. His dad found it easier to give Harry small tasks to do to 'help' him as he cleaned, rather than trying to occupy Harry to free himself up to clean. So, we have a lot of photos which involve Harry 'helping' – like this one, when he was using the floor wipes. As he got older, we bought him some utensils for smaller hands – a mini dustpan and brush and small broom – which he loved.

As they get older, children's play refines into a more sophisticated role-taking pretence which can be related to real or fictional characters (German & Leslie, 2001). From about 18 months onward, children engage in more imaginary play as they use objects and resources and engage in symbolic play, where they can use a wooden block as a phone or have some imaginary ice cream in a bowl. They can also take on a role in their play and imitate that character – for example, announcing "I'm a doctor" and playing the doctor role or saying "Quick, get the hose, the house is on fire!" Children can also engage in make-believe situations – for example, "Let's pretend we're climbing" – or fantasy scenarios – "Pretend I'm Spider-Man and I can climb up walls!" There may be times when the lines between fantasy and reality are blurred (Grimmer, 2020), and when children are engaged in role play they often 'become' the character and move beyond pretending to 'being'. Lobman and Clark state, "Pretending is at the heart of what it means to be human" (2015:92). If we consider how we, as adults, like to get lost in a book or TV series or enjoy the escapism of a film, role play offers children a similar opportunity.

As educators, we can support our children by observing them as they play, sometimes joining in when invited. We can also provide an enabling environment which may enhance their role-play – for example, by adding some props and resources or providing lots of open-ended resources, such as large boxes or pieces of material, for the children to use as they wish. Sometimes our role will be to ask questions or comment on what they are doing; however, we must resist the urge to take over their play or hijack it as an opportunity to teach them about the role they have taken on. Our role may simply be to stay quiet and continue observing (Fisher, 2016).

Playing in imaginative ways can involve many executive function skills as children develop rules, plan a narrative, adopt a role and act in a particular way. It requires them to be mentally flexible as they use props and resources and adapt to changes as they develop in the game, or even inhibit actions if they don't fit in with the role they have assumed (see Chapter 5).

By about two-and-a-half to three years old, children tend to play more socially and move from playing alongside each other to more associative and cooperative play where they share the same goal in their play (Parten, 1932). In the preschool age range, we can sometimes see children regulate their own behaviour as well as that of their peers as they play together, negotiating rules and compromising on storylines. Educators can support children by talking about the roles they adopt, providing any props or resources they need or ensuring they have the necessary ingredients to create their own. When children create their own, they need to plan ahead, gather resources and continually problem-solve or adjust their plans as their creations take shape. This is executive functioning in action. In addition, when children repurpose an object or use something in a new way that is different to its original purpose, it demonstrates their ability to be flexible in their thinking – for example, when they turn a basket upside down and pretend it is the till in a shop.

Using role play – Nursery teacher Kate Bate, Cinnamon Brow CE Primary School Nursery

We believe role play is vitally important to enhance and develop early communication skills. Before their child begins at nursery, I ask parents to email me a photograph of their child during the summer holidays. These are then laminated and displayed in our role-play area, specifically designed to promote Personal, Social and Emotional Development and Communication and Language skills for the children's first few weeks in nursery. We Velcro the photos to the sides of the role-play arch, enabling the children to talk about them and move them around. The area is furnished with fake grass, wooden toadstools, a children's camping chair, books about different families and a sofa, with lots of greenery encouraging and promoting a safe communication space. We also display photographs of holiday-themed activities with words, like *caravan, tent, a local play area* and *seaside*. We then, as practitioners, are able to use these pictures as talking prompts to get to know our new children and to encourage the more reluctant speakers. It is really important to us that they feel safe and valued, and we have found that this approach gives the children something to talk about together as they begin to make new relationships with each other.

We change our role-play area usually twice a half-term to follow children's interests and support their learning. In addition to a themed role-play area, we believe it is important to have a permanent home corner, situated near the role-play area and close to our mark-making and reading areas. We continually incorporate many different opportunities for reading and writing/mark-making in this space. We also ask for a family photograph from each child, which we display in the home corner all year. Children regularly talk about their families in this area and it really helps with their sense of identity. We also include jigsaws and books about families along with familiar things from their home to aid their communication skills – like local takeaway menus, a phone book, diary, calendar and computer. We have also found that having phones throughout the classroom is a wonderful way to get children talking – more than one is best, so they can have a conversation together. Adults modelling good practice is an absolutely fabulous way to encourage speaking – we write shopping lists with the children and take telephone messages or orders from Asda. Children learn so much from interacting with us as practitioners.

Finding common ground with children is really important to gain their trust and to build a relationship. We encourage our children to bring in objects or photos from home which they can talk about and show to their peers. We sometimes add these to our floorbooks, which we use to document children's learning and make it visible throughout the school. A lovely example of this was when a shy little boy who was mad about dinosaurs brought in a photo-graph of him and his dad next to a T-Rex skeleton. This was a wonderful way to open up communication, and he absolutely loved talking all about his favourite subject to his friends. Now, he is one of our most lively talkers!

There are several links between executive functions and language development as children use language to plan, communicate their needs and problem-solve. As adults, we often need to talk things through or think aloud when thinking critically, and the same is true of children. So, role-modelling this – providing a running commentary of what we are doing and why – can sometimes be helpful in making our own thinking and decisions visible to our children. Also, adopting a problem-solving approach to resolving conflict, which talks through an issue and sees incidents as opportunities to learn, is helpful and is described in Chapter 4.

There are many ways that role play supports self-regulation – for example, it:

- Provides children with real-life scenarios within a safe environment.

- Offers an opportunity to empathise and take on the perspective of others.

- Encourages mental flexibility and problem-solving.

- Enables children to play with their feelings and practise emotional control.

- Allows children to resolve conflicts.

- Provides a social context within which they can learn how to interact with others, cooperate and negotiate rules together.

- Offers an opportunity to explore identity and counter stereotypes in a safe environment – for example, boys can play at being a mummy or wear a dress and girls can play at being a daddy or Superman.

- Nurtures children's dispositions such as resilience, perseverance and a 'can-do' attitude.

- Builds children's language and communication skills as children talk through scenarios and possibilities.

- Offers opportunities for children to use executive-functioning skills.

Some schools (albeit not many) promote role play beyond early years and have a role-play area in each class throughout the school, whereas some continue until children are six or seven years old. Within England, role play is usually seen within early years settings and EYFS classes in schools and occasionally into Key Stage 1; however, as Chapter 2 highlighted, in most countries around the world children do not enter formal schooling until the age of six or seven, which is the second year of formal infant classes in England. Therefore, around the world, children have access to role play until they are much older than in England. We believe that role play is an essential pedagogical approach for supporting children's self-regulation and therefore ask why it does not have a higher profile throughout our schools at an older age.

Collaborative play – Year One Class Teacher

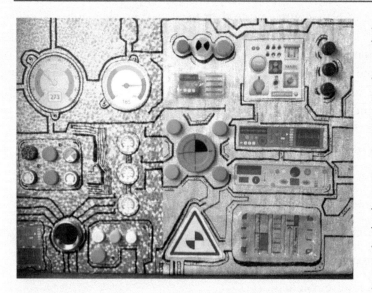

A class teacher talked about how she worked with a large class of year one children who were predominantly boys, and their passion and interest at the time was space, the planets and what it would be like to go to another planet. The teacher asked the children what they would like the role-play area to be, and the unanimous decision was to create a spaceship with windows and planets hanging around.

Once the children had chosen the material and built the area, they used it collaboratively to plan trips to outer space, read stories about going to space and dress up as astronauts. Often one child (not always the same child) would take on the role of the lead astronaut, telling their fellow astronauts what the mission was. The children were observed saluting and saying, "Yes captain!", asking questions about the different types of aliens they might encounter and what they should do. They were observed moving in slow motion with their feet slowly and carefully touching the surface, as if walking on the moon. They talked about looking after each other and how they would need breathing masks to stay alive. The children demonstrated real care and empathy for their peers as they went off into space by zooming around the classroom with their peers waving goodbye and wishing them well.

The role-play area enabled them to become someone else and consider how that character might behave, what they might say, what actions and mannerisms the character might adopt.

Social and dramatic play

Children regularly recreate events and situations that they have experienced, often taking on character roles and imitating grown-ups – for example, through being the teacher and reading to the teddies, being a shopkeeper in the role-play area or being a builder in the construction area. This is a type of role play described as socio-dramatic play or social-and-dramatic play and is often seen during free play and tends to be child-led. Children's play becomes more complicated in terms of themes and negotiated rules at about 4–5 years. This often develops cooperatively and collaboratively, and it supports children's self-regulation skills as they practice empathy, negotiate problems and take on roles linked to their interests and real-life experiences.

The role of the adult in this play is the same as within role play – observing, participating (when invited), modelling roles and resourcing. We do not need to provide props for every aspect of their play because children are very resourceful, imaginative and creative and can adapt or source materials and resources themselves. Therefore, providing open-ended materials and resources is a better way of supporting their play, because the children can use these things flexibly or symbolically – for example, a large box could be a table for a shop one day and then transformed into a car during the next session. It is also helpful to provide real objects rather than plastic or pretend ones. We could ask for donations of old mobile phones or a keyboard and mouse for children to use in their play. A few props can be helpful at times; however, we need the children to lead this play, so our role is listening to them and allowing them to enhance their play area themselves – for example, through making signs or creating labels or resources.

Once children have shown an interest in a particular role, we can widen children's experiences by offering them opportunities to find out more. For example, if a child has just taken their pet to the vet, we may see them playing 'vets' with their friends; therefore, we may arrange a vet to visit us or take the children to a local vet surgery and then perhaps create one in our room. This allows us to extend the narrative, share vocabulary relating to the play theme and offer ideas to extend their play. It is important that we value socio-dramatic play because through this play children are learning how to act and behave in their world.

Social and dramatic play develops children's self-regulation skills through:

- Providing an opportunity for social interaction.

- Practising social etiquette and developing children's understanding of rules.

- Using long- and short-term memory.

- Developing their ability to problem-solve and think critically.

- Practising their language and communication skills.

- Helping children to understand the world and how it works.

- Allowing children to be creative and use their imagination.

Rough and tumble play

Within ECEC, educators are usually very responsive to the needs of their children – for example, if a child cries, we will try to find out why, or if a child is missing their parent, we might ask if the child needs a cuddle. This is because we understand the importance of building secure attachments with children and responding sensitively in all situations. However, sometimes when children engage in rough and tumble play, educators distract or attempt to redirect the children's attention elsewhere to discourage them from engaging in this play.

If we take a moment and reflect upon our own childhoods, we might remember playing games that involved running, chasing, being chased, tickling, wrestling and fighting 'baddies'. Perhaps our play made links with the popular culture of the time – for example, through taking on the role of a TV or cartoon character. We were learning a lot through this play – from the skills we were practising to learning about rules and how to behave in social situations. We might have been learning about how to take risks or set limits or exploring friendship and family roles. Many of these games come under the umbrella of rough and tumble, which is a very natural way for children to play. Children will tend to giggle and laugh frequently during this play, and we will observe them smiling and generally looking OK. Often these games involve role play, pretending and imaginative storytelling. Children need to negotiate rules with each other and concepts of fairness, justice, right and wrong, and 'goodies' and 'baddies' often underpin the storyline.

Grimmer (2020) notes there are many benefits to rough and tumble play, and the majority of these are linked with self-regulation – therefore, we can conclude that encouraging rough and tumble play will help children to develop this. In fact, Jarvis and George (2010) suggest that rough and tumble play is vital for healthy child development. However, despite these benefits, many ECEC educators are not comfortable with permitting this play. They may feel concerned that if a child gets hurt, they will be held responsible, or perhaps that allowing children to play aggressively will lead to real fighting and violence. Research suggests that this is not the case, with one study showing that rough and tumble play led to real fighting in less than 1% of the observed time (Scott & Panksepp, 2003).

An analogy of this is how puppies develop and learn bite control by play-biting with their siblings. They are practising biting in order to find out when to stop. To someone who is not used to puppies, this biting may be rather frightening; however, it could be argued that if a puppy didn't have the chance to chew everything and play-bite its siblings, it may never learn its own strength of bite. Educators need to be able to tell the difference between aggressive play and real violence. Tamsin shares some useful ideas about this in her book, *Calling All Superheroes* (Grimmer, 2020). Rough and tumble play can help children to develop self-regulation, and the role of the educator is to permit this play within a safe environment. They will need to observe closely, supervise and ensure that children are consenting to the play.

Empathy

Empathy can be described as understanding how someone else feels – frequently the phrase "putting yourself into someone else's shoes" is used. Often educators expect young children to be able to empathise, forgetting that this involves Theory of Mind and knowing that others think or feel differently, which is beyond the developmental capabilities of most children under the age of four or five (see Chapter 5). Empathy involves responding emotionally to someone else and the situation they are in and imagining how they must feel in that situation.

Developing empathy is a part of children's social development linked with Theory of Mind (see Chapter 5). Empathy is a pro-social behaviour and one we want to foster in our children; however, in order for children to develop empathy, they need to feel safe, secure and loved themselves. Young children develop empathy over many years, and it is difficult to say developmentally when all children will be able to empathise. Despite this, it is a skill that is part of our ability to self-regulate because empathy is all about considering how someone else might feel, and understanding how our behaviour, words and actions might impact someone else can help us to maintain control or inhibit our impulses.

The term *mental states* tends to refer to our emotions, bodily feelings or thoughts and perceptions (Oosterwijk et al., 2012), and one way to promote empathy with children is to consider how we highlight or acknowledge these states in the moment. Telling a child what we are feeling and why is explaining and exemplifying that emotion. When we do this, it is helpful to highlight that we don't know what other people are thinking or what they would like, for example, but we can find out by asking them. We also need to explain to children that sometimes other people's thoughts and feelings will be different from our own.

Promoting empathy through our interactions

Use the language associated with thinking and feeling

"We could collect some leaves and make a picture for your mummy. I think she would like that. What colours do you think she might like?"

"I saw Ezra at the park today. I was surprised to see him, as I thought he was still at his Grandma's house."

Link concrete objects with thinking and feeling words

Share objects with the children and explain why you like them or how you feel about them. Invite the children to imagine which object their friend/parent would like.

Talk about past experiences

Look through photographs of our time together – for example, in a floor book, learning journeys or in a learning story – and talk about what we did.

"Do you remember visiting the zoo? We saw a penguin eating a fish."

Talk about upcoming events

Talk to the children about what you intend to do at the weekend or who you might see that evening. Explain how you feel and why.

"I would like to go on holiday with Sarah. She loves to visit hot countries. What should we suggest Sarah takes with her?"

Use and name the mental states as they happen

Talking about our thoughts, feelings and emotions in the moment will help children to reflect on this themselves.

"Which cup do you think John would like? Should we ask him? Which cup would you like, John?"

Reading books and stories

Share books and stories with children where we talk about how the characters are feeling or what they are doing and why.

"I wonder how the crocodile felt when his brothers and sisters were swimming and he didn't like water?"

Incorporate jokes and humour

Often when we joke with children or use humour we can release tension and inject fun or playfulness into the situation. For example, when children watch a character like Mr Tumble fall over, we can laugh but also say, "Oh no! Poor Mr Tumble!"

However, we need to be wary of using sarcasm, being self-deprecating or teasing children as, due to their age and stage of development, they may take this seriously and will not understand.

In summary

In our view, what really makes the difference for children in the long term is encouraging them to develop the dispositions and attitudes that enable them to interact with others socially and learn effectively. If all children have the opportunity to become self-regulated learners, it will enable them to build relationships with others and prepare them for future success in life. Thus, these dispositions support children to be life-ready. They learn how to socialise, how to persevere if things do not go their way and how to be resilient if they ever receive a knock back. They become adept at turning conflicts with others into problems to solve and noticing patterns and links in their learning. They are able to stop themselves from lashing out at a friend or hiding if they feel overwhelmed, upset or angry with someone else. This is where developing self-regulation empowers children and enables them to grow as part of a community and within society.

In the next chapter we consider the important role the adult plays when supporting children to develop self-regulation.

Questions for reflection

1. In what ways do we promote children's social development and confidence?

2. Consider the role-play area in our setting or classroom – does it reflect the children's interests? How could we improve it to promote self-regulatory skills?

3. To what extent do we use language to role-model being empathetic with others?

References

Asuquo, S. (2020) *Shine*. Market Harborough: Troubador Publishing Ltd.

Bronfenbrenner, U. (1979) *The Ecology of Human Development: Experiments by nature and design*. Boston, MA: Harvard University Press.

Fisher, J. (2016) *Interacting or Interfering?: Improving interactions in the early years*. London: Open University Press.

German, T. & Leslie, A. (2001) 'Children's inferences from "knowing" to "pretending" and "believing"', *British Journal of Developmental Psychology, 19*(1), pp. 59–83.

Glazzard, J. & Trussler, S. (2020) *Supporting mental health in primary and early years: a practice based approach*. London: Sage.

Gravett, E. (2018) *Monkey and Me*. Basingstoke: Two Hoots.

Grimmer, T. (2020) *Calling All Superheroes: Supporting and Developing Superhero Play in the Early Years*. London: Routledge.

Hopgood, T. (2015) *Walter's Wonderful Web*. Basingstoke: Macmillan Children's Books.

Jarvis, P. & George, J. (2010) 'Thinking it through: Rough and tumble play', in J. Moyles (Ed.), *Thinking about play*, pp. 164–178. Maidenhead: Open University.

Lee, T. (2015) *Princesses, Dragons and Helicopter Stories: Storytelling and story acting in the early years*. London: Routledge.

Lobman, C. & Clark, K. (2015) 'From the dress-up corner to the stage: Dramatic activities for early childhood classrooms', *Young Children, 2*(3), pp. 92–99.

Mathieson, K. (2007) *Identifying Special Needs in the Early Years*. London: Paul Chapman.

Oosterwijk, S., Lindquist, K. A., Anderson, E., Dautoff, R., Moriguchi, Y., & Barrett, L. F. (2012) 'States of mind: Emotions, body feelings, and thoughts share distributed neural networks', *NeuroImage, 62*(3), pp. 2110–2128.

Parsons, S. & Branagan, A. (2021) *Word Aware 1: Teaching Vocabulary Across the Day, Across the Curriculum*. London: Routledge.

Parten, M. (1932) 'Social participation among preschool children', *Journal of Abnormal & Social Psychology, 27*(3), pp. 243–269.

Rosen, M. (1993) *We're Going on a Bear Hunt*. London: Walker Books.

Scott, E. & Panksepp, J. (2003) 'Rough-and-tumble play in human children', *Aggressive Behavior, 29*(6), pp. 539–551.

Thoutenhoofd, E. & Pirrie, A. (2015) 'From Self-Regulation to Learning to Learn: Observations on the Construction of Self and Learning', *British Educational Research Journal, 41*(1), pp. 72–84.

Vygotsky, L. (1978) *Mind in society: The development of higher psychological processes*. Boston, MA: Harvard University.

8 The role of the adult

Tamsin Grimmer

Introduction

The way we act and react to children and their behaviour is perhaps the most important aspect of our role when considering self-regulation. We can either escalate the situation or calm things down, and it can be easy to make things worse unintentionally. For example, whilst visiting a castle, Tamsin was queuing for the toilets and overheard a parent talking to their toddler. The facilities were a long way from the castle. The parent, obviously annoyed at having to run all that way with a child desperate for the toilet, found her daughter couldn't go once they were in the cubicle. As the parent got increasingly stressed and cross, the child got more and more upset, and it ended with the parent saying, "No castle – we won't go back into the castle unless you do your wee!" The child, obviously learning to use the toilet, was sobbing, "Castle – me go castle mummy!" As her whimpering began to ease, she then changed tactics and started saying, "Sorry, mummy!" over and over again, to which the parent replied, "It's too late to say sorry now. I told you to go to the toilet before. Now we can't go to the castle and you've made mummy sad." The child began to cry even more, and it really escalated things. It must have taken a while to calm her down.

There are times when adults escalate an issue, usually by not acting like the adult in the situation. For example, by trying to get the last word, saying, "I told you so" or being so adamant they are right that they will not let a subject or situation go. In the castle situation, it would have been easy for the parent, annoyed as she was, to say, "You thought you needed a wee – well done for trying. Let's go back to the castle now." As it was, the child didn't have a full understanding of the situation. She didn't realise how frustrating toilet training a child is and how much effort her mum had to go through to get her to the toilet on time. She is also learning to use her interoceptive skills to work out when she needs to go to the toilet, and she won't always get it right.

DOI: 10.4324/9781003162346-9

This chapter explores the role of the adult in building relationships and secure attachments with our children and considers our own wellbeing and regulation and how we can become co-regulators of our children, supporting them to develop self-regulation. It also shares the importance of the learning environment we provide and the role it can play in emotional literacy. This chapter will finish by exploring how we can adopt a restorative approach when moving forward.

Relationship

In order to respond to children mindfully and support their self-regulation, we first need to build a strong, trusting, reciprocal relationship with them. Children need to feel loved, accepted and valued by us in order to trust us. A key person in a school or setting offers a child an opportunity to build a secure attachment with someone other than their parent or main carer. This also gives them a reassuring link with home and helps them to know that there will always be someone available to look out for, care for and love them.

Adults have a special role to play in providing an emotionally enabling environment within which children will thrive and flourish. As Chapter 3 explained, this is about our ethos and the nurturing environment we create, not just the physical space. Developing a warm, loving and friendly atmosphere where we build effective and close relationships with the children will enable them to feel safe and secure and will provide a basis for self-regulation skills.

Here are a few ideas of how to build authentic relationships and attachments with children in our care:

■ Get down to the children's level – or lower – as this will be non-threatening to them.

■ Observe children closely and pay attention to their language, interests and fascinations.

■ Tune in to what they say, their body language and their interactions with others.

■ Comment on something they are doing or something we can relate to.

■ Adopt a loving pedagogy with warm and affectionate interactions.

■ Use positive body gestures, facial expressions and eye contact.

■ Remain calm and use a warm and friendly tone of voice.

■ Listen and respond sensitively to the child and with empathy.

■ Offer opportunities for children to be involved in decision-making.

■ Value what children say and do.

■ Be trustworthy and show genuine interest in the children and their activities.

- Have realistic expectations of behaviour and ensure a consistent approach with regular reassurance from adults.

- Allow specific toys or comforters to help children feel secure.

- Create a sense of belonging in our setting or school.

- Spend time with the children and enjoy their company!

The 4 S's of attachment

Siegel and Bryson (2020) talk about the four S's of attachment – safe, seen, soothed and secure – to simplify how parents (and we would suggest educators) interact with their children. Children are dependent on us and need to be protected, so *safety* is the first S. No one would want to deliberately scare a child; however, within our settings, we need to be aware that there is a power dynamic at play. We are big and our children are much smaller. Sometimes, when we raise our voices or snap at children, we can come across as very frightening. In an online interview Siegel explains this puts our brains into a quandary. Usually, when we feel afraid, we would return to our main caregiver for support and protection; however, if it is our main caregiver who is the cause of the fear, we are unsure how to react or where to go for support. One half of us will want to return to our carer, and the other half tells us to stay away from the source of the fear (Siegel in Gaddis, 2020). This gives us increased cortisol as we go into survival mode, as Chapter 1 explained. We want our children to feel safe; therefore, we should never frighten them and should actively avoid using fear as an incentive for compliance.

The second S is *seen*. This is not only about noticing what children say, do and are interested in, but also tuning in to what children are thinking and feeling. When we are attuned to their emotional states, we can truly empathise, which will help children to feel valued and understood. Adults can do this by holding children in mind, thinking about them and putting their needs first. This is part and parcel of developing a loving pedagogy (Grimmer, 2021).

The next S is *soothed*, which is about adults co-regulating children's emotions and helping them to regain feelings of calm. When adults use emotion-coaching strategies and respond mindfully in the moment to children, they help them know how to respond appropriately. In addition, they act as a role model, demonstrating effective ways of how to respond in similar situations and strategies children can use in the future.

Feeling safe, seen and soothed leads to children who feel secure and can use their adult as a 'secure base' (Ainsworth et al., 1978), which is when a child feels comfortable and secure enough to leave the adult's side in order to explore and investigate or take risks in their surrounding environment. This is the forth S and Siegel calls this the adult becoming a "launching pad", so that children feel able to go off and explore independently (Siegel in

Gaddis, 2020). We could argue that this is what we are aiming for as educators: children who are confident, capable and willing and able to be independent, safe in the knowledge that they are loved and cared for. When adults are emotionally available to children, sensitive and responsive to their signals, they are creating this secure attachment (Siegel, 2012). Research shows that children who are securely attached grow into adults who achieve more academically, have better self-regulatory skills and can function more effectively in a social context, building effective relationships with others (Siegel, 2012; Bergin & Bergin, 2009).

The 4 S's	What it means for the child	Implications for the role of the adult
Safe	Feeling safe and secure, able to make mistakes, not frightened by adults.	Adults who are available to the child, never frighten them, offer a secure base and practise acceptance of children, even if they make mistakes.
Seen	Feeling empathised with and understood. Being held in mind and feeling valued.	Adults who not only see with their eyes, but who are able to become attuned to children's emotional states and empathise. Adults who adopt a loving pedagogy and hold children in mind.
Soothed	Being able to regain feelings of calm, feeling soothed.	Adults who are able to be a calming influence, accept children's feelings and be there for the child. Adults who co-regulate children's emotions by coaching and supporting 'in the moment' and by role-modelling how to act and react when we feel certain ways.
Secure	Knowing that an attachment figure will be there. Feeling safe, seen and soothed leads to feeling secure and having a sense of belonging. Being resilient and having a high level of wellbeing. Being able to use the adult as a 'launching pad' to take risks and explore independently.	Adults who are available to the child and who build strong relationships where children can use them as a secure base.

The 4 S's of attachment, inspired by Siegal & Bryson (2020)

Being the adult in the room

The strategy of acting like an adult and smoothing things over is sometimes called 'partial agreement'. This is when we stop arguing or we deliberately partly agree – for example, saying, "I'm sure you didn't mean to", "I see what you mean" or "I would feel that way too". These sorts of phrases demonstrate understanding and our desire to resolve matters. They avoid the argument being extended by the adult and usually de-escalate the situation, rather than adding fuel to the fire. They seek to restore the relationship and value this over being right or knowing more. Building loving relationships should be at the heart of the role of the adult and being able to regulate ourselves is a vital part of restoring and maintaining these relationships.

As the example of the blue teapot illustrates, it would have been easy to chastise the child for breaking it, and doing so would perhaps have curtailed his curious nature. Bit by bit children's natural ways of enquiring can be worn away by the response of adults, until we have children who fit our mould or who conform, and those who do not conform are often labelled as disobedient. So, the way the adult acts and reacts has a lot to answer for!

The blue teapot – Elaine Brown, Childminder

We used to have a big, shiny-blue porcelain teapot in our outdoor area. It had a lovely happy smiley face on the front, and the children loved to play with it. Now and again, I would spot a child carrying this teapot across the grass towards the path and I would quickly say, "Please keep the teapot away from the path because it might break!" That big, shiny-blue teapot survived a couple of summers, but one day he was no more. This particular day, I happened to turn around just at the precise moment that a two year old dropped it – right there on those flags. Oh dear, give a two year old a teapot and it is bound to break at some point, right? Of course – but, this was not an accident. This child purposely walked across the grass with the teapot in his little chubby hands, he got to the edge of the grass where the flagstones were and he just stopped, dropped and watched. In slow motion the blue shiny teapot smashed. He stood transfixed, the broken smile in pieces by his feet. Now, I knew this child really well, and I knew this was not him misbehaving or being mischievous. What I did know was this child was curious, he was an experimenter, he was always trying to work things out, and I know he desperately wanted to see – in his two-year-old little world – what would happen to that blue teapot if it was actually dropped on those flags. It made me reflect that when children do things like this, we as adults might have a knee-jerk reaction and automatically think that they are acting up or misbehaving, but sometimes it's not what it seems. Observation and knowing the children in our care really well – and also understanding how their little minds work – is key. Most importantly, our own ability to regulate our responses and reactions to behaviours is fundamental to their learning and confidence. This lovely little boy continued to be full of curiosity and wonder of the world, and I hope that my gentle and calm reaction gave him a little more confidence to continue on this journey. Hopefully, though, he hasn't broken any more teapots!

This will mean putting aside our ego, forgetting any reference to who is right or wrong in any given situation and ignoring the urge to say, "I told you so!" – even if you did tell them only seconds before. Instead, the role of the adult is to remain calm, non-judgemental and rational and put the emotional needs of the child first. At this moment, we need to defuse the situation, not make a point. The learning will follow once tempers have eased and everyone is calm again. Remember, as Chapter 1 explained, when we are full of emotion we are not able to think rationally, so lectures or long explanations about what should have happened are pointless.

We need to pre-empt situations and think about how we will respond when or if certain situations arise. This is partly about knowing and understanding our policies and procedures as well as talking about our response as a team. Tamsin often suggests having a script ready, so that all educators remain consistent in their approaches to supporting children with their emotions and behaviour. Chapter 9 thinks about how we can use our policy to share our ethos and practice with parents and carers. Responding sensitively is also about becoming a co-regulator for our children and helping them to deal with their big feelings in the moment.

Using social stories (Gray, 2015) can help younger children to understand their feelings and empathise with others. These are short descriptions of situations written from a child's perspective (see example below) to help children to know what to expect in that situation and how to respond appropriately. They are a great strategy to have up our sleeves because we can tailor them to the needs of our individual children. As Mainstone-Cotton (2021) suggests, although social stories can be bought, they are best when they are written by us, as educators, so that they address the exact issue or situation that needs to be covered.

Feeling cross social story – Lisa Gibbons, Denmead Infant School

We use social stories with the children which we have printed with pictures, photographs and clip art to help illustrate the words. This is an example of the social story we use when children are feeling cross:

> When I get cross I feel a spikey feeling in my tummy. It can be an uncomfortable feeling. The feeling makes me want to push other people or want to screw up my work. An adult will help me stay safe when I have this feeling.
>
> If I am feeling cross, my teachers will try to help me and I can ask my teachers for help.

Sometimes I need to calm down first. An adult will help me know when I am cross and ask me to go to my safe space. I will do a quiet activity to feel calmer. The adult will help me calm down.

My teachers will be happy that I have calmed down, and I will feel happy instead of cross.

Our own regulation and wellbeing

It is impossible to co-regulate a child if we are dysregulated ourselves. We need to be in touch with our own emotions and notice the various behaviours or situations that press our buttons so that we can find ways of dealing with them that avoid our overreacting or getting overly upset. Remaining calm ourselves is important because if we have 'flipped our lids', we will not be thinking straight or be able to remain rational and neutral. If we can recognise the situations that stress, upset or wind us up, we can then avoid them, be prepared for them or ask for help.

Mainstone-Cotton (2021) reminds us of the impact that stress has on our bodies and wellbeing. A small amount of stress and cortisol is natural and can even help us to remain focused; however, too much stress has a damaging impact on our body and mental health. We need to become aware of the signs of stress on our body so that we can help reduce these levels. According to Mainstone-Cotton (2021), there are many strategies we can use to support us – for example, eating well, exercising, sleeping well, mindfulness, self-compassion and partaking in activities that bring us joy.

Co-regulation

Co-regulation is a supportive process that relies on a foundation of a warm, responsive and trusting relationship between adults and children. It is about adults who interact in the moment, coach and role-model instruction to scaffold learning as well as provide a safe and stable environment, consistent routine and predictable boundaries. The routine actually helps children to be on autopilot in relation to their own behaviour, which aids self-regulation because it makes it easier for the child to know how to act at any given time. In this environment, adults help children to regulate their emotions and teach them strategies to use in the future.

Ways that we can support children's self-regulation include:

- Following the child's lead and reacting and interacting sensitively.

- Using language associated with feelings and emotions.

- Avoiding reprimanding children for having big emotions, instead offering calm and continuous reassurance, emotional support and warmth.

- Acknowledging and accepting children's feelings.

- Using any incidents that arise as opportunities to use conflict-resolution and emotion-coaching techniques.

- Engaging in role play and pretend play, e.g., role-modelling calming strategies.

- Using books and stories to talk about a character's thoughts and feelings.

- Developing emotional intelligence and praising children when they successfully manage big emotions.

- Encouraging children to recognise other people's feelings.

- Focusing on fostering dispositions and attitudes that enable children to be resilient and persevere in the face of challenges.

- Playing listening and attention games.

- Supporting children to problem-solve and develop creative approaches to learning.

- Being readily available to the children, alongside them and able to support if needed.

Babies and young children rely on external sources of self-regulation – that is, their care-givers are co-regulating them from day one. We might sing to a baby whilst gently rocking them or stroking their back to help them feel calm or distract a toddler by pointing out an aeroplane to avoid a tantrum. As they grow, children may still rely on adults to help them feel calm and strengthened, but they are also developing other strategies, such as self-talk or private speech, which is when a child talks to themselves as they meet challenges. For example, if we notice a young child building a tower, they may say to themselves, "It's tall … be careful", perhaps repeating what they have heard an adult say, but in doing so they are coaching themselves. Sometimes adults do this too – we talk to ourselves when completing a tricky task and become our own greatest cheerleader!

Children can also use objects to self-soothe or help themselves to calm down – for example, having a special teddy or blanket can provide the child with comfort at a stressful or upsetting time (see Chapter 3). Our role as adults is to allow, accept and value these objects as a supportive strategy that helps our children to feel more secure. In addition, we need to provide an enabling environment within which children can feel safe so that they have the confidence to explore, investigate and take risks.

Learning about self-regulation and co-regulation – Cassie Hartley, Thrive Childcare and Education

Building my knowledge around self-regulation has been fascinating and vital to my role working with children and staff. I feel this has definitely improved my practice and I understand children better. It's amazing how knowing this information can help support children throughout their early years and how it shapes their future. I wish I'd known this sooner!

For example, there was a child that used to become very upset, seemingly without warning, and 'flipped his lid' quite often. I would show the staff how to support him by using the cosy space (our self-regulation space) to ensure he was safe and comfy as he would kick his legs, thrash his arms around and be vocal. I would reassure him that I was there and sit close by (as he didn't want me to touch or talk to him). Once he had regulated himself, bringing his breathing down to a calm level, I would talk to him, and we would read books together until he was ready to go and play.

After a few weeks of staff using this strategy, the child would take himself over to this space whenever he could feel himself getting worked up, and he would lie down looking at the ribbons moving, look out the window or sit and look through books. Giving him the space, acknowledging his feelings and not attempting to reason with him when he was in the middle of an 'episode' really worked, and eventually we could see him thriving in areas that we wouldn't have seen before. His parents were really happy and relieved with his progress, especially as he was due to transition to school soon.

I love sharing and giving support to staff and parents about neuroscience and self-regulation. Seeing that light-bulb moment when they understand the reasons why children have tantrums and flip their lids is amazing, and knowing that the child will be better supported in the future makes my role worthwhile.

Enabling environments

Our learning environment can have a big impact on how children develop self-regulation. For example, we need to consider room layout because large open spaces will naturally encourage children to run, whereas smaller spaces clustered into zones or divided up with furniture will encourage more sustained attention. Can we organise our learning environment so that it encourages independence and autonomy by ensuring accessible resources – for example, through labelled or open containers, free-flow indoor and outdoor provision and outlines or silhouettes to show children where resources should be stored?

We need to provide different areas for children to access that are calm spaces or safe spaces – that is, places in our setting or school where children can go to calm down, hide, cuddle up or be alone and recharge so they are ready to learn and generally feel safe and secure. Cosy corners, dens, tents or teepees are great ideas for how to create these spaces, and they could be temporary or permanent features in the environment. In the case study, Sarah uses soft furnishings and lights to create a magical and inviting space where children can relax or escape the busy-ness of the day.

Calming areas – Sarah Brady, Childminder

Having moved from working in a school environment to working within my own home, I've really had to work hard to consider how to make the most of the available spaces whilst still wanting to create 'cosy corners' and dens for the children. I try to make my whole setting calming so it feels like a second home for the little ones. I often use a travel cot tipped onto

its side, which is very easy to set up and convert when needed. I've noticed that the children really appreciate having a comfortable space where they can explore and be calm but not 'feel seen', especially when they're still settling in and the environment is new to them. Sometimes the expanse of an unfamiliar room can seem overwhelming. I know my children well and try to set these spaces up with resources that I know will interest them and encourage them to explore inside. I like to add cushions, throws, lights and sensory sounds/music too. I've also had some children who have chosen to use these spaces when they've needed a little time to calm down or when they've felt the need for a nap.

We can include or provide specific resources in our environments that help the children to feel calm, and we need to ensure these resources are freely accessible during the day. Chapter 1 shares more ideas about calming strategies. One idea is to make worry dolls or worry monsters for children to share their worries with, which links with the theme that a problem shared is a problem halved. We need to talk about our worries to help them get smaller and disappear. We can also check in with each child on a daily basis, finding out how they are feeling and making time to talk to them one-to-one.

Worry monsters – Tracy Clark, Brentford Day Nursery & Pre-School

The worry monsters have arrived at Brentford Day Nursery to support with our children's emotional wellbeing and mental health.

We first introduced the worry monsters as we had some children who were worried about the change from nursery to school.

So, we sat the older children down in a group, and we talked about what their biggest worries were. Some said not liking the food or not knowing where to hang their coats.

We modelled how to use the worry monster, explaining how they can write or draw their worry, put it in the monster's mouth and zip it away.

The children were so excited about this – they couldn't wait to write down or draw their worries and zip them away!

Once we introduced the monsters, we looked at some books about worries and being anxious.

These really helped the children understand it's ok to have these worries, and we have created that safe space in the room for them to feel secure.

We want to ensure our environment meets the needs of our children in relation to their emotional development. We can reflect upon the following questions.

Does our environment:

- Offer access to sensory toys and fiddle or fidget toys to help children feel calmer?

- Contain areas for quiet and noisy play?

- Provide places to rest, sleep or calm down?

- Ensure equal access to activities and resources?

- Reflect different cultures and our local community?

- Enable children to see themselves and their families reflected within it?

- Provide resources and books that promote an understanding of emotions?

- Ignite children's interests and cater for individual children?

- Have clearly defined areas?

- Remain safe, yet challenging, clean and tidy with resources that are monitored, maintained and replenished?

In addition, we want to ensure our environment promotes emotional literacy and supports our children's emotional development. So, we can display photographs of children expressing different emotions and provide mirrors for children to access so they can see their facial expressions. We can then refer to these and use them as and when it becomes appropriate. Using a chart that encourages children to put their name or picture next to a specific emotion is not helpful – children will not always know how they feel, or their feelings will not fit neatly into a box. While using photographs is useful, limiting children to specific emotions or using a very closed activity board is not. Instead, we can talk to children about how they are feeling – perhaps using images or photographs of feelings, but not limiting it to one or two and keeping the activity open ended.

This reminds Tamsin of a story her colleague tells: She was visiting a setting with a self-registration system that involved children choosing where to post their names. There were several boxes – each labelled with words and pictures for the specific feelings happy, sad and angry. On this particular day, she witnessed two little girls spending a long time looking at the boxes and finding it hard to decide where to put their names. In the end they pushed the happy and sad boxes apart and put their names in between. They weren't feeling particularly happy or sad – they just felt normal and found the whole process of choosing how they were feeling rather frustrating.

Our calming basket and emotions display – Childminder

We have gathered some sensory materials and mirrors and put them in a basket for children to freely access. We displayed photos of emotions around the basket. Under the small table is a box of books, which contains some picture books about feeling calm, anxious or worried. Children are free to access these resources at any time.

Part of our role as educator is to plan our environment and ensure that it is supporting and not hindering children. For example, research into the use of bright colours suggests that colourful play surfaces can interfere with young children's play, even disrupting it at times because it can be "excessively stimulating" (Stern-Ellran et al., 2016). With this in mind, we may want to use bright colours sparingly and be aware that some children might struggle with over stimulation in an overly bright or colourful environment. In addition, when the walls of our settings are highly decorated with stimulating displays, research has found that kindergarten children find it harder to focus and maintain attention, and their learning may actually be disrupted (Fisher et al., 2014).

This idea fits within the thought that some children may be hyper- or hypo-sensitive to sensory stimulation. If a child is hyper-sensitive, they are extremely responsive and reactive to sensory input, whereas if a child is hypo-sensitive, they are not very sensitive or responsive to sensory input. Many neurodiverse children may also have sensory processing difficulties; however, educators need to be aware that several neurotypical children will also struggle in this area. *Neurodiverse* is the term given to a child who learns differently due to conditions such as autism, ADHD, dyslexia or dyspraxia. If a child is neurotypical, they learn in a typical way and do not have any intellectual or developmental differences. Our role as an adult could be to simplify the sensory environment, which could also be referred to as creating a low-arousal environment.

Low-arousal environments

We need to be aware that, for some children, our lovely learning environments will be too much. In order to remain fully inclusive in our approach – and specifically if we identify that we may have a child in this situation – we may want to create a space which could be described as low arousal. These are environments where all aspects have been considered and any stressors identified have been minimised – for example, light, noise, colour and clutter.

We can consider the following points when creating low-arousal environments:

■ How cluttered are our surfaces, displays, walls and ceilings?

■ Can we use bright colours sparingly, opting instead for more neutral colours?

■ What is the level of background noise? Can we reduce it by using soft furnishings or turning off any unnecessary music/radio?

■ Can we use rugs or carpets under spaces where chairs will scrape to help limit noise?

■ Can we increase the amount of natural light and decrease fluorescent lighting?

■ Is it possible to dim our lights?

■ Do we have blinds or nets which allow light but can block direct sunlight if needed?

■ Are there any strong smells in our setting – think perfume, cleaning chemicals or food? Can we minimise these?

■ Are children able to move about frequently during the day?

■ Can we minimise sedentary times?

■ Where can children go to calm down?

■ Do we have any soft spaces or cosy areas with cushions and covers?

■ Are resources such as sensory and fidget toys available to access at all times?

■ Do we have ear defenders available?

■ Do we have a selection of books and stories that teach children about feelings and emotions?

- Do children have access to mirrors and photographs of emotions?

- Is a visual timetable displayed? To what extent do we use it?

- Can we place some resources out of sight, in cupboards or in boxes with lids?

- To what extent do we allow enough personal space for children to sit next to each other without being crammed together?

- Can we use pictures, symbols and objects of reference to label the environment?

Arousal levels and the environment – Early Years Teacher Charlie Swan

I trained as an Early Years Teacher in the Reception class of a special needs school, where emotional regulation was a priority. In particular, we aimed to create a low arousal environment. I ensured the activities and classroom I planned for were not over-stimulating and supported an enabling environment (e.g., clear visual supports, key vocabulary used, visual and auditory 'clutter' reduced). Those children who displayed self-injurious behaviours and were highly dysregulated had a calmer space, which allowed them to process and access the co-regulatory supports on offer. However, this did not mean it was a 'no arousal' environment, particularly where some children had more moments of under-arousal. We worked collaboratively with the occupational therapists through sensory integration principles to construct an environment that was 'just right' for each unique child. We supported individual movement breaks and sensory circuits, which were designed around the sensory inputs we needed to regulate. We used activities which alerted, organised and calmed (e.g., trampette, balance beams, weighted blankets). These were useful for supporting the vestibular and proprioceptive regulation of children in a safe way. I feel this collaborative approach meant we could co-regulate with children through modelling and offering emotional and arousal modulation within the environment. This environmental co-regulation was vital while the self-regulation and metacognitive skills of our young learners were still developing. Essentially, constructing together a space and environment that helps an individual thrive.

When our proprioceptive, vestibular and interoceptive senses (mentioned in Chapter 6) are on overdrive, we can feel dysregulated – for example, if an area is too cluttered, it can make a child feel overstimulated, or if a child does not recognise they need the toilet, they may appear jittery and out of sorts. Mckaskie (2018:12) shares that "If an individual is finding it challenging to regulate their sensory input due to sensory processing difficulties, then they may require additional support and strategies to support self-regulation." If we notice that one of our children has difficulty with sensory processing, we may want to talk to a specialist in order to fully support them.

Zones of regulation

Many schools and settings have chosen to use the *Zones of Regulation* framework and strategies (Kuypers, 2011) to help children in their provision with self-regulation. The framework consists of four different coloured zones, each which relates to different states of emotional energy or alertness. They compare these zones to traffic signs reminding the child how to manage their feelings when they feel that way. For example, the red zone could be compared to a 'stop' sign, suggesting the child needs to stop and recover; the yellow zone is like a 'caution' or 'warning' sign, reminding the child that they need to be aware of their heightened emotions; the green zone would be a 'go' sign, expressing a calm feeling; and the blue zone is a 'rest' sign, reminding the child to take a break.

When using this approach, the children are reminded that all of these zones are natural ways to feel and experience; however, sometimes we may need support in knowing how to deal with those feelings. They are taught how to recognise when they are in each emotional state and given suggested ideas of how to act and react when they are in that particular zone. This reminds me of the ideas around using regulation scales with children, as explored in Chapter 1 – children are invited to compare their feelings with a sliding scale of emotions in the hope they can follow the advice of the scale and learn how to regain feelings of calm independently.

Zones of regulation – Early Years Teacher Charlie Swan

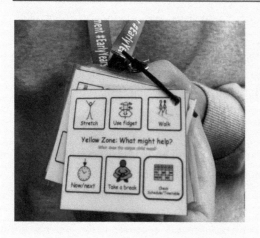

I completed my Early Years teacher training at a special needs school and have supported children in the Reception class through our SCERTS framework [Social Communication, Emotional Regulation and Transactional Supports]. This framework is all about having the most effective sensory, visual, interpersonal and learning supports in place to build

spontaneous and functional communication and maintain a well-regulated emotional state. Through this we have drawn upon another approach called the 'Zones of Regulation' to support emotional regulation through colours. In practice, I created emotion lanyards to acknowledge and validate children's feelings on the go! They correlated to the Zones of Regulation colours (Blue, Green, Yellow, Red) and on the back had suggested ideas of ways to overcome dysregulation (e.g., if angry to take some deep breaths or space, if worried to check our schedule or have a hug and other ideas such as movement breaks, having a drink and creating low-arousal environments).

During my mainstream pre-school placement these lanyards also worked effectively, almost like emotional Sustained Shared Thinking where the children and I reflectively worked together to validate a feeling and together found a safe route to equilibrium. I was proud of one child who eventually learnt to find the emotion card 'Angry' and state "I need space" as an alternative to pushing peers.

Adopting a restorative approach

Restorative practice within education stems from the concept of restorative justice, which considers wrongdoing and criminal activity as something that impacts on others within a community and empowers the victims of crime by attempting to restore relationships rather than simply punishing or focusing on rule/law breaking. The focus is on conflict resolution and healing relationships and communities. In education, the term *restorative practice* tends to be used rather than justice, although the ideas are similar. The approach is growing steadily, with more schools and settings choosing to work in this way.

According to Hopkins (2003:44), the following ideas are at the heart of this approach:

■ Mutual respect and appreciation.

■ A belief in people's ability to resolve their own problems given time, support and a chance to tell their story.

■ Acceptance of diversity.

■ An inclusive approach to problem-solving, so that the feelings, needs and views of everyone in a given community are taken into account.

■ Congruence between beliefs and actions – 'walking the talk'.

This approach empowers children to take responsibility for their actions and also to learn how to resolve problems for themselves. It works best when the whole setting or school adopts this approach at policy level so that everyone works in the same way with the children. It relies on the adults having empathy and compassion, remaining non-judgemental whilst dealing with any challenges they face and ensuring we end each day at peace with each other.

There is an acronym consisting of 5 R's (Title, 2021) which is helpful when summing up this concept:

■ Relationship – this focuses on restoring relationships that may have broken down or become damaged. Building strong relationships and being trauma and attachment aware provides a good foundation for this.

■ Respect – everyone should be trusted and their opinions should be valued and actively listened to. The respect should be mutual, and all parties should show respect for each other as well as for themselves.

■ Responsibility – taking responsibility for our own actions is vital, and all parties should do this.

■ Repair – this is the next step in healing the relationship. Talking about repairing a relationship is very different from talking about punishment or taking revenge. It involves positive action, which will ultimately resolve the situation and demonstrate that we will not repeat the behaviour.

■ Reintegration – this is when a child is accepted back into their friendship group, setting or community with no strings attached, although the process of accepting responsibility and repairing the relationship has enabled this to happen. This is counter to a more punitive approach, which could end in exclusion or a child being suspended from a setting due to their misbehaviour.

Research shows there are many benefits to restorative practice, and it can even enhance children's academic achievement and provide an emotionally and physically safe environment (Short et al., 2018). Restorative approaches are ideal for settings and schools in supporting children of all ages and can also inform our adult relationships with our families and social circles. The methods dovetail with the use of emotion coaching, problem-solving and the principles of nurture mentioned in Chapter 4.

Relationships using restorative approaches – Headteacher Rachel Tomlinson, Barrowford Primary School

At Barrowford, we recognise that most children self-regulate their behaviour and behave very well every day and never need reminding about how to do so appropriately. We want to encourage these children and thereby encourage the children who may not behave appropriately sometimes to manage their behaviour positively. Our relationship policy is not primarily concerned with rule enforcement. It is a tool used to promote good relationships, so that people can work together with the common purpose of helping everyone learn.

Our school uses restorative approaches to enable everyone to take responsibility for their behaviours. All staff have attended training and apply this approach when resolving situations in the school. This approach starts with a restorative enquiry if conflict arrives over low-level issues, i.e., friendship breakups, disputes over games, running in the corridor and not responding to reasonable adult requests.

At Barrowford School, we have the following underpinning principles:

- Positive relationships are imperative to our practice between all members of our school community.
- Children and adults have a sense of belonging, feeling safe, secure and valued.
- People learn to cope with all aspects of their lives with support from others.
- The importance of fostering social relationships in a school community of mutual engagement.
- Responsibility and accountability for one's own actions and their impact on others.
- Respect for other people, their views and feelings and circumstances.
- Empathy with the feelings of others affected by one's own actions.
- Fairness.
- Commitment to an equitable process.
- Active involvement of everyone in school with decisions about their own lives.
- A willingness to create opportunities for reflective change in pupils and staff.

Our aims in relation to behaviour include:

- Students will be encouraged to develop positive behaviour for learning in recognition of its importance as a life-long skill.

- To provide a safe, happy and friendly environment which encourages each individual to achieve their own potential through a desire for excellence, using challenging, active and creative personalised learning.
- To enable staff to support children with their behaviour through providing students with strategies to manage their own behaviour.
- To maintain a calm and purposeful working atmosphere.
- To ensure that all children and adults have a sense of belonging, feeling safe, secure and valued.
- To provide a clear, fair and consistent approach to behaviour.
- To foster, nurture and value strong and healthy relationships.
- To ensure that our children are intrinsically motivated to do the right thing because it is the right thing to do.

We work closely with parents/carers, with regular informal meetings taking place to discuss progress, share any concerns and to plan next steps. We offer nurture provision and additional support, if needed, including play sessions, play therapy, Lego therapy and counselling and sensory-room time.

A restorative approach invites children to talk about the situation after everyone has calmed down. Within the early years, this is slightly harder as, depending on the age and stage of development of the children involved, we may need to simplify the questions or seek answers using a mosaic approach. Some of the following questions may be beyond our children's capabilities developmentally but could provide a starting point for a discussion or conference with a child:

- What happened?

- How were we feeling?

- What were we needing?

- What were we thinking?

- Who did the situation affect?

- How might they be feeling?

- What have we learned?

- What could we do differently next time?

- How can we repair the relationship?

Adopting this approach enables the adult to co-regulate children's emotions and focus on the child in terms of their needs and feelings when dealing with behaviour or emotional outbursts.

Summary

When we consider the role of the adult in supporting children's self-regulation, we firstly need to focus on relationship building. Once we have developed loving attachments with our children, we will be better placed to act as a co-regulator and coach them, in the moment, through their big feelings and emotions. We must remain calm and regulated ourselves in order to de-escalate any problems. Another part of our role is to develop enabling environments where we support children's emotional development, being aware that some children may find our environments too stimulating. The adult can also directly teach children how to recognise the things that stress them and teach strategies of how to respond when they feel that way.

The next chapter will explore how we can share our approach and ethos with parents and carers and support their role as co-regulators for their children.

Questions for reflection

1. To what extent have we prioritised relationships and building secure attachments with our children?

2. Does our environment welcome questions and risk-taking, accept mistakes and allow children and adults to change their minds or have different ideas, thoughts and beliefs?

3. Do we have any calm areas and how are they used?

References

Ainsworth, M., Blehar, M., Waters, E., & Wall, S. (1978) *Patterns of attachment: A psychological study of the strange situation.* Hillsdale, NJ: Lawrence Erlbaum.

Bergin, C. & Bergin, D. (2009) 'Attachment in the Classroom', *Educational Psychology Review, 21*, pp. 141–170.

Fisher, A., Godwin, K., & Seltman, H. (2014) 'Visual Environment, Attention Allocation, and Learning in Young Children: When Too Much of a Good Thing May Be Bad', *Psychological Science, 25*(7), pp 1362–1370.

Gaddis, J. (2020) 'The 4 S's of Attachment-Based Parenting – Dan Siegel – 276', *YouTube.* Available at https://www.youtube.com/watch?v=7zV2nLEeh0c.

Gray, C. (2015) *The New Social Story Book.* Arlington, TX: Future Horizons Firm.

Grimmer, T. (2021) *Developing a Loving Pedagogy in the Early Years: How Love Fits with Professional Practice.* London: Routledge.

Hopkins, B. (2003) *Just schools: A whole school approach to restorative justice.* London: Jessica Kingsley.

Kuypers, L. (2011) *The Zones of Regulation.* Santa Clara, CA: Think Social Publishing Inc. Available at https://www.zonesofregulation.com/index.html.

Mainstone-Cotton, S. (2021) *Supporting Children with Social, Emotional and Mental Health Needs in the Early Years: Practical Solutions and Strategies for Every Setting.* London: Routledge.

Mckaskie, A. (2018) *Sensory Pre-Referral Graded Approach.* Manchester: Trafford Children's Therapy Service. Available at https://mft.nhs.uk/app/uploads/2019/09/sensory-processing-pre-referral-advice-oct18.pdf.

Short, R., Case, G., & McKenzie, K. (2018) 'The long-term impact of a whole school approach of restorative practice: The views of secondary school teachers', *Pastoral Care in Education, 36*(4), pp. 313–324.

Siegel, D. (2012) *The Developing Mind: How relationships and the brain interact to shape who we are.* New York: Guilford Press.

Siegel, D. & Bryson, T. (2020) *The Power of Showing Up: How Parental Presence Shapes Who Our Kids Become and How Their Brains Get Wired.* London: Scribe Publications.

Stern-Ellran, K., Zilcha-Mano, S., Sebba, R., & Levit Binnun, N. (2016) 'Disruptive Effects of Colorful vs. Non-colorful Play Area on Structured Play: A Pilot Study with Preschoolers', *Frontiers in Psychology*, 7, pp. 1–9. doi: 10.3389/fpsyg.2016.01661.

Title, B. (2021) 'Restorative Practices in Schools: The 5 Rs', *ReSolutionaries Inc.* Available at https://www.resolutionariesinc.com.

9 Enabling parents to support their children

Tamsin Grimmer

Introduction

Working with parents is an important part of our role as educators. Children are not born with a manual, and many families find they are learning how to respond to their children at each developmental stage as they grow together. This has certainly been true for Tamsin. Despite being a teacher, having a family of her own was a baptism of fire in terms of her lived experiences, particularly around supporting her own and her children's self-regulation – or sometimes lack of it.

As discussed in this book, self-regulation is a complex notion and certainly not a term many parents would use in relation to their children – although, as parents become more aware of trauma and attachment-based parenting approaches, like therapeutic parenting, they may be exploring this area. We feel enabling parents to support their children in developing self-regulation, is actually about enabling parents to approach their parenting and discipline in an alternative way, changing the way they view their role as parent, how they view their child and their behaviour and, ultimately, changing the way they impact society! This chapter offers our thoughts around an approach to parenting which, we feel, will fully support children in developing self-regulation. We share the important influence that parents have and also consider some practical ways of supporting them to understand behaviour as communication and reinterpret things like schematic play. As mentioned in the Introduction, we are using the term *parents* to include all main carers, not just birth parents.

The importance of the home learning environment and influence of parents

There is a wealth of evidence that demonstrates the important influence that parents and the home learning environment have on children in their early years, with some research indicating that parents are the single most important factor that

DOI: 10.4324/9781003162346-10

has a positive impact on children's future achievement (Field, 2010; Desforges & Aboucher, 2003). The Field report states, "Parental involvement has a significant effect on children's achievement and adjustment even after all other factors (such as social class, maternal education and poverty) have been take[n] out of the equation" (Field, 2010:86).

Research has shown that it tends to be parental involvement in the little things that can make an enormous difference to children – for example, reading a bedtime story regularly to their child will have a big impact on their future literacy skills (Hunt et al., 2011). We can encourage parents to get involved with their children's learning and make suggestions that are free, do not take up too much time and will have a large impact on their child – such as, cuddle up for a story before bedtime, count steps when out walking together or collect some different coloured leaves or pebbles while at the park. We need to share our approach and help parents to see themselves as significant and important in relation to their children's learning and development.

Self-regulation from a parent's perspective – Holyrood Nursery Salford Royal, Thrive Childcare and Education

The nursery's approach is that they value all children's abilities and stages and support all developmental changes. They are willing to adjust routines to fit in with each child. Ethan is at a stage where he is really trying to understand his emotions and can sometimes find this difficult to express. The nursery are supporting Ethan by giving him space. He has his own little teepee in the nursery that he can go to whenever he feels he needs to be on his own, which really helps support his needs.

The nursery's approach to supporting children's developing self-regulation skills is very helpful. I have sat with Ethan's key worker and am reassured that they will support my child wherever needed. Ethan is learning to manage his emotions, but as a two year old this can be very difficult, and I'm happy the nursery can be there for him when I'm not.

The approach of supporting children's self-regulation is helpful for me too. I was aware of self-regulation, but it certainly made me more aware of how my reactions can impact on my child, and the nursery has given support to both myself and my child. I'm thankful that Ethan has such an amazing key worker in Jane. He absolutely adores her and speaks about her when he isn't at nursery. As a parent, all you want is your child to be supported and happy. As a first-time parent, it's reassuring to know I can also speak to the nursery staff for any advice, and I trust the staff at the nursery.

Early childhood educators will want to work in partnership with parents with regard to supporting their child to develop self-regulation at home. However, many parents get stuck in a rut around discipline, rewards and punishment and miss the important message that their own responses to their children will have the biggest impact.

We all know that children learn through imitation, and parents around the world are often bringing up miniature versions of themselves. In order to raise children who are excellent at regulating their behaviour, their role models – that is, their parents – also need to practise what they preach! As parents, when we respond to our children, are we being proactive in supporting them to understand why certain behaviours may be unacceptable or are we being reactive in our discipline?

At this point, it might be helpful to unpick the term *discipline*, which in modern-day English is linked with the practice of training people to obey a set of rules and can be associated with punishment, which is unhelpful and far removed from its original meaning. We understand that *discipline* actually means instruction and training, and it is derived from a root word meaning 'to learn'. If our aim as parents is to help children learn, this needs to involve role-modelling and motivation, not punishment or rewards.

All behaviour is communication

We need to impress on parents that all behaviour is communication and share the important impact they have on their children. For example, the Parent-Infant Foundation (2021) highlights the importance of the first 1001 days of a child's life and explains to parents that they make an enormous difference. One way to do this is to share information and simple ideas about how to better communicate with children from birth.

Sharing a few Top Tips with parents can also help remind them what is important when it comes to communication:

- All children are unique and will learn language at different rates.

- Avoid comparing children's language and communication development with each other.

- Tune in to the child's signals and cues to engage in meaningful talk.

- Use pictures, objects, gestures, signs, rhymes, songs and play to encourage communication.

- Value all attempts at communication and remember to listen too!

Partnerships with parents – Jennie Holloway, Noah's Ark Nursery

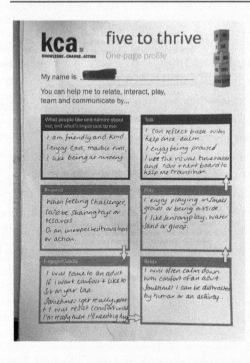

We are a small setting so are able to have really good partnerships with parents. It all starts when the parent makes their first enquiry. We enable them to look around at a time that is suitable for all the family members that need to visit. This has meant the visits can be personal, relaxed and allow plenty of time for the child to explore and parents to ask questions.

Settling in for children has been really tough since COVID-19, but we have found having the family visit first has really helped relax the parents and to some extent the child too. However, flexibility has been vital as all children are different and some need to attend for one hour at a time whilst others feel able to stay all day. The Keyperson manages this for each individual child, and this really helps develop the partnership and the child's self-regulation as we are working at a pace they can manage and achieve.

Communication with parents is daily. Every family receives short feedback about the child's day, and this continues to build the partnership. Families are aware how they can contact key people or the manager, and it is often two-way communication. We work hard to identify any needs and have signposted or referred many families to support agencies when required.

We continuously support self-regulation at Noah's Ark Nursery using Five to Thrive (Knowledge Change Action, 2021). This framework uses a strengths-based approach to support children. We are always at the children's level. We listen and we support. Showing the children this level of interest allows them to reach high levels of engagement, and we see great learning and development.

We have encouraged a variety of activities during school holidays to help the families continue to support their children's wellbeing and self-regulation at home – for example, through suggesting simple play activities, how to promote independent self-help skills and some ideas of local places to visit. We have used private social-media platforms to connect with our families and invited them to share the activities they have tried, demonstrating that we value their comments. We have had lots of engagement and built a really warm, caring and supportive environment for the families to share, comment and meet each other.

We must also demonstrate to parents that we value their input ourselves and we see their role as vitally important in helping children to develop self-regulation. We can share the idea that the behaviour we see is only the tip of the iceberg, explaining that children are communicating their needs and wants through the way they behave. The seen behaviours do not explain why the child is acting in this way – we need to unpick this further and really seek to understand.

However, as Montessori observed, "It is easy to judge every puzzling reaction, every difficult phase as naughtiness" (1936:78), and we may find, as educators, we are introducing the concept of being a behaviour detective to parents and suggesting that we view behaviour as, "A problem that must be solved, an enigma that must be deciphered" (Montessori, 1936: 78). This is more challenging for the adult, as they become more of a student with the child than a judge, which can be contrary to the way we, as parents, want to be. We must be open to learn and observe and have a yearning to decipher and understand our children.

Schematic play

This is certainly true when we consider schematic play, because during this play children regularly behave in interesting and unusual ways that are sometimes confusing or even frustrating, such as lining up the toy animals, climbing inside boxes or repeatedly playing with the taps. As early childhood educators, we recognise these play patterns as children learning through schematic play. This is when children are investigating and exploring the world through first-hand experiences and engagement in repetitive play. Tamsin's book, *Observing and Developing Schematic Behaviour in Young Children* (Grimmer, 2017), considers 12 different types of schematic play that we see in practice and interprets the behaviours, offering ideas of how to further extend each type. It also considers how schematic play can be occasionally mis-interpreted as poor behaviour.

We may notice children repeatedly throwing toys or resources, kicking or hitting others, jumping on and off furniture, pulling all the tissues out of a tissue box or emptying all the contents of containers on the floor for no apparent reason. Children may have an urge to play with doors or windows, dismantle toys, knock towers over or post resources down the back of the radiator! These sorts of behaviours can upset others, appear destructive or make us feel the children are lacking in self-regulation. However, many of these behaviours are schematic, and we need to reinterpret what they are doing using schematic play as a lens and then respond differently. As Nutbrown explains, "Many professional educators use what they know of schemas to divert children from disruptive activities and to focus them on more worthwhile endeavours" (Nutbrown, 2011:22).

The families of our children might not know anything about schematic behaviour, and we may find we are regularly asked by parents why their child is doing these things. Therefore, it is important to share our understanding with them, as many parents can be concerned that their child's new game of throwing everything, for example, is disobedience or defiance. Part of our role is reassuring them that schematic play is a common occurrence in early childhood and nothing to be concerned about. We can then offer them practical ideas of how they can support their children's development at home in ways that link into the schema they are interested in.

Here are some ideas of how to support parents to better understand schematic behaviour:

- Help them to recognise and identify schemas and play patterns.

- Talk about behaviours that could be described as schematic.

- Reassure them that schematic behaviour is a common way many children learn and develop.

- Explain that children repeatedly behaving in unusual, odd or frustrating ways is how they are learning about the world around them.

- Display photos of children engaging in schematic play – for example, display pictures of children spinning wheels, playing with balls, drawing circles, etc., to illustrate a schematic interest in rotation.

- Share how repeating actions help children's brains to develop.

- Provide ideas of how to extend children's play, including simple games or activities that they can play together at home.

- Plan a workshop to share ideas about schematic behaviour.

- Set up your room with lots of schematic activities and add posters stating what children are learning through this repetitive play.

- Create a series of little information leaflets, each focusing on one type of schematic play at a time.

Building relationships with parents

Offering parents ideas of how to support their children at home relies on our having built a successful and authentic relationship with them in the first place. Parents need to know that we love looking after their children and want the very best for them. This links with Tamsin's ideas around developing a loving pedagogy (Grimmer, 2021) as she talks about holding the carers in mind. Seeing our children from their parents' perspective can help us to understand what parents are going through and offer us insight so we can respond sensitively and empathetically.

Here are some general ideas for effective communication with parents:

- One size will not fit all, so we need to think about the 'Unique Family' just as we would the 'Unique Child'.

- Make policies available and easily accessible in different formats, considering how easy they are to read and understand. Using simple, plain language like "When a child … " or "Adults will … " can help.

- Use a variety of methods to engage and communicate with families, e.g., face-to-face, communication books, phone, email, texts, website, leaflets, notice board, etc.

- Ask parents about their preferred means of communication. If any of our families need information to be provided in different formats or languages, communicate with parents this way from the outset.

- Have an information board for parents that is updated daily and is as visible as possible. Avoid overloading it with information; instead, keep information simple and clear.

- Remain sensitive in the way we communicate. Parents are the child's first educator, and we must avoid any blame or judgement.

- Include home visits as part of our settling-in procedure.

- Find out as much as we can about our children and families – ask about interests, likes, dislikes and the way their child responds emotionally.

- Offer opportunities to have regular meetings with the child's key person.

- Ensure that discussions between parents and educators are confidential and private.

- Share positive stories and feedback about their child every day.

- View families as a resource – for example, involve parents by using their talents, experience and backgrounds to enhance our provision and their children's learning.

- Offer parents the contact details of support groups to indicate our appreciation of the difficulties parents experience at times.

- Invite parents to attend workshops which summarise new ideas we have gained from training and offer ideas of what to do at home.

- Share with parents how they can become co-regulators of their children's emotional states.

- Respect parents and how they choose to respond to their child, while sharing how we respond in the setting to try to aid consistency between home and setting.

- Ensure that up-to-date information and reading materials about child development are available for both parents and educators.

Partnership with parents – Chloe Webster, Pebbles Childcare

In order to adequately support children in managing and regulating their emotions and understanding their behaviours, it is imperative that we have the support of the child's parents and family so that the child feels and experiences a consistent approach between home and the setting.

We recently experienced a child suddenly using aggressive behaviour towards their peers and caregivers within the setting, and Mum also shared that this was happening at home as well as more frequent emotional and unexplained outbursts, where the child would lay on the floor and scream. We have an open line of communication between ourselves and parents in the setting and do our best to ensure we are up to date with the children's lives and experiences away from the setting. Therefore, we discovered after lengthy chats with Mum that the child had begun their settling-in sessions at a new setting in preparation for the new term. They were finding the transitional period between the two settings both challenging to understand and cope with, and they were feeling more tired (having recently dropped a nap prior to increasing their days in childcare).

Together we decided that this was a natural reaction to the level of change the child was experiencing and, despite being an incredibly articulate child, they were struggling to process and digest this change. So, we were able to focus more on preparing the child for his next setting during his sessions with us in the week and talking positively about his key people, resources and peers at the additional setting so it felt less intimidating and he was more prepared each week for the change of routine and the additional day at a different setting. Mum was on board and supported us with this and replicated these conversations and discussions at home, and we quickly saw the child's mood and behaviour change positively once he had been supported in grasping a better understanding and felt that his emotions were understood and supported in a way that was relevant to him.

Partnership or engagement with parents

It has been argued that working in partnership with parents is not enough, and settings and schools should be looking towards parental engagement instead. This idea "moves from parental involvement with school to parental engagement with children's learning. This movement represents a shift in emphasis, away from the relationship between parents and schools, to a focus on the relationship between parents and their children's learning" (Goodall & Montgomery, 2014:399). We need to be engaging parents with their children's learning instead of simply building effective relationships.

This is an interesting take and one which fits well when thinking about how to enable parents to support their children's self-regulation. It takes more than a good relationship with parents to help them do this. We must have built their trust, but also we need them to have an interest in developing their children's learning themselves. This requires both parents and educators to see themselves as working towards the same aim – supporting their children's learning. Goodall and Montgomery (2014) make the important point that engagement with learning is not the same thing as engagement with the setting or school. In fact, a parent can fully engage with their child's learning without being very involved in the day-to-day practices of the provider at all. However, they see engagement as more of a continuum, with parents being involved with the setting or school at one end and engaged with the learning process at the other. The process of engaging parents with learning may be gradual, but it will have a bigger impact on outcomes for their children longer term.

Offering parents practical ideas of how they can support their children at home is a good place to start. Many settings create parent leaflets or newsletters that include information, and some providers plan information evenings or workshops where parents can attend to find out about things they can do at home. However, when parents are invited to learn alongside educators, powerful learning takes place. Parents and educators get a lot out of attending together – it helps to encourage a consistent approach between home and setting and enables all parties to hear the same message at once.

Self-regulation space – Happitots Boddam Nursery, Thrive Childcare and Education

We have a child who, after transitioning to the preschool room, began to show signs of frustration and appeared to struggle with his emotions and expressing how he felt. He would shout in a very angry tone, his facial expressions showed anger and he would throw toys or equipment and kick. This would not be directed purposely at his peers. After gathering information from observations and tracking on an ABC chart, there appeared to be no specific triggers.

We were trying to improve how he coped with his feelings in order for him to be able to communicate and regulate his emotions. So, we developed a self-regulation area to include emotion books, sensory toys and soft furnishings in a quiet part of the room. Staff were using calming tones when supporting this child. One member of staff would go into the area with him and encourage and show him how to use the 'breathing star', a technique we use to help calm children down. We held a meeting with mum, and she said she was struggling at home with him and any ideas we had would be beneficial. We gave her a parent leaflet about self-regulation and demonstrated how to use a 'breathing star' so that she could try this at home. During a review with mum she said that the family were all using the information and guidance given, and she felt it was working.

The self-regulation area has been a real support for this little boy. He still requires guidance from staff when he needs to access the area but now recognises when he feels calmer and is able to rejoin his peers. His periods of frustration appear to be decreasing.

We have learnt through practice the benefits of using our self-regulation area and how this can support children dealing with their emotions. We are also more aware of our tone of voice and facial expressions.

PACE (Playfulness, Acceptance, Curiosity, and Empathy)

PACE stands for *Playfulness, Acceptance, Curiosity*, and *Empathy* (Golding & Hughes, 2012) and is a parenting strategy which reminds us how to interact with children in a way that helps them to feel safe and secure and build positive attachments. It was designed with children who may have experienced trauma in mind; however, the authors are clear that PACE, combined with love, is an invaluable tool to support all children's development. Chapter 3 explored how developing a loving pedagogy (Grimmer, 2021) can support children to develop self-regulation, and Golding and Hughes call love the "essential ingredient that makes PACE work" (2012:20). In fact, we recently found out that in early writing PACE was called PLACE, with the *L* standing for 'love', because love is so essential; however, the authors settled on PACE as the acronym because, as Golding told Tamsin on Twitter, "PACE is a way of being, delivered with love", so love surrounds the whole concept.

Although PACE was created for parents, educators can also learn a lot from this approach whilst sharing it with parents as a great strategy to use at home. Early childhood educators and parents alike would agree that play and playfulness are important parts of children's lives, and Article 31 of the United Nations Convention on the Rights of the Child (UNICEF, 1989) mentions the right of the child to engage in play and recreational activities. Using playfulness with children allows us to connect with them on an emotional level, build close bonds, inject joy into these relationships and generally respond with humour and fun. Tamsin sometimes uses playful parenting at home to try to address issues in a non-threatening way – for example, in the summer one of her children was hesitant to get into the paddling pool, and Tamsin offered to get in with her but suggested she might turn into a big iceberg if it's cold. Then she joked that there was already an iceberg (lettuce) in the fridge. Adding humour in this way helped to resolve the issue.

The *A* of PACE stands for acceptance, and it refers to our acceptance of children's feelings and emotions as well as childen's wishes and views about a situation. This begins with the premise that children are entitled to their own thoughts and feelings, and we love and accept them regardless of their behaviour. This reminds us of unconditional love, which says to a child, "We love, value and accept you for who you are, and how you act and react will not change that." This is linked with the first and most important step in emotion coaching when we acknowledge, label and validate feelings, which was mentioned in Chapter 4.

Curiosity within the PACE approach relates to a parent being curious about their child, wanting to discover their uniqueness and grow together. As educators, we are also curious about our children, wanting to get to know them well and using our knowledge of their interests and fascinations to plan effective environments and understand how to interact sensitively with them. Having curiosity about our children can enable us to become the behaviour detective mentioned in Chapter 1 and be less judgemental about why a child acts the way they do. It helps us to seek to understand, look for the unseen needs under the surface and listen to what the child is communicating to us.

The last element of PACE is empathy, which is discussed in more detail in Chapter 7. Baron-Cohen (2011:11) describes empathy as "our ability to identify what someone else is thinking or feeling, and to respond to their thoughts and feelings with an appropriate emotion." Therefore, empathy is what helps to connect us with our children. Sometimes empathy is confused with sympathy, which is when we feel sorry for someone or are moved by their situation, whereas true empathy is about sharing the emotion they feel and responding sensitively.

Using PACE within our settings and schools and encouraging parents to use PACE at home can help us support children in regulating their behaviour and responding with more consistency between home and setting. It builds on our connection and relationships with children so we are better equipped to co-regulate and offer understanding. PACE is an example of a nurturing approach that we can adopt and fits really well with developing a loving pedagogy.

Here are some suggestions of ideas that may help parents to understand their children's behaviour developmentally:

- Introduce the iceberg model so they can see children's behaviour as communication.

- Encourage them to be behaviour detectives and seek to understand why their children behave a certain way.

■ Introduce how to respond with PACE and adopt an emotion-coaching approach.

■ Demonstrate how they can be a role model for their children and practise acceptance of all emotions.

■ Encourage parents to respond mindfully rather than react emotionally.

Boundary setting

Most parents are aware that setting boundaries and having rules in place helps their child to understand the expectations placed upon them. However, sometimes parents confuse this with trying to control their child through rules and regulations. Although parents have a certain amount of influence over their child, they do not have full control over what their child does, says, thinks and feels. Adults control many aspects of a very young child's life – for example, when and where they go, what they wear and who they meet. As children get older, they themselves begin to gain more control over many of these elements. As parents, we accept children's short-term dependency in the hope that our children grow to be independent in the future; however, sometimes we don't like to give up this control.

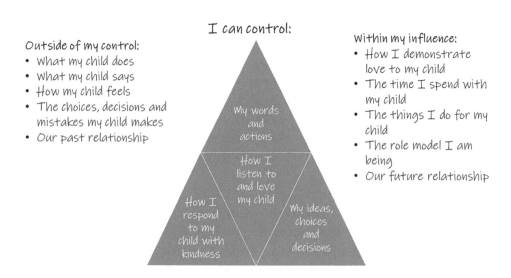

Parents will need to understand that they cannot control what their child does and says, nor can they control how the child feels or the individual choices the child will make every moment of the day. Seeking to control these elements will only lead to stress and frustration. Instead, parents need to focus on the elements that they do have control over, which are their own responses, thoughts, actions and feelings. For example, if a parent tries to put a rule in place that their child cannot do a certain thing, they may set themselves and their child up to fail because they cannot control whether their child does this thing. However, if they put a boundary in place that relates to what the parent will do, it clearly sets limits on the behaviour, but it is within the parent's control. For example, saying "If you throw food, we will put the snack away" will work better than saying "Do not throw food" because we cannot always stop a child from throwing the food.

We are not suggesting that we throw away the rule book, but we may need to rephrase our rules and focus on things within our influence and control. Keeping our rules positive can also help to remind children what they should be doing rather than what they should not be doing. So, reminding a child to have "kind hands" is better than saying "Don't hit others!" These ideas fit within an emotion-coaching response too, as described in Chapter 4. We need to empathise with our children, acknowledge the underlying emotions involved and then set limits, if needed, on their behaviour.

Loving kindness

Sometimes being totally loving is not the easiest way to act. Parents sometimes need to respond with 'tough love' – or, as Tamsin refers to it, 'loving kindness', which is when the loving response offers warmth but also clear boundaries (Grimmer, 2021). Parents can remain assertive without being aggressive in their parenting style, offering high levels of both empathy and guidance. Lexmond and Reeves (2009) found that children whose families adopted this approach had higher levels of self-regulation and were more socially responsible.

In addition to this, parents also need to ensure that their children's emotional cups are filled up with love so that their children 'feel' loved which, in turn, helps them to feel safe and secure. This links with Chapman and Campbell's (2012) work around love languages – the idea that we have different ways that we like to give and receive love. As part of their research, Chapman and Campbell asked young people how they knew they were loved by their parents. They often heard responses such as, "Well, my mum tells me she loves me, but she never spends any time with me" or "My dad plays with me but he has never hugged me." They organised loving into five languages: Words of Affirmation, Quality Time, Physical Touch, Receiving Gifts, and Acts of Service. They suggest that if parents identify their children's love languages and the ways they prefer to feel loved, then they can speak the same language as their child and reassure them that they are loved. "By speaking your child's own love language, you can fill their 'emotional tank' with love" (Chapman & Campbell, 2012:17).

Sharing information with parents – Alena Szczuczko

During lockdown in 2020, as part of mental health week, Alena wanted to share some information with parents about how they could enable their children to manage their feelings and emotions, which she sees as crucial for their mental health. She sent them the following information:

> In "any normal day" children can feel overwhelmed with their feelings and emotions, which can cause them to feel sad, confused, anxious, angry or even tired. Depending on their age their response may vary. Some may become overly attached or even withdrawn, whilst others may become hyperactive, may feel bored, scared or teary.

Here are my five tips to help manage feelings and emotions in children:

1. **Breathing exercises** – Ask your child to focus on their breathing and take five long and deep breaths. They can inhale, wait five seconds and exhale. Or, ask your child to blow out a candle, reminding them not to touch the candle. Perhaps you can also play relaxing/mindful music. The increased oxygen helps their brain to calm and relax. ☺
2. **SPOT, STOP, SWAP** (Shetty, 2020) – Help your child to recognise how to **spot** when they feel a negative thought or feeling. This will help them to accept the feeling and give them an opportunity to decide what to do next. Stopping the activity or moving to a different environment or place will help them to **stop** that negative thought or feeling that bothers them. Next, they can **swap** the feeling for a positive thought – for example, if a child gets very upset because they miss their friend from school, whenever they feel this way they can talk about it. This will change the environment, and after the conversation they can record a short video for their friend to say hello, or they can write a letter or draw a picture for their friend. ☺
3. **Listen and talk** – Listen to their concerns and show them your support. Talk to them and explain what's happening and reassure them that it is OK not to feel OK sometimes. ☺
4. **Love and understanding** – Show them how much you love them and care for them as you always do! ☺ Ensure they know you understand their feelings and spend quality time with your child by playing their favourite game or organising a treasure hunt at home or in the garden.
5. **Coping strategies** – Children can distract themselves by talking, creating art, colouring, mindfulness exercises, writing about their feelings or expressing their feeling through dance, sport or drama. This is also called

self-expression. Remind them to think positively and plan something to look forward to when lockdown ends! ☺

Top tip of what not to do:

Avoid negativity in the house, such as complaining, comparing and criticising, because these are contagious and can create more negative thoughts. Instead, share love and positivity – for example, at dinner every member of the family can share what they liked about that day and what made them smile – and ensure you praise each other at least once a day.

Sharing our policy and approach with parents

When working with parents we need to ensure that our policy is transparent and informative in sharing our approach. The summary and conclusion of this book suggests we should reconsider how we frame our policy and, instead of looking at behaviour management, focus on adopting an ethos around self-regulation that will underpin our whole approach. This is helpful when working with parents because it clearly outlines how we will support our children in day-to-day practice. We can also share specific ideas about how we respond to children in our setting and suggest parents try some of the ideas at home.

Sharing the 'Keep Your Cool Toolbox' with parents – Marlis Juerging-Coles, St John's Pre-School

We recommend parents use the 'Keep Your Cool Toolbox' (Conkbayir, 2020). Listed below is how we use some of the toolbox ideas in preschool:

Name it to tame it

- When a child displays behaviours which suggest that they are dysregulated (such as aggression, shouting, or destructive behaviours), we help the child by remaining calm, staying with them, helping them return to a calmer place and naming the emotions we detect to help the child label what is going on.
- Once the child is calmer, we offer them play materials which help them remain calm and, where appropriate, talk with the child about their triggers whilst supporting them in finding things that may help them calm themselves in a similar situation.

Mindful moments

■ We practice yoga at Pre-School, supporting children to become aware of their own bodies, their breathing and paying attention to how their environment feels.

■ In moments of distress, we encourage children to practice their calm breathing to slow their heartbeat and allow them to return to a physically calmer space.

■ To support mindful moments in acute situations, we may offer children calming music, nature sounds or support them in using deep breathing, which are all techniques from the toolbox.

Get active

■ We start our day in the garden to allow children to use gross motor skills and engage in very energetic play. This, in turn, allows children's minds to calm and become more focussed in play and learning.

■ If we are unable to access the garden or allow highly energetic play due to safety restrictions, we will use music and movement to allow children to experience this energetic outlet.

Questions, questions

■ We strongly believe that children should be encouraged to ask questions to learn and to experience an honest response from adults. This should encourage them to feel valued and also to be honest themselves.

■ We pay attention when children ask questions – we listen with intent and answer questions as truthfully as possible whilst bearing in mind children's level of understanding. This builds a relationship of trust and encourages children to express themselves in situations where they feel unsure, enabling us to co-regulate and help sooner.

■ By allowing and encouraging questions from children and using the 'name it to tame it' technique, we are able to use our relationship of trust to address behaviours and situations with children where dysregulation occurred.

Puzzle power

■ We use puzzles/jigsaws in the setting as a self-regulation tool for children who benefit from structured activities. Jigsaws have a clear concept and ending and can help children practice problem-solving in a non-threatening environment.

- We use specific emotions jigsaws to encourage talk about how emotions can look and when we have experienced such emotions ourselves.
- Whilst we may use emotion puzzles as a communication aid, we also appreciate that some children may need to figure out their own emotions without disruption, and we respect a child's wishes in this.

Tap it out

- Similar to our mindful moments, we may use tapping in our sessions to calm anxieties and feelings of dysregulation as well as to feel well-grounded in our own bodies.
- We use a concept of imaginary glitter being spread over your head, face and shoulders by tapping.
- Children are encouraged (where appropriate) to use this technique to self-regulate.

Act it out

- We have several small-world resources, including a doll's house, available to children at all times.
- We encourage children to use small-world resources to help them engage with their lived experiences and act out situations, anxieties and worries in their own way.
- Where appropriate, practitioners will engage in such play to offer co-regulation strategies through cooperative play, but always allowing children to take the lead in their play and respecting their boundaries.

Troublesome triggers

- We have several resources at hand to support children with their calming techniques. These will generally be things we have found through experience will work for individual children or things that parents/guardians have informed us about.
- We have weighted teddies to help children return to a calm place and potentially aid their breathing exercises; we have a disco light which changes colour and other sensory resources.
- We encourage children to access these resources, either as part of their normal routine or to help them in situations where dysregulation has caused them to 'flip their lid'.

Take a break

■ Where children become overwhelmed and/or over-stimulated, we encourage them to 'take a break' in a quiet area of the room. This can be particularly helpful when physical signs show a child becoming tense but they have not yet 'flipped their lid'.

■ It is important to note that this is NOT time-out. It is not to punish children for their behaviour.

■ This strategy is used to support children to reach a calm and safe place where co-regulation of their emotions is possible again.

■ This is also a very important technique for children who do not like physical contact as a calming strategy but prefer to have their own personal space.

■ 'Take a break' can be supported by an adult, who may offer to put some calm music on or read a story, but it can also be used independently if children need time to reconnect with their sense of self.

Many schools and settings aim to keep their families up to date and informed about how to support their children. There are various websites and organisations which can support us and our families in our role and settings, and schools can signpost these to parents. Asking families what they already do is vital, and knowing how they support their child at home can help us in our settings to individualise provision and tailor our strategies to specific children. We can learn from parents just as much, if not more, than parents can learn from us. Having said that, we can still share our ideas with families and role-model our approach.

Home-school liaison – Jess Gosling, International School Early Years Teacher

One child was struggling with following instructions, which was also a significant problem at home. So, we created a home/school record, discussing through issues we had and triumphs the child accomplished. I also discussed with the parent the positive methods we were using at school, and she replicated these at home. The record helped us spend valuable minutes together talking through what went well and what the child's struggles were that day. I found it interesting the extent to which the child did not realise how his actions affected others, which made me reassess just how much we can presume that children are aware of what 'good' choices are. It took a significant period of time for the child to be aware when he had a very positive day, but we did get there!

Calming strategies to suggest parents try at home, which may help children to develop self-regulation:

- Being physically active together.
- Star breathing and other breathing techniques.
- Having a home calming toolbox.
- Yoga and mindfulness techniques.
- Playing counting games.
- Singing songs or nursery rhymes.
- Playing some calm music.
- Engaging in puzzles or jigsaws together.
- Copying rhythmic actions together.
- Giving their child a bear hug.
- Playing with sensory activities or putting lavender essential oil or smelly bubbles in a bath.
- Sharing photos of emotions.
- Making silly faces in the mirror and talking about emotions.
- Reading books and stories about feelings.
- Having worry dolls and worry monsters.
- Using small-world play or role play to express their thoughts and emotions.
- Massaging their child's back or rubbing hand lotion into their hands or feet.
- Creating safe spaces or dens.
- Having a break or time away if needed (both parents and children).
- Dimming lights and limiting background noise – for example, turning off the radio or TV.

My calming toolbox for home

One strategy Tamsin's children were invited to create at school and use at home

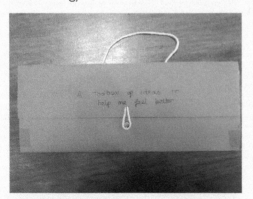

was a toolbox of ideas of things that help them feel better. As part of an intervention group at school, they created two toolboxes – one for home and one for school. They stuck pictures in of people who help them to calm down – for example, family members or pets – places they can go to feel calm – for example, their room or garden – or activities they can do which help them feel better – for example, reading or playing with Blu-Tack.

Tamsin has noticed her children using these toolboxes at times and reminding themselves who they can talk to, where they can go or what they can do to help them to regulate their emotions. Although designed to be used with older children, this idea would still work well as an aide-memoire for younger children and would also remind parents of strategies to use and calming things to try.

Summary

This chapter highlighted the importance of working closely with parents and considered how we might encourage them to engage with their children's learning and development rather than simply getting involved in our settings. We have thought about how we can encourage families to practise acceptance of their children's behaviour and emotions and how we can offer ideas of strategies to use at home, which will support their children's development of self-regulation. We have also considered how our ethos should underpin our practice and how our policies should share this with parents.

The next section will build on this idea and focus on how we might adopt an ethos around self-regulation that will act as the foundation for our practice. It will also summarise the key points within the book and challenge educators to reflect upon their practice in the light of their learning.

Questions for reflection

1. Are we consistent when boundary setting in partnership with parents and across all age ranges?

2. How do we share our ethos around self-regulation with parents?

3. To what extent have we shared strategies such as PACE and the 'Keep Your Cool Toolbox' with our families?

References

Baron-Cohen, S. (2011) *Zero Degrees of Empathy: A New Theory of Human Cruelty.* London: Allen Lane.

Chapman, G. & Campbell, R. (2012). *The 5 love languages of children.* Chicago, IL: Northfield Publishing.

Conkbayir, M. (2020) *Keep Your Cool Toolbox.* Available at https://keepyourcooltoolbox.com.

Desforges, C. & Aboucher, A. (2003) *The impact of parental involvement, parental support and family education on pupil achievement and adjustment: A literature review,* DfES Research Report 433.

Field, F. (2010) *The Foundation Years – Preventing poor children becoming poor adults.* London: Cabinet Office. Available at https://webarchive.nationalarchives.gov.uk/ukgwa/20110120090141/http:/povertyreview.independent.gov.uk/media/20254/poverty-report.pdf.

Golding, K. & Hughes, D. (2012) *Creating Loving Attachments: Parenting with PACE to nurture confidence and security in the troubled child.* London: Jessica Kingsley Publishers.

Goodall, J. & Montgomery, C. (2014) 'Parental involvement to parental engagement: A continuum', *Educational Review, 66*(4), pp. 399–410.

Grimmer, T. (2017) *Observing and Developing Schematic Behaviour in Young Children: A Professional Guide for Supporting Children's Learning, Play and Development.* London: Jessica Kingsley.

Grimmer, T. (2021) *Developing a Loving Pedagogy in the Early Years: How Love Fits with Professional Practice.* London: Routledge.

Hunt, S., Virgo, S., Klett-Davies, M., Page, A., & Apps, J. (2011) *Provider Influence on the Early Home Learning Environment (EHLE),* Research Report DFE-RR142, Department for Education (DfE).

Knowledge Change Action (2021) *Five to Thrive.* Available at https://kca.training/five-to-thrive.

Lexmond, J. & Reeves, R. (2009) *Building Character Report.* London: Demos. Available at www.demos.co.uk/files/Building_Character_Web.pdf.

Montessori, M. (1936). *The secret of childhood.* London: Longmans, Green and Co.

Nutbrown, C. (2011) *Threads of Thinking* (4th ed.). London: Sage.

Parent-Infant Foundation (2021) *1001: First 1001 Days Movement.* Available at https://parentinfantfoundation.org.uk/1001-days.

Shetty, J. (2020) *Think Like a Monk: The secret of how to harness the power of positivity and be happy now.* London: Thorsons.

UNICEF (1989) *United Nations Convention on the Rights of the Child.* Available at www.unicef.org.uk/Documents/Publication-pdfs/UNCRC_PRESS200910web.pdf.

Summary and conclusion

Tamsin Grimmer and Wendy Geens

This book has considered self-regulation within the context of ECEC. We thought about it as broadly as possible and tried to tie in some of the wealth of research and theory that has been documented in this area. We both found, in writing this book and delving deeper into some of the themes, that our core beliefs about early childhood have been challenged as we came to the realisation that self-regulation underpins everything. This book made us both consider what we believe to be important and highlighted the vital role educators play in co-creating a new vision for future society. In supporting children to develop self-regulation and consciously responding and reacting mindfully to them, whilst fostering positive dispositions, we can help this vision become a reality. This chapter summarises our thoughts on this and draws themes from the book together. It also challenges educators and policymakers to consider self-regulation more holistically and look towards the future, offering suggestions and recommendations.

Ethos and approach – not just a policy

We have talked about having a policy that reflects our practice, however, as we have explained, it's bigger than that – it's actually about our whole ethos supporting children's self-regulation. So, our policies and procedures will reflect this, but underpinning everything will be the ethos we adopt. Therefore, embedded in our ethos needs to be our beliefs about what we want for children, bearing in mind our children today shape society tomorrow.

Some schools and settings are rethinking the whole idea of behaviour management because it can give the wrong message to children, parents, carers, staff and other professionals. Tamsin suggests in her book, *Supporting Behaviour and Emotions in the Early Years* (Grimmer, 2022), that we should reframe behaviour management as 'supporting behaviour' or 'promoting positive behaviour'. This is because talking about managing children's behaviour introduces a power dynamic that is both unhelpful and

DOI: 10.4324/9781003162346-11

unnecessary. It doesn't see the child as competent but, rather, as someone needing managing. Therefore, thinking about behaviour in terms of relationships, our pedagogical approach and our role in co-regulating children is more helpful and supportive. Chapter 2 shared how an international school has self-regulation at the heart of its whole ethos, and a school in Chapter 8 adopted a restorative approach that underpins everything they do. We believe thinking about managing behaviour generates negative connotations rather than listening to the child communicate how they are feeling and responding sensitively.

Another school swapped the role of 'Behaviour Management Coordinator' for a 'Self-regulation Champion', which puts the emphasis on the adult co-regulating children instead of managing their behaviour. In addition, adapting the title and content of the policy in this area can give a clear message about ethos and values. For example, having a 'Relationships' policy or a 'Supporting Children's Self-regulation' policy, rather than a 'Behaviour Management' policy, is subtle but demonstrates a clear change of emphasis. Although a change of title can demonstrate our priorities, it is important to change our practices too.

Policy on 'Promoting self-regulation through co-regulation and a loving pedagogy' – Marlis Juerging-Coles, St John's Pre-School

Policy statement

We believe that children flourish best when their personal, social and emotional needs are understood, supported and met and where there are clear, fair and developmentally appropriate expectations for their behaviour.

As children develop, they learn about boundaries, the difference between right and wrong, and to consider the views and feelings, and needs and rights, of others and the impact that their behaviour has on people, places and objects. The development of these skills requires co-regulation from an adult to help encourage and model appropriate behaviours and to offer intervention and support when children struggle with conflict and emotional situations. In these types of situations, key staff can help identify and address triggers for the behaviour and help children reflect, regulate and manage their actions.

Procedures

In order to help children self-regulate in an appropriate way, we will:
- Create an environment where children feel loved, appreciated and important.
- Approach each situation individually and empathetically because we understand that not every situation fits the same resolution.

- Get to know our children and families well to enable us to understand what environmental factors may be influencing a child's behaviour (both long-term and short-term) and what needs the child is expressing.
- Use the 'keep your cool toolbox' (Conkbayir, 2020) to help children self-regulate through co-regulation.
- Attend relevant training to help understand and guide appropriate models of behaviour.
- Have the necessary skills to support other staff with dysregulation issues and to access expert advice, if necessary.
- Undertake an annual audit of our provision to ensure our environment and practices support healthy social and emotional development. Findings from the audit are considered by management and relevant adjustments applied.

We also share with parents and carers what we do if a child appears consistently dysregulated and how we respond if, despite intervention, concerns remain. This means that parents are aware, from the outset, how we will respond to their child.

What do you believe?

Tamsin and Wendy often challenge their students to consider what they believe about children and what they want children to learn whilst attending their schools and settings. As educators, how we view children and our image of the child will underpin our pedagogical approach and values. With this in mind, Tamsin recently wrote her own 'creed' clearly stating her beliefs about young children.

- Firstly and most importantly, I believe that children should be **loved**.

- Children need to grow and develop in **relationship** with others.

- Children are **competent, capable** and **rich in potential.**

- Children are **important in their own right** and should have a recognised place in society as a group in themselves. I believe **childhood** to be a vitally important phase in our lives.

- Children can and do **make a positive contribution** and should be **valued and listened to.**

- Children should be allowed to **play, be free to explore** and **investigate** and be given **time** to do so.

- Children should be **respected, protected and kept safe,** whilst being allowed to take **risks and challenged** as they grow and develop.

- Children should be able to **direct their own learning** at times and their **views should be taken into consideration** within their education.

#lovingpedagogy

If we are striving for a more peaceful society, we need to help children learn how to resolve conflict and interact with others peaceably today. If we want leaders who can make decisions, prioritise and problem-solve solutions, we need to enable our children to develop executive functioning skills. If we want to be greeted by a smile rather than a frown in our future interactions, we need to role-model this and help our children become more socially confident.

In terms of the children, we want them to have the confidence to ask for help or to ask questions about what they or others are doing. We would like them to be able to engage in conversations and know what they say is being listened to and that they have a voice. We want children to be able to make friends and be considerate towards others – for example, when playing a game, we want them to invite another child to go first and know how to wait their turn and bounce back, even if they lose.

Reflecting on what we believe – Allie Thorne, Malthouse Nursery School

I found Tamsin's creed incredibly powerful and thought-provoking. Consequently, I began to reflect on my own creed. Whilst I know my own beliefs and ethos for my nursery setting, I felt that giving myself the time to reflect enabled me to really focus on the type of culture and environment I wish for the children in my care to experience.

Subsequently, this sparked numerous discussions within my team, who reflected on their own beliefs, as well as promoting independent research on shared beliefs and how having a shared culture of strong beliefs and values makes for a strong team, which in turn, of course, benefits all our children. Additionally, we discussed why this should also be considered when employing new staff members.

Furthermore, discussions between staff members over the following days were invaluable, consequently prompting a staff meeting with creed as our focus. The meeting gave us time as a team to reflect on our beliefs and values together and to concisely write our own creed for our nursery, providing us with a clear ethos.

Fostering dispositions

We don't know what jobs will be needed when the children we teach are older. In fact, according to the McKinsey Global Institute (2017), many of the jobs that they will end up doing probably don't exist yet: "If history is any guide, we could also expect that 8–9 percent of 2030 labor demand will be in new types of occupations that have not existed before".

How can we prepare children and educate them for a world that we find it difficult to imagine? We need to move away from trying to fill children's brains with knowledge and instead focus on executive function and learning dispositions that are flexible and can be stretched and applied to any industry. Skills that require the working memory and dispositions that develop resilience – for example, being able to bounce back from challenges or difficulties – are essential attributes in the development of self-regulation. We think there is a much bigger debate at play here. We want our children to grow into confident citizens who have fulfilling lives and contribute to society. We want our children to care, to put themselves in the place of others and to articulate their views but also have respect for others who may not hold the same views. The only way to achieve this is to give children opportunities to develop and extend their skills and dispositions and, rather than being driven by a knowledge-based curriculum, be driven by the desire to achieve the attributes mentioned above.

This book has discussed key aspects of self-regulation, such as empathising, being organised and managing feelings. The more we investigated the whole area of self-regulation and the relationships children have with adults, the more important the role of the adult became – the impact educators can have on a child's self-regulation was magnified. We cannot shout it loudly enough that educators make hugely significant contributions to a child's development. Whilst other themes emerged, which are shared later in this summary, it is key to remember the co-regulator role.

So, all these dispositions – and more – make up self-regulation. It is not about trying to raise passive, compliant children who do what adults tell them or children who are able to control their behaviour – it is about raising confident and competent children who speak because they have something to say and are also able to listen to others. It's about children who can inhibit their impulses because they are growing up in settings and schools where they are supported emotionally and where they are learning to be empathetic. It's about children who are ready, eager and excited to learn!

Key messages in this book

There are several key messages in this book:

- Prioritising self-regulation involves adopting a whole setting/school ethos that underpins practice.

- This ethos should be trauma-informed and attachment-aware, and it should value wellbeing more than academic skills.

- When all children feel valued and their differences are respected, it creates an inclusive environment.

- Everyone feels dysregulated at times, and the way we respond to stress is important.

- Dysregulation is not a choice for children, it is the natural way our brain responds to stressors.

- The 'self' in self-regulation should be redefined and refocused on co-regulation.

- The role of the adult is pivotal in supporting self-regulation, and we must remain calm and regulated ourselves.

- Schools and settings should avoid rewards-based systems when supporting children's self-regulation.

- Executive functioning begins very early in life, and these skills are grown through positive experiences.

- Expecting children to sit still is unrealistic and counterproductive.

- Positive dispositions support children to be life ready.

- We can encourage families to practice acceptance of their children's behaviour and emotions and offer ideas of strategies to use at home to support their children's development of self-regulation.

- Educators need to act now for the sake of our children's futures.

Recommendations for education policy makers

1. Ensure that curriculum focuses less on learning knowledge and more on growing skills and dispositions so the children are better equipped to cope with what the future holds.

2. Uphold the UN Convention on the Rights of the Child (UNICEF, 1989) and keep children central to decisions made.

3. Reflect upon school starting age and review it in countries where children start at 4 or 5 years old, which has no academic advantage.

4. Have due regard for how the world is changing and ensure curricula are flexible, able to adapt to changing perspectives and grounded in humanitarian values.

Recommendations for school and setting leaders

1. Decide what you what for children and what you believe about society.

2. Adopt an ethos in which self-regulation is not only the foundation on which children learn and develop but is at the heart of all the setting offers.

3. Establish a loving pedagogy where relationships are valued and attachments with children built.

4. Prioritise growing dispositions as part of your curriculum – for example, children who want to learn, who are not frightened of making mistakes, who are resilient and who have a go.

5. Embed emotional literacy so that children become attuned to their own emotions and learn how to respond.

6. Ensure your approach is respectful of cultures and takes into accounts children's backgrounds.

7. Ensure your work supports parents and adopts a collaborative approach to the child's development.

8. Show you care and smile!

Our mission

In this book we have talked about the skills that constitute self-regulation, but actually self-regulation is a way of life and a way of being! We challenge educators to change the way we think about children and about society as a whole. As Jarvis (2020:11) warns,

> It cannot be too strongly emphasised that the provision of appropriate infant care is one of the most important issues for contemporary Anglo-American social policy, as it is now increasingly clear that the mental health and productivity of our future population depend upon our current actions.

It is our hope that this book will encourage settings and schools to promote good well-being and create citizens for the future who have a positive mental health. The development of self-regulation is fundamental in promoting this.

The schools and settings that get this right have children with emotionally literacy, resilience, good mental health and a positive sense of self. These providers develop warm, loving relationships with children and families and engage parents in their children's learning. We have shared case studies and examples from international schools that get this right and have the flexibility to embed their ethos throughout their provision as well as from UK schools and settings that have been brave enough to put their beliefs into practice and stand firm in their ideals about what is right for young children. Their children are the lucky ones. In these schools and settings, self-regulation underpins everything they do, they say and they are – it provides the foundation for their whole approach.

This is not just a different take on a behaviour policy or a change in the title of the coordinator, although these things may highlight a shift in thinking – it's a whole ethos. It's an ethos that aims to develop children into citizens who care, who have empathy and understanding and who are growing positive dispositions, enabling them to not only cope but thrive within their daily lives. By adopting an ethos in which self-regulation underpins our practice in the context of a loving pedagogy, we really can change the world, one child at a time!

We will end this book where we began: For the sake of our children's futures and for wider society as a whole, we must support children in developing self-regulation. As educators, we should be ready, willing and able to respond to this challenge. This is our mission, should we choose to accept it!

References

Conkbayir, M. (2020) *Keep Your Cool Toolbox*. Available at https://keepyourcooltoolbox.com.

Grimmer, T. (2022) *Supporting Behaviour and Emotions in the Early Years: Strategies and Ideas for Early Years Educators*. London: Routledge.

Jarvis, P. (2020) 'Attachment theory, cortisol and care for the under threes in the twenty-first century: Constructing evidence-informed policy', *Early Years: An International Journal of Research and Development*, pp. 1–15. doi: 10.1080/09575146.2020.1764507.

McKinsey Global Institute (2017) *Jobs lost, jobs gained: What the future of work will mean for jobs, skills, and wages*. November 28, 2017. Available at https://www.mckinsey.com/featured-insights/future-of-work/jobs-lost-jobs-gained-what-the-future-of-work-will-mean-for-jobs-skills-and-wages.

UNICEF. (1989) *United Nations Convention on the Rights of the Child*. Available at www.unicef.org.uk/Documents/Publication-pdfs/UNCRC_PRESS200910web.pdf.

Index

Milton Keynes UK
Ingram Content Group UK Ltd.
UKHW050637081023
430150UK00004B/4